Reality by Design

365 Principles for Transforming Your Mind & Reality

Daily Wisdom Inspired by the Masters of Mind and Manifestation

RUSSELL L. POWERS

This book is intended for informational and inspirational purposes only.
It is not intended as a substitute for professional medical, legal, financial,
or psychological advice. The author and publisher disclaim any liability
arising from the use or application of the ideas contained herein.

ISBN: 979-8-9943130-0-8

Published by Reality by Design Publishing
RealityByDesign.net

Printed in the United States of America

First Edition, 2026

DEDICATION

To my family

For supporting me through all the trials and tribulations.
For believing in me when doubt crept in.
For standing beside me during all of life's challenges.
For celebrating with me in the victories.

And specifically, to my wife, for always pushing me to keep chasing my dreams, even when the path seemed impossible.

Your love and encouragement are the foundation upon which this book was built.

With all my love and gratitude,

Shelley, Jackson, Mason, and Michael

CONTENTS

ACKNOWLEDGMENTS

No book is written alone, and this one exists because of the people who refused to let me quit on myself.

To my wife, Shelley

You're my best friend and my anchor through every storm. Thank you for your unwavering support, for protecting my creative time on countless late nights, and for believing in me, even when I couldn't believe in myself. This book—and this life—wouldn't exist without you.

To my sons, Jackson, Mason, and Michael

You are my greatest teachers and my deepest motivation. Everything I've learned, I've learned so I could attempt to show you a better way. I am endlessly proud to be your father.

To my parents

Thank you for never giving up on me, even in the darkest moments I created for our family. From the time I was a child through getting sober and beyond, you've loved me unconditionally and believed in me when I couldn't believe in myself. You always encouraged me to chase my dreams and supported me every step of the way. Your love during my lowest moments gave me the foundation to start over and rebuild. I wouldn't be here without you, and I am eternally grateful.

To the men in recovery who mentored me

You showed me a new way to live when I had no idea such a way existed. Your example, your time, and your willingness to walk beside me in recovery gave me the tools I still use today. I am here because you were there.

To all my mentors and teachers

Though most of you I've never met, your wisdom illuminated the path when I was lost in darkness. This book is my attempt to honor your teachings by passing them forward to others who are searching as I am.

To you, the reader

Thank you for choosing this book. Thank you for committing to a year of transformation. Thank you for believing you can change. Your willingness to do the work matters more than you know. I'm honored to walk this journey with you.

Finally, I'm grateful for every trial, every failure, and every moment of suffering that brought me to this point. Without the darkness, I would never have appreciated the light. Without the chaos, I would never have learned to create. Everything—all of it—was necessary.

Preface

This book exists because I nearly died at twenty-seven.

By that age, I had run out of places to hide. Drugs, alcohol, gambling, codependency—I used anything to escape the chaos in my mind. I used to describe it as three radio stations and two TVs all playing at once, and I'd do anything to turn down the volume. A failed marriage. A lost business opportunity. Jail. Homelessness. I moved from city to city trying to outrun myself, but no matter where I went, there I was.

I was always mad at the world for what it was doing to me, failing to see I was doing it to myself. I was terminally negative, constantly doubting myself. The critical self-talk and the endless replaying of past events were constant companions I couldn't escape.

Then came the moment that changed everything. Alone, broken, and out of options, I cried out to God and surrendered completely. For the first time in my life, I asked for real help. Within two hours, I was on my way to detox at my parents' house, shaking violently in an upstairs bedroom for a week, terrified but certain something had shifted. For the first time since I was thirteen, I believed I might actually make it.

The next few years in recovery rebuilt me. Through the 12 steps and the men who mentored me, I got sober and stayed sober. I met my wife Shelley after eight months. I bought the business I'd once lost. I built a family—three sons I adore more than anything in this world. From the outside, I had the dream life.

But inside, I was still struggling. The anger that had plagued me since I was thirteen wouldn't let go. I was lying to my wife about money and gambling, vaping behind her back, repeating old patterns with new "substances". Even worse, I was my own worst enemy—beating myself up with relentless negative self-talk. My mind was a constant battleground—why I wasn't good enough, why I didn't deserve the life I had, why everything would eventually fall apart. Six years sober with everything I'd ever dreamed of, and I was still a wreck internally, still creating problems. My wife gave me an ultimatum: counseling or divorce.

For two years, a skilled counselor pulled things out of me I didn't know were there, things I didn't realize were crushing me that I had been holding onto since I was a kid, buried deep down inside me. The work was exhausting and transformative. When the sessions ended, I was slightly terrified to be without the counselor there to guide me—I'd seemed to always mess things up before given enough time.

Shortly after, I relapsed into vaping. Full of fear and unable to tell my wife, I hid it from her and fell back into dishonesty. This time, I sought out a different kind of help—a hypnotherapist. Around the same time, I'd started exploring meditation as a way to quiet my relentless mind. During a month-long meditation challenge with a friend, I had a profound experience that opened my eyes to what meditation could offer. The synchronicities were impossible to ignore—the hypnotherapist practiced meditation, mindfulness, and breathwork, exactly what I'd been discovering. That's when I encountered Joe Dispenza's work.

From that moment, my life truly began to transform. I dove deep into reality creation, manifestation, frequency, vibration, and consciousness. I built a library and consumed everything I could about meditation, yoga, mindfulness, and breathwork. I studied the masters of thought—Joe Dispenza, Vadim Zeland, Napoleon Hill, Jim Rohn, Earl Nightingale, James Allen, Neville Goddard—and began daily practices to transform myself. I was desperate not to lose my marriage, my family, or my business. My life changed dramatically. The anger began to dissolve. The resentment against myself lifted. The constant self-judgment quieted.

I learned that I emit my highest frequency when I'm being my authentic self, pursuing my true desires. Meditation and daily practice didn't just heal me—they healed my marriage and my family, building on what the counselor had started years before. I discovered that I could change, that I could create the life I wanted if I was willing to follow simple direction and apply daily disciplined action.

Why I Wrote This Book

I wrote this book to gather in one place all the teachings that transformed my life. I needed constant reminders and repetition to change—one reading wasn't enough. The same principles had to show up again and again until they became part of me. This book is designed that way intentionally: the most critical principles repeat throughout, over and over, because repetition is how transformation happened for me.

I also wrote this for my three sons. I wanted to create something I could pass on to them—an operating system for life, a guide to becoming their authentic selves without having to learn everything the hard way like I did. But more than that, I hope this book helps one other person find what I found through these teachings. If your life and mind improve even a fraction of how mine has, then every hour spent writing was worth it.

Today, as a certified holistic life coach, I work with people navigating similar transformations. I've seen firsthand how powerful these principles are when applied consistently with support and accountability. That's why I'm building a community where we can interact, support each other, and navigate this journey together. Because while transformation is personal work, it doesn't have to be done alone.

What Makes This Book Different

This isn't a book about one teacher or one philosophy. It's an integration of wisdom from multiple masters who illuminated the path for me—principles of neuroscience, meditation, consciousness, reality creation, achievement through goal setting, personal development, and timeless philosophical wisdom. This book weaves their teachings together into a daily practice format because I learned that transformation doesn't come from reading once—it comes from daily engagement.

The format is simple: 365 daily readings, one per page, organized into twelve monthly themes that build progressively from foundational principles to mastery and integration. This is how lasting change happens—not through a weekend seminar or a single inspiring book, but through consistent daily practice over time.

A Final Word

As Itzhak Bentov said: "I speak from my present level of ignorance. The more you know, the more ignorant you become, because ignorance grows exponentially—the more answers you get, the more new questions arise." I was once told that once you know you don't know, then you know. I'm still learning. I'm still growing. I'm still discovering how much I don't know.

But what I do know is this: we can change. We can create the life we want. We can heal our minds, our relationships, and our reality. It requires willingness, simple direction, and daily discipline. The masters who came before us illuminated the path. This book is my attempt to pass their light forward.

Thank you for choosing to invest a year in your transformation. Thank you for your commitment to becoming who you're meant to be. I'm grateful you're here, and I'm honored to walk this journey with you.

With gratitude,

Russell L. Powers

Introduction

How This Book Works

This book contains 365 daily principles designed to transform how you think, act, and create your reality. Each day offers one page—a single principle, insight, or practice to contemplate and apply. The structure is intentional: 365 days, 12 monthly themes, building progressively from foundational concepts to mastery and integration.

The Twelve Monthly Themes

1. **January: The Power of Thought** - Foundation principles

2. **February: Reprogramming the Subconscious** - Changing your mind

3. **March: Faith & Mental Equivalents** - Building Belief systems

4. **April: Personal Responsibility** - Taking ownership of your life

5. **May: Reality Transurfing & Intention** - Conscious creation principles

6. **June: Visualization & Future Self** - Mental rehearsal techniques

7. **July: Creating Abundance** - From scarcity to prosperity

8. **August: Daily Disciplines** - Consistent practices for growth

9. **September: Breaking Old Patterns** - Release and transformation

10. **October: Desire & Definiteness of Purpose** - Clarity and focus

11. **November: Gratitude & Present Moment** - Appreciation practices

12. **December: Mastery & Integration** - Bringing it all together

Each month builds on the previous ones. The early months establish foundational understanding—how your mind works, how to reprogram limiting beliefs, how to develop faith in your ability to create. The middle months introduce practices and principles for conscious reality creation. The final months focus on integration, helping you embody these principles until they become your natural way of being.

How to Use This Book

Read one entry per day. This is the recommended approach. Each entry is designed to give you something meaningful to contemplate and apply for 24 hours. Reading ahead could possibly diminish the impact—these aren't concepts to consume quickly; they're practices to live daily.

That said, you can also work at your own pace. If you're drawn to spend multiple days with a single entry, do so. If you need to revisit earlier months, go back. The goal isn't completion; it's transformation.

Reflect on the "Today" prompts. Most entries end with a "Today" section offering specific actions or reflections. These aren't just suggestions—they're the bridge between knowing and doing. Reading without practice is entertainment. Practice is what creates change.

Revisit entries that resonate. Some days will hit differently than others. When an entry strikes you deeply, mark it. Return to it. Let it sink in over days or weeks. Transformation isn't linear—sometimes you need to hear the same message ten times before it penetrates.

Create a daily ritual. Use this book as part of your morning or evening routine. Many people find morning reading sets the tone for the day, priming their mind with empowering principles before engaging with the world. Others prefer evening reading as reflection and integration practice. Choose what works for you, then make it consistent.

Resources to Support Your Journey

At the back of this book, you'll find a comprehensive Resources section with tools to deepen your practice. This includes recommended books from the masters referenced throughout these pages, downloadable worksheets for goal setting and daily reflection, apps, meditation and breathwork resources, and links to communities where you can connect with others on similar journeys. These resources are entirely optional—the daily entries contain everything you need for transformation. But if you're drawn to explore specific principles more deeply or want structured tools for practices like a gratitude journal, goal setting or habit tracking, the Resources section provides guidance. Use what serves you. Leave what doesn't.

Why Repetition Matters

You'll notice certain principles appearing multiple times throughout the year. This is intentional.

The most critical principles—the ones that create the deepest transformation—are repeated from different angles across different days and months. You might encounter the principle of taking responsibility in April, then again in September when learning to break patterns, and once more in December during integration. Each time, the principle is explored differently, revealing new facets and applications.

Repetition serves transformation. Reading a principle once plants a seed. Encountering it again waters that seed. By the third or fourth appearance, the principle begins taking root in your subconscious, shifting from intellectual understanding to embodied knowing.

This is how lasting change happens—not through a single dramatic insight, but through repeated exposure that gradually rewires your thinking until new patterns become automatic.

The Masters Behind the Teachings

This book weaves together wisdom from multiple teachers and traditions. Rather than presenting one philosophy, it integrates complementary insights from masters who approached transformation from different angles:

Joe Dispenza brings neuroscience and meditation to conscious creation. His work on breaking the habit of being yourself, rewiring neural pathways through mental rehearsal, and becoming your future self forms the foundation for many entries about personal transformation and meditation practice.

Vadim Zeland's *Reality Transurfing* offers a unique model for understanding how reality works—the alternatives space, pendulums, importance, and intention. His concepts appear in May and in days addressing how to navigate the infinite field of possibilities and choose your own variant of reality.

Napoleon Hill contributed timeless principles from *Think and Grow Rich*—definiteness of purpose, burning desire, faith, specialized knowledge, organized planning, and the mastermind principle. His work heavily influences October's focus on desire and purpose.

Jim Rohn's personal development wisdom—particularly around goal setting, disciplines, and personal responsibility—shapes August's daily disciplines theme and appears in practical life application throughout the year.

Earl Nightingale and **James Allen** provide philosophical grounding, especially around thought as the primary creative force and personal responsibility for one's circumstances.

These teachers each illuminated different aspects of how consciousness creates reality. This book integrates their wisdom into a coherent system you can practice daily.

What to Expect

Months 1-4 (January-April): Foundation

The first four months establish how your mind works and how you may have been creating your reality unconsciously. You'll learn about thought as creative force, how to reprogram limiting beliefs, the role of faith and mental states, and the critical importance of taking responsibility. These months may challenge comfortable beliefs about how reality works. Stay open.

Months 5-8 (May-August): Active Creation

The middle months shift from understanding to application. You'll learn specific techniques for conscious reality creation—intention-setting, visualization, mental rehearsal, and daily disciplines that compound into transformation. These months emphasize practice over theory. You'll be doing, not just reading.

Months 9-12 (September-December): Integration & Mastery

The final months help you break old patterns that resist change, clarify your deepest desires, cultivate gratitude and presence, and integrate everything into a cohesive practice. December's focus on mastery emphasizes that true transformation comes from embodying these principles until they become who you are, not just what you know.

The Commitment Required

This journey requires commitment. Not perfection—commitment. You'll miss days. You'll forget to apply principles. You'll fall back into old patterns. This is normal and expected. Don't beat yourself up. What matters is returning and continuing.

Transformation isn't about doing everything perfectly. It's about showing up consistently, applying what you learn imperfectly, and trusting that small daily actions compound into profound change over time.

A Note on Practice

This isn't just a book to read—it's a practice manual. The difference is crucial.

Reading gives you information. Practice gives you transformation. You can read every entry, understand every concept intellectually, and change nothing in your life. Or you can apply the principles and transform completely.

Daily application matters more than perfect understanding. You don't need to grasp every concept fully before taking action. Apply what resonates. Practice imperfectly. Let your understanding deepen through experience rather than trying to understand everything before starting.

Progress over perfection. Some days you'll apply principles powerfully. Other days you'll barely remember to read. Both are part of the journey. What compounds into transformation isn't perfection—it's the willingness to keep practicing, keep returning, keep choosing growth over comfort.

Begin

You're about to spend a year transforming your mind and your reality. Thank you for making this commitment. Thank you for choosing growth. Thank you for believing you can change.

The journey begins with a single day, a single page, a single principle applied. Everything else builds from there.

JANUARY

THE POWER OF THOUGHT

Foundation principles

January 1

You are what you think.

Your entire life is a reflection of the thoughts you habitually hold in your mind. Like a garden that yields whatever seeds are planted in it, your consciousness produces results according to the mental seeds you sow. Most of what you experience in life—your circumstances, relationships, and outcomes—began as a thought. When you think a thought repeatedly, you create neural pathways that become your automatic responses, your habits, and ultimately your destiny.

It's common for people to go through life never once examining their thoughts. They accept whatever thoughts arise as truth, never questioning where these thoughts came from or whether they serve them. But you are not your thoughts—you are the awareness that observes them. This distinction changes everything.

Today, begin the practice of thought observation. Throughout your day, pause and ask yourself: "What have I been thinking about for the last hour?" Notice the dominant thoughts. Don't judge them, just observe. Are these thoughts about problems or possibilities? About what you fear or what you desire?

Then, consciously choose one empowering thought to replace your most frequent limiting thought. If you catch yourself thinking "I never have enough," immediately replace it with "I am learning to create abundance." The key is not to fight the negative thought but to redirect your mental energy toward what you want to create.

Observe, recognize, and redirect. You cannot change what you do not see, and you cannot create a new reality with old thinking. Choose thoughts that serve your highest vision of yourself.

January 2

Circumstances do not make the person; they reveal them.

When difficulties arise, it's easy for people to blame their circumstances for their unhappiness. Yet circumstances are neutral—it's our interpretation and response that determines their meaning.

Two people can face identical challenges: one sees an insurmountable obstacle, the other sees an opportunity for growth. The difference lies not in the circumstances but in the consciousness observing them. While not every difficulty originates from your thinking, sometimes life simply happens, your current situation often reflects patterns of past thought. If you find yourself in difficulty, pause and honestly assess: has my thinking been aligned with this outcome? What role, if any, has my mental state played in creating or perpetuating this circumstance?

Here's the liberation: even when circumstances arise beyond your control, you can still influence what comes next through new thinking. External conditions are temporary and malleable; your inner state of consciousness shapes how you move through them and what emerges on the other side.

Today, begin to take absolute responsibility for your life. Not blame, but responsibility—the ability to respond consciously rather than react automatically. When you accept that you are the co-creator of your experience, you reclaim your power to shape what happens next.

January 3

Every thought is a cause; every condition is an effect.

The universe operates according to laws, and cause and effect play a powerful role in shaping our experience. While not everything in your life traces back to your thinking, some circumstances arise from factors beyond your control. Your thoughts, beliefs, and habitual emotional states create patterns that significantly influence what you attract, how you interpret events, and which opportunities you recognize or miss.

Your present moment reflects, at least in part, the mental patterns you've been running. This might seem overwhelming, but it's actually empowering. While you can't control everything that happens to you, you have tremendous influence over how you respond and what patterns you perpetuate or break. The person experiencing poverty consciousness can shift their relationship with abundance—not through forced positivity, but by mentally rehearsing prosperity and seeing all their needs met until that reality begins to manifest. The person feeling isolated can transform their beliefs about connection and worthiness by consistently feeling connected and worthy before circumstances change. Your body doesn't know the difference between an actual experience and one you vividly imagine, especially with an elevated emotion attached. When you mentally rehearse a new state daily, you broadcast that frequency, and reality mirrors it back to you.

Today, explore whether your current conditions connect to mental causes. What beliefs might be influencing this situation? What habitual thoughts could be maintaining it? Not because you're "doing it wrong," but because identifying these patterns gives you power to change them. Once you see the mental causes you can control, you can replace them with new causes that produce different effects. This isn't magical thinking—it's recognizing where you actually have power to change things.

January 4

Your mind is a garden; you are the gardener.

Imagine a beautiful garden that has been neglected for years. Weeds have taken over, choking out the flowers, creating chaos where there was once order. This is the state of many minds—overrun with negative thoughts, limiting beliefs, and destructive mental patterns that were never consciously chosen.

The good news is that you are the gardener, and starting today, you can begin the work of renovation. First, you must pull the weeds—identify and remove the thoughts that do not serve you. Worry, resentment, fear, self-doubt: these are mental weeds that drain your energy and prevent growth. But removal is not enough; nature abhors a vacuum. You must immediately plant new seeds—thoughts of confidence, gratitude, possibility, and purpose. Water these seeds daily with attention and emotion. Protect them from the harsh winds of criticism and doubt.

In time, your mental garden will flourish, and the fruits of your inner cultivation will manifest in your outer world. Remember: a gardener cannot plant corn and expect to harvest wheat. You cannot think thoughts of lack and expect abundance. You cannot dwell on illness and expect health. The garden yields what you plant.

January 5

As you think, so you become.

The process of becoming is not mysterious—it follows a precise sequence. Thought crystallizes into habit, habit solidifies into character, and character determines destiny.

If you want to know what you will become five years from now, examine the thoughts you are thinking today. Are you thinking thoughts of mediocrity or excellence? Scarcity or abundance? Fear or courage? The tragedy is that attention often settles on what isn't wanted rather than what is truly desired. They replay past failures, imagine future disasters, and wonder why their lives don't improve.

But the masters of thought understand this principle and use it consciously. They guard their thoughts zealously, allowing only those mental images that align with their desired future. They know that they cannot think one way and live another.

Beginning today, become aware of the dominant thoughts that occupy your mental space. Are these the thoughts of the person you wish to become? If not, gently but firmly redirect your attention. It will feel awkward at first—like learning a new language. But persist, and within weeks, you will notice subtle shifts in your perception, your energy, your circumstances. This is not wishful thinking; this is the scientific application of mental law.

January 6

Change your thinking, and you change your world.

It's common for people to try to change their lives by changing external conditions—getting a new job, moving to a new city, entering a new relationship. And while these changes may provide temporary relief, they rarely produce lasting transformation because the root cause remains untouched: the thinking that created the dissatisfaction in the first place.

Wherever you go, there you are, carrying the same patterns of thought that created your previous experience. True change must begin at the level of consciousness. When you transform your thinking, you transform your perception. When you transform your perception, you transform your experience. And when you transform your experience consistently over time, you transform your reality.

This is not to say that external action is unimportant—action is essential. But action without transformed thinking is merely motion without direction.

Today, identify one limiting belief that has held you back. Perhaps it's "I'm not good enough" or "Success isn't for people like me" or "It's too late for me to change." Now consciously replace this belief with an empowering truth. Every time the old thought arises, gently redirect to the new thought. This is the work of transformation, and it begins with a single thought, repeated with intention until it becomes your new reality.

January 7

The mind moves in the direction of our dominant thoughts.

Your subconscious mind is like a ship's autopilot system—it moves constantly in the direction programmed by your dominant thoughts. If your dominant thoughts are of limitation, your life will move toward limitation. If your dominant thoughts are of possibility, your life will move toward possibility. The key word here is 'dominant.'

It's not about having a positive thought once in a while when you're feeling good. It's about the persistent, habitual, repeated thoughts that occupy your consciousness throughout the day. What do you think about during idle moments? What mental movies play when you're driving, showering, or falling asleep? These dominant thoughts are programming your autopilot, setting the course for your life's journey.

The good news is that you can reprogram this autopilot at any time. It requires vigilance, consistency, and patience, but it is absolutely possible. Begin by selecting one dominant thought you want to install—perhaps "I am becoming more capable every day" or "Opportunities flow to me easily" or "I am worthy of success and happiness." Then, deliberately think this thought dozens of times per day. Write it down. Say it out loud. Feel it emotionally. Gradually, this new thought will become dominant, and your life will automatically adjust course toward this new direction.

January 8

You cannot rise higher than the level of your own thinking.

There is an invisible ceiling in every person's life, determined not by circumstances but by the quality of their thoughts. If you give a million dollars to someone whose thought life hasn't expanded to match that level of wealth, within a short time they will return to their previous financial level. Why? Because their thinking creates a comfort zone, and anything beyond that comfort zone can subconsciously feel unsafe, unfamiliar, and threatening. This is why lottery winners often end up bankrupt, and why some children of wealthy individuals struggle despite every advantage. The external resources don't match the internal consciousness.

If you want to expand your life, you must first expand your thought life. This means challenging the limitations you've accepted, questioning the beliefs you've inherited, and deliberately constructing a mental framework that can accommodate the life you desire. Read books that stretch your mind. Associate with people who think bigger than you do. Expose yourself to ideas and possibilities that make your current thinking feel small. This expansion of consciousness is uncomfortable. It requires you to acknowledge that your current thinking has been somewhat inadequate. But this discomfort is the price of growth.

Today, ask yourself: What level of thinking would be required for me to achieve my goals? Then begin thinking at that level, even before you have evidence that it's working. Faith precedes the miracle.

January 9

Your thoughts are the architects of your destiny.

Just as an architect creates detailed blueprints before construction begins, your thoughts create the blueprint for your life experience. Every building, every relationship, every achievement exists first as a thought before it becomes a reality. The architect doesn't just wish for a beautiful building, they design it with precision, considering every detail, every measurement, every function.

Similarly, you must become the conscious architect of your life, designing your days with intention rather than accepting whatever random thoughts happen to drift through your consciousness. Many lives are built without a blueprint, shaped by unexamined thoughts, inherited patterns, and unconscious habits. The result is often instability, confusion, and the lingering sense that something isn't quite working.

Today, take control of this process. What structure do you want to build with your life? What are the specifications? What materials—which thoughts, beliefs, and attitudes—will you use? Remember that just as a building can only be as strong as its foundation, your life can only be as magnificent as the thoughts that support it. Begin each day with this question: What thoughts will I think today that will contribute to the life I'm designing? Then think those thoughts deliberately, persistently, expectantly, knowing that your mental architecture is determining your destiny.

January 10

The quality of your thoughts determines the quality of your life.

There is a direct correlation between the elevation of your thoughts and the elevation of your life experience. Low-quality thoughts—those characterized by fear, worry, resentment, and victimhood—produce a low-quality life experience. High-quality thoughts—those characterized by gratitude, possibility, purpose, and growth—produce a high-quality life experience. This is not a moral judgment but a practical observation.

What are high-quality thoughts? They are thoughts that energize rather than deplete, thoughts that open rather than close, thoughts that build rather than destroy. They are thoughts that acknowledge challenges while focusing on solutions, thoughts that honor the past while creating a better future, thoughts that see the humanity in others while maintaining healthy boundaries.

Today, conduct a quality audit of your thinking. Throughout the day, pause periodically and ask: Is this a high-quality thought? Would I be proud if others could hear my internal dialogue? Does this thought move me toward my goals or away from them? When you catch yourself thinking low-quality thoughts, don't judge yourself—simply upgrade the thought. Replace "This is too hard" with "I'm capable of doing hard things." Replace "Nothing ever works out for me" with "I'm discovering what works through this process." Small upgrades in thought quality, repeated consistently, lead to massive improvements in life quality.

January 11

Your thoughts are either building your future or repeating your past.

Every moment presents you with a choice: think thoughts that replicate your past experiences, or think thoughts that create new future experiences. Often, people become trapped in a mental loop, replaying the same thoughts they thought yesterday, which are the same thoughts they thought last week, which are the same thoughts they've been thinking for years. This mental repetition creates predictable results—the past simply recycles itself endlessly.

But when you consciously interrupt this pattern and introduce new thoughts, you inject new possibilities into your timeline. This is not about denying your past or pretending difficulties didn't happen. It's about refusing to let your past dictate your future. The person you were yesterday does not have to be the person you are today. The limitations you accepted last year do not need to be accepted this year.

Today, become aware of the difference between past-oriented thinking and future-oriented thinking. Past-oriented thoughts sound like: "I always…" "I never…" "That's just how I am…" Future-oriented thoughts sound like: "I'm becoming…" "I'm learning…" "I'm creating…" Every time you catch yourself in past-thinking mode, shift to future-thinking mode. This simple practice, done consistently, will literally change the trajectory of your life.

January 12

Where attention goes, energy flows.

Your attention is your most valuable resource, and whatever you give attention to grows in your experience. If you constantly focus on your problems, your problems will expand and multiply. If you focus on possibilities, possibilities will expand and multiply. This is not because of some mystical law but because attention directs your mental and physical energy toward specific outcomes.

When you focus on your problems, your mind becomes a problem-finding machine, generating more evidence of problems and more reasons why they're insurmountable. When you focus on a possibility, your mind becomes a possibility-generating machine, noticing opportunities, making connections, and discovering resources.

People often scatter their attention across hundreds of concerns, worries, and distractions, wondering why they never achieve significant results. Mastery begins with the consolidation of attention. Choose one goal, one aspiration, one vision that truly matters to you. Then give it your sustained, focused attention—not just occasionally, but daily, deliberately, emotionally. Think about it in the morning. Visualize it throughout the day. Plan for it in the evening. As you consolidate your attention in this way, you'll notice something remarkable: the universe begins to reorganize itself around your focus. People, resources, and opportunities are drawn into your life path, matching your thought energy.

January 13

You become what you repeatedly think about.

Repetition is the mother of learning and the father of transformation. A single positive thought has little power to change your life, but a thought repeated hundreds of times becomes a belief. A belief repeated thousands of times becomes a conviction. A conviction repeated hundreds of thousands of times becomes your identity. This is how transformation occurs—not through dramatic moments of insight, but through the quiet, consistent repetition of empowering thoughts.

Consider the person who thinks, once per day, "I am capable and strong." This thought has minimal impact. Now consider the person who thinks this same thought fifty times per day, who writes it down every morning, who says it out loud throughout the day, who feels it emotionally before sleeping. Within weeks, this thought has reshaped their neural pathways, their self-perception, their behavior, and inevitably their circumstances. This is the power of repetition. It's not enough to know the truth intellectually; you must repeat the truth until it becomes your lived reality.

Today, choose one empowering thought about yourself or your life. Then commit to thinking this thought repeatedly—not casually, but deliberately, with feeling, with conviction. Set reminders on your phone. Write it on sticky notes. Say it during idle moments. Let repetition do the work that willpower cannot.

January 14

> *Your mind is either your greatest asset or your greatest liability.*

The same mind that can lift you to extraordinary heights can also trap you in perpetual misery. The difference lies entirely in how you use it. An undisciplined mind is like a wild horse—powerful but dangerous, running wherever impulse leads, creating chaos and exhaustion. A disciplined mind is like a trained horse—equally powerful but directed, controlled, harnessed toward purposeful action.

It's common for people to never attempt to train their minds, assuming that thoughts just happen randomly, like weather. But the masters know better. They understand that the mind can be trained, directed, focused, and cultivated. They spend as much time developing their mental discipline as an athlete spends developing physical discipline.

How do you train your mind? Through consistent practice. Meditation teaches you to observe thoughts without being controlled by them. Visualization teaches you to direct imagination toward desired outcomes. Affirmations teach you to replace automatic negative thinking with intentional positive thinking. Reading teaches you to expose your mind to elevated ideas. All of these practices work, not because they're magical, but because they're exercise for your mental muscles.

Today, commit to treating your mind as your most important asset. What would happen if you invested as much time in mental development as you invest in entertainment? Begin with just 10 minutes of deliberate mental training, and watch your life transform.

January 15

Thoughts held in mind produce after their kind.

This principle is absolute and unchanging: you will always harvest what you plant in the garden of your mind. If you plant thoughts of abundance, you will harvest abundant circumstances. If you plant thoughts of scarcity, you will harvest scarce circumstances. If you plant thoughts of health, you will harvest healthy conditions. If you plant thoughts of illness, you will harvest illness. There are no exceptions to this law, no special cases, no lucky breaks. The universe is impersonal—it doesn't care about your excuses, your history, your reasons. It simply responds to the dominant mental seeds you plant.

This might seem harsh, but it's actually the most liberating truth you can embrace. It means you are not a victim of circumstances; you are the creator of circumstances through your habitual thinking. Many people resist this principle because it requires them to take complete responsibility for their current situation. It's easier to blame the economy, the government, their parents, their circumstances. But blame keeps you powerless. Responsibility grants you power.

Today, examine the harvest you're currently reaping in your life. Is it what you want? If not, trace it back to the mental seeds you've been planting. Then consciously choose new seeds. Plant them daily. Water them with attention and emotion. And trust the law: thoughts held in mind will produce after their kind.

January 16

You are the sum total of your thoughts.

Look at your life honestly and you will see your thinking patterns made visible. Your relationships reflect your thoughts about connection and worthiness. Your finances reflect your thoughts about money and value. Your health reflects your thoughts about your body and wellbeing. Your career reflects your thoughts about your capabilities and potential.

Everything in your external world is an accurate mirror of your internal world of thought. This is sometimes uncomfortable to acknowledge because it means you cannot blame circumstances for your current situation. But this discomfort is the doorway to freedom. If you created your current reality through your past thinking, you can create a new reality through new thinking. You are not stuck, not limited, not destined to repeat your history. You are the sum total of your thoughts, which means as your thoughts change, you change. As you change, your circumstances must inevitably change to match your new level of consciousness.

Begin today by taking inventory. What am I the sum total of right now? What thoughts have I been thinking that produced this result? Be honest but not harsh with yourself—this is observation, not judgment. Then ask: What do I want to become the sum total of? What thoughts must I begin thinking now to create that new reality? The answers to these questions contain your roadmap forward.

January 17

Your outer world mirrors your inner world.

A great deal of what you experience externally is a reflection of what exists internally. If you feel chaotic inside, your external life will reflect chaos. If you feel peaceful inside, your external life will reflect peace. If you feel abundant inside, your external life will reflect abundance. This is not mysticism—it's the natural operation of consciousness. Your inner state determines your perceptual filters, your decisions, your actions, your energy, and therefore your results.

Two people can be in identical circumstances—same job, same income, same city—and have completely different experiences based solely on their inner world. One feels trapped and miserable; the other feels grateful and content. The circumstances aren't creating the experience; the consciousness is creating the experience. This means that any attempt to fix your outer world without first addressing your inner world is doomed to fail. You might achieve temporary changes, but you'll quickly recreate the same problems because the consciousness that created them remains unchanged. Real transformation begins within.

Today, instead of trying to fix external circumstances, work on cultivating your internal state. Practice gratitude to shift from scarcity to abundance. Practice self-compassion to shift from harsh judgment to acceptance. Practice presence to shift from anxiety about past and future to peace in the now. As your inner world transforms, your outer world will naturally and automatically follow.

January 18

Guard your mind as you would guard your most precious possession.

If someone tried to break into your home and steal your possessions, you would take immediate action to protect your property. Yet many people allow negative thoughts, limiting beliefs, and destructive mental patterns to infiltrate their minds without any resistance whatsoever. They consume news designed to trigger fear and outrage. They engage in conversations filled with gossip and complaint. They expose themselves to entertainment that glorifies violence, cynicism, and degradation. Then they wonder why they feel anxious, depressed, and hopeless.

Your mind is infinitely more valuable than any physical possession, yet it receives far less protection. Beginning today, become a guardian of your mental space. Be selective about what you allow in. Before watching that show, reading that article, or engaging in that conversation, ask yourself: Will this elevate my consciousness or diminish it? Will this strengthen my vision or weaken it? Will this add to my peace or subtract from it? This doesn't mean living in a bubble of toxic positivity, ignoring real problems, or avoiding all challenging content. It means being intentional rather than passive about what you expose your mind to.

Every input creates an output. Every idea you encounter either reinforces your highest vision or undermines it. Guard your mind with the same vigilance you would guard your greatest treasure, because that's exactly what it is.

January 21

What you think about expands in your experience.

There is a mysterious but reliable principle at work in consciousness: whatever you focus your attention on multiplies. If you think about problems, you'll experience more problems. If you think about solutions, you'll experience more solutions. If you think about lack, you'll experience more lack. If you think about abundance, you'll experience more abundance.

This happens through multiple mechanisms. First, your attention acts as a filter, causing you to notice evidence that confirms your focus while ignoring evidence that contradicts it. If you're thinking about how difficult life is, you'll notice every difficulty while overlooking every ease. Second, your focus directs your energy and actions toward manifesting more of what you're focused on. If you're constantly thinking about debt, your decisions will be made from scarcity consciousness, creating more debt. Third, your dominant thoughts broadcast a frequency that attracts matching circumstances, people, and opportunities. The key to using this principle deliberately is to focus on what you want to expand rather than what you want to eliminate. Don't think about poverty—think about prosperity. Don't think about illness—think about health. Don't think about loneliness—think about connection. This isn't about denial; it's about direction.

Today, audit your mental focus. What are you expanding through your attention? If you don't like what's expanding, redirect your focus immediately. Think about, talk about, and imagine what you want more of, and watch it grow.

January 22

You cannot solve a problem with the same thinking that created it.

As Dr. Joe Dispenza teaches, "Your personality is made up of how you think, act, and feel. It is your state of being. Therefore, your same thoughts, actions, and feelings can keep you enslaved to the same past personal reality. However, when you as a personality embrace new thoughts, actions, and feelings, you will inevitably create a new personal reality in your future."

Most problems persist not because they're difficult to solve, but because you keep trying to solve them from within the same personality that created them. You cannot think your way out of a problem using the same level of thinking that produced it. You must rise above the problem entirely by becoming someone new—someone for whom that problem simply doesn't exist.

This requires a shift in consciousness. Instead of focusing on fixing what's wrong, focus on becoming the person who lives above that problem. See yourself as already being that person. How does that version of you think? What do they believe? How do they act throughout their day? What emotions do they embody?

The key is to mentally rehearse being this new person before your external reality reflects it. Spend time each day visualizing yourself as the person you want to become—not hoping or wishing, but actually experiencing the thoughts, feelings, and actions of that elevated personality. When you do this consistently, you're no longer the old personality trying to solve old problems. You're a new personality creating a new reality.

Today, identify one recurring problem. Then ask: Who would I need to become to live beyond this problem? Practice being that person in your mind until it becomes your natural state of being.

January 23

> *Your thoughts are the tools with which you shape your reality.*

A sculptor starts with a block of marble and uses tools—chisel, hammer, file—to reveal the form within. You start with the raw material of infinite possibility and use thoughts to shape your reality. The sculptor cannot blame the marble for the final form; the form is entirely determined by how the tools are used.

Similarly, you cannot blame circumstances for your life; most of your life is determined by how you use your thoughts. But here's the critical insight: without awareness, people are using their mental tools unconsciously, randomly, and carelessly. They pick up whatever thought happens to be available—worry, fear, resentment, doubt—and chip away at their reality without any awareness of what they're creating. Then they step back and wonder why their life doesn't look like what they wanted.

The master sculptor is intentional with every strike of the chisel. The master thinker is intentional with every thought. They choose their mental tools deliberately, knowing that each thought is either carving their vision or defacing it.

Today, recognize that you are constantly sculpting your reality through your thoughts. Are you using your tools consciously or unconsciously? Are you creating what you intend or accepting what randomness produces? Pick up your mental tools with awareness, and use them to deliberately shape the reality you desire.

January 24

The thoughts you think most often become your beliefs.

A belief is simply a thought you've thought so many times that you've stopped questioning it. At some point, it moved from "I'm thinking this" to "This is true." This is how both empowering and limiting beliefs are formed—through repetition, not through evidence. You weren't born believing you're not good enough, that money is hard to come by, or that success isn't for people like you. You thought these thoughts repeatedly until they hardened into beliefs.

The liberating realization is that if repetition created these beliefs, repetition can also dissolve them and install new ones. You don't need to wait for circumstances to change to change your beliefs. You don't need permission, proof, or validation. You simply need to think new thoughts repeatedly until they become your new beliefs. This requires patience because you're working against years or decades of mental conditioning.

The old beliefs won't surrender without resistance. But every time you choose the new thought over the old belief, you weaken the old neural pathway and strengthen the new one. Eventually, the new thought becomes automatic—in other words, it becomes your new belief.

Today, identify one limiting belief you're ready to release. What new belief would you like to install in its place? Write it down. Then begin the practice of repetition: think this new thought first thing in the morning, throughout the day, and last thing before sleep. Let repetition do its work.

January 25

Your mind is always working, either for you or against you.

Your mind never rests, never takes a vacation, never goes offline. Even while you sleep, it continues to process, organize, and integrate information. The question is not whether your mind is working—it's always working. The question is whether it's working for your benefit or your detriment.

When you allow your mind to run on autopilot, it absorbs whatever the world feeds it—and the world is feeding you fear through the news, inadequacy through social media, and constant distraction designed to harvest your attention for profit. An untrained mind becomes a dumping ground for everyone else's agenda, creating anxiety and stress that serve no purpose in your life.

When you train your mind intentionally, it becomes your greatest ally, working tirelessly to solve problems, identify opportunities, and move you toward your goals even when you're not consciously thinking about them. A well-trained mind will wake you up with insights, surprise you with solutions, and guide you toward beneficial actions automatically.

The difference between these two modes—the mind working for you versus against you—is entirely within your control. It comes down to what you consistently feed your mind. When you feed it constantly from external sources—news, social media, other people's opinions—it tends to produce fear, limitation, and lack. But when you feed your mind from within yourself, consciously choosing what to create and holding a vision of possibility and purpose for the future you want, it will work just as diligently to manifest that instead. Choose consciously.

January 26

Every thought is a seed planted in the garden of tomorrow.

The thought you're thinking right now won't manifest immediately—there's always a lag between cause and effect, between seed and harvest. This lag can be both a blessing and a curse. It's a blessing because it means your past negative thoughts don't have to define your future; you can plant new seeds today that will produce different results tomorrow. It's a curse because it can create the illusion that your thoughts don't matter, that there's no connection between what you think and what you experience.

But the master understands that every single thought is consequential. Today's worry is tomorrow's anxiety. Today's doubt is next week's setback. Today's gratitude is next month's abundance. Today's vision is next year's achievement.

You're always planting seeds, whether you're aware of it or not. The question is: What kind of garden do you want to walk through tomorrow, next week, next year? If you want a garden of peace, plant thoughts of peace today. If you want a garden of prosperity, plant thoughts of prosperity today. If you want a garden of health, plant thoughts of health today. Don't make the mistake of planting weeds—thoughts of fear, lack, and limitation—then wondering why your future garden is overrun with problems.

Today, be intentional about every seed you plant. Your future self will thank you for the garden you're creating right now.

January 27

The quality of your life is determined by the quality of your questions.

Your mind is a question-answering machine. It will always find an answer to whatever question you pose. But the quality of the answer depends entirely on the quality of the question. Ask "Why does this always happen to me?" and your mind will generate a list of reasons why you're a victim. Ask "What can I learn from this situation?" and your mind will generate insights and growth opportunities. Ask "Why am I so stupid?" and your mind will provide evidence of your inadequacy. Ask "How can I improve?" and your mind will generate strategies for development.

Much of the time, disempowering questions are asked unconsciously throughout the day: Why is life so hard? Why can't I ever catch a break? What's wrong with me? Why doesn't anything work out? These questions direct your mind to search for evidence of hardship, bad luck, personal defects, and failure—and your mind, being an excellent servant, will find exactly what you've asked it to find.

The transformation begins when you become conscious of your questions and deliberately upgrade them. Instead of "Why is this happening to me?" ask "What is this teaching me?" Instead of "Why can't I do this?" ask "How can I learn to do this?" Instead of "What's wrong?" ask "What's possible?" Your mind will work just as hard to answer empowering questions as disempowering ones. Give it better questions, and it will give you better answers.

January 28

Your thoughts are electromagnetic signals that attract corresponding circumstances.

Modern neuroscience confirms what mystics have known for millennia: thoughts are not ephemeral, insubstantial things—they are real, measurable, electromagnetic events in your brain. Every thought generates a specific frequency, a pattern of neural activity that radiates outward. This might sound mystical, but it's physics. You are literally broadcasting your consciousness into the world around you through the thoughts you think. These broadcasts attract circumstances, people, and opportunities that match their frequency.

Think thoughts of scarcity, and you'll attract scarce circumstances. Think thoughts of abundance, and you'll attract abundant circumstances. This is how resonance works. Like frequencies attract and amplify each other; unlike frequencies repel. This is why positive people tend to surround themselves with other positive people and opportunities, while negative people seem to attract drama and difficulty. They're broadcasting different frequencies through their habitual thoughts.

The exciting implication is that you can change what you attract by changing what you broadcast. Begin by becoming aware of the frequency you're currently transmitting. If your dominant thoughts are fearful, worried, and negative, you're broadcasting a low-frequency signal that will attract matching low-frequency experiences. Shift to thoughts of possibility, gratitude, and purpose, and you automatically begin broadcasting a higher frequency that attracts better matching experiences. You don't need to believe this principle—just experiment with it and observe the results.

January 29

The thoughts you entertain become the life you live.

The word entertain comes from the Latin roots *inter* and *tenere*, meaning "to hold between." To entertain something is literally to hold it in your consciousness, to give it attention, to keep it company. Every thought you entertain—whether positive or negative, empowering or limiting—is something you are holding within your mind, allowing it to take up space and influence your inner world. Over time, the thoughts you repeatedly entertain shape your perceptions, your emotions, and ultimately your reality.

In many cases, people don't carefully consider which thoughts they entertain. They allow any random thought to move in and stay as long as it wants. A worry walks through the door, and they offer it a seat and a meal. A fear knocks, and they invite it to stay the night. A doubt arrives, and they give it a permanent room. Then they wonder why their mental house feels crowded, chaotic, and uncomfortable.

The master thinker is selective about which thoughts receive the privilege of attention. Not every thought that arises deserves to be entertained. Some thoughts should be acknowledged briefly and then dismissed. "Thank you for visiting, but you're not staying here." Others should be welcomed warmly and invited to stay. "Yes, come in and make yourself at home."

Today, pay attention to which thoughts you're entertaining. Are you giving your best mental hospitality to worry, fear, and doubt? Or are you entertaining thoughts of possibility, gratitude, and growth?

Be selective. Your mind is valuable real estate—only entertain thoughts worthy of living there.

January 30

You are not your thoughts; you are the observer of your thoughts.

One of the most liberating realizations possible is this: you are not your thoughts. You are the consciousness that witnesses thoughts. There is a part of you—your awareness—that stands apart from the stream of thoughts, able to observe them without being controlled by them.

It's common for people to be so identified with their thoughts that they believe "I am thinking" means "I am my thoughts." But this is an illusion. If you can observe your thoughts, you must be something other than your thoughts. This distinction is transformative. When you identify as your thoughts, you're trapped by them. A negative thought feels like truth, an identity statement, a limitation. When you recognize yourself as the observer of thoughts, you gain freedom.

A negative thought is just a thought—you can observe it, consider it, and choose whether to believe it or not.

Today, practice this distinction. When a thought arises, instead of thinking "I am anxious" or "I am not good enough," notice "I'm having the thought that I'm anxious" or "I'm observing the thought that I'm not good enough." This subtle linguistic shift creates psychological space between you and the thought. From this space, you can choose: Which thoughts will I believe and act on? Which thoughts will I simply observe and release? This is the beginning of true mental freedom.

January 31

Master your thoughts and you master your life.

This is the culmination of everything we've explored this month: life mastery begins and ends with thought mastery. Not time management, not money management, not people management—thought management.

Because when you master your thoughts, everything else falls into place naturally. Your time organizes itself around your priorities. Your money flows more easily. Your relationships improve. Your health strengthens. Your opportunities multiply. Why? Because thoughts are the source code of your reality. Every other area of life is downstream from consciousness. The person who cannot control their thoughts cannot control their life, no matter how many external strategies they employ.

Conversely, the person who has mastered their thinking can create success in any circumstance. This doesn't mean you'll never have negative thoughts or face difficulties. Mastery doesn't mean perfection; it means sovereignty. It means you're no longer at the mercy of random mental patterns. You've become the conscious director of your mental state, choosing thoughts intentionally rather than accepting whatever thoughts happen to arise.

As you close this month, reflect on your journey. Have you become more aware of your thinking patterns? Have you begun to choose your thoughts more consciously? Have you noticed any shifts in your external circumstances as your internal consciousness has shifted?

This is just the beginning. The practice of thought mastery is lifelong, but every moment of conscious thought selection is a moment of life creation. Continue building this foundation, for everything else depends on it.

February

Reprogramming the Subconscious

Changing your mind

February 1

Your brain is programmable.

You are not stuck with the brain you have. Neuroscience has shattered the old belief that the brain is fixed and unchangeable after a certain age. The discovery of neuroplasticity reveals that your brain physically rewires itself based on how you use it. Every thought you think, every action you take, every experience you have is literally reshaping your neural networks.

This means the programming you received in childhood—the limiting beliefs, the fear-based patterns, the inherited conditioning—is not permanent. You can reprogram your brain at any age. But here's the catch: your brain will be programmed either deliberately or accidentally. If you don't take conscious control of this process, your brain will be programmed by your environment, your past experiences, and your unconscious patterns. Many walk through life with outdated software running their lives—programs installed decades ago that no longer serve who they are or where they're going.

Let today mark the beginning of your conscious reprogramming. You're going to update your mental software, install new programs that serve your current goals, and delete old programs that hold you back. When you consistently think new thoughts and practice new behaviors, your brain physically changes. New neural connections form, old ones weaken, and gradually, your automatic responses shift. The person you're becoming is being physically constructed in your brain right now through your thoughts and choices.

February 2

What you practice, you become.

Your brain allocates resources based on what you do most frequently. If you practice worry, you become skilled at worrying. If you practice gratitude, you become skilled at finding things to appreciate. This isn't motivational philosophy, it's neurobiology. Every time you repeat a thought or behavior, you strengthen that neural pathway, making it easier to repeat in the future. Repeated often enough, and it becomes automatic, effortless, your default mode.

For many, unconscious patterns are quietly undermining their success. Past hurts are rehearsed until victimhood becomes familiar. Worst-case scenarios are imagined until anxiety feels normal. Attention stays fixed on what's wrong until limitation becomes habitual. Then it's surprising when suffering feels effortless and thriving feels difficult.

Transformation begins with intention. What do you actually want to become excellent at? Peace? Confidence? Focus? Resilience? Choose one quality, and then practice it deliberately. If you want peace, practice peaceful thoughts and responses throughout the day. If you want to become confident, practice confident posture, confident self-talk, confident actions. Don't wait until you feel ready. Practice creates the feeling, not the other way around.

Today, identify one mental or emotional quality you want to develop. Then create small opportunities to practice it repeatedly throughout the day. Remember: you don't rise to the level of your goals; you fall to the level of your practice.

February 3

Repetition rewires the brain.

The key to lasting change lies in consistent repetition. When you repeat a new thought or behavior consistently over time, you create new neural pathways that eventually become stronger than the old ones. This process, called neuroplasticity, means you're literally reconstructing your brain through repetition.

The first time you think a new empowering thought, it feels awkward and forced. The hundredth time, it feels more natural. The thousandth time, it becomes automatic. This is your brain rewiring itself to support your new identity. Many times, people give up too soon, before the new pathway has had time to solidify. They try a new pattern for a few days, don't see immediate results, and revert to old habits. But the brain requires sustained repetition—typically 60 to 90 days—before new patterns become established.

Today, commit to one new thought or behavior you'll repeat daily for the next three months. Write it down. Set reminders. Track your consistency. Trust that with each repetition, you're physically changing your brain, even when you can't see or feel the changes yet. The transformation is happening at the neural level long before it becomes visible in your life.

February 4

Your subconscious accepts whatever you consistently tell it.

Your subconscious mind is like a faithful servant—it doesn't question, doesn't judge, doesn't argue. It simply accepts as truth whatever your conscious mind tells it repeatedly. This is both the danger and the opportunity.

If you consistently tell yourself "I'm not capable," your subconscious accepts this as fact and works to prove it true. If you consistently tell yourself "I'm becoming more capable every day," your subconscious accepts this equally and works to make it true. The subconscious cannot distinguish between real experiences and vividly imagined ones, between truth and repeated lies. It operates on the principle of acceptance and manifestation.

Many unknowingly program their subconscious with limiting beliefs through repetitive negative self-talk. "I'm so stupid." "I never get lucky." "I can't do anything right." Repeated thousands of times, these statements become the subconscious operating system, directing behavior and creating matching circumstances.

Today, become aware of what you're consistently telling your subconscious. Then begin consciously programming it with empowering statements. Use present tense affirmations with emotion and repetition. Your subconscious is listening to every word, make sure you're giving it instructions that serve your highest good.

February 5

You must become the person
who has what you want before you can have it.

This principle reverses how most people approach success. They think: "When I have the money, then I'll feel abundant. When I have the relationship, then I'll feel loved. When I have the success, then I'll feel confident." But the universe works in reverse.

You must first embody the consciousness of the person who has what you want, and then the external manifestation follows. This isn't pretending or faking—it's aligning your internal state with your desired external state. The person who has financial abundance thinks differently, feels differently, and acts differently than the person experiencing scarcity. They're not worried or desperate; they're relaxed and confident about money. To become financially abundant, you must first adopt this consciousness, even while your bank account may show otherwise. This feels counterintuitive and even dishonest to many people, but it's actually how reality creation works.

Your external world is always reflecting your internal world. Change the internal first, and the external must follow.

Today, identify who you would need to become to have what you want. How would that version of you think? Feel? Act? Speak? Then begin embodying that identity now, not after the success arrives. Be it first, then you'll see it.

February 6

Breaking the habit of being yourself requires conscious effort.

You have an established identity—a habitual way of thinking, feeling, and acting that feels like "you." But this identity is not fixed; it's simply a pattern you've repeated so many times it feels permanent. Your current identity created your current life. To create a different life, you must become a different person.

Breaking free from your habitual self is challenging because the known, even when uncomfortable, feels safer than the unknown. Your body is addicted to the emotions you've been feeling for years. Your mind is attached to the thoughts you've been thinking. Stepping into a new identity means experiencing discomfort, uncertainty, and unfamiliarity. This is why it's common for people to return to old patterns even after making progress—the pull of the familiar is powerful.

But transformation requires you to become comfortable being uncomfortable. You must consciously override your automatic patterns, again and again, until the new pattern becomes your new automatic.

Today, notice when you're being your habitual self—the same reactions, the same thoughts, the same choices. Then consciously choose differently. Do something your old self wouldn't do. Think a thought your old self wouldn't think. Feel an emotion your old self wouldn't feel. Each conscious interruption of the old pattern weakens it and creates space for the new you to emerge.

February 7

Your emotions are the language of your body.

Every emotion you feel creates a cascade of chemical reactions throughout your body. When you feel stressed, your body releases cortisol. When you feel joyful, your body releases endorphins. These chemicals don't just affect your mood—they affect your immune system, your digestive system, your cardiovascular system, and your brain function.

Repeated emotional patterns create habitual chemical states that your body becomes addicted to. If you've spent years feeling anxious, your body has become chemically dependent on anxiety. Even when circumstances improve, your body will crave the familiar anxiety chemicals and will unconsciously create situations that justify feeling anxious again. This is why people often unconsciously self-sabotage just when things are going well—their body is demanding its familiar emotional chemistry.

Breaking free requires you to feel new emotions, even when circumstances haven't changed yet. You must teach your body a new chemical state—abundance instead of scarcity, peace instead of anxiety, excitement instead of dread. At first, this feels fake or forced because your body is screaming for its familiar chemistry. But persist. Generate the elevated emotions of your desired future every day, how you will feel in that future, and gradually your body will become addicted to these new chemical states instead and pull your desired future into your life path.

Today, choose one elevated emotion—gratitude, joy, inspiration—and deliberately cultivate it for 10 minutes, regardless of circumstances. You're chemically reprogramming your body.

February 8

Practice becoming greater than your environment.

People tend to allow their environment to control their internal state. Bad traffic makes them angry. A rude comment makes them upset. An unexpected bill makes them anxious. They've become stimulus-response machines, giving complete power to external circumstances.

Elevated Emotion Meditation is the practice of deliberately generating and sustaining elevated emotional states independent of external circumstances. When you sit quietly and consciously direct your thoughts and emotions regardless of what's happening around you, you're training yourself to become greater than your environment. You're proving to yourself that you have sovereignty over your internal world. This isn't about escaping reality or bypassing problems. It's about claiming your power to choose your state of being independent of circumstances.

The person who can maintain peace amidst chaos, abundance amidst scarcity, and love amidst hostility has true power. This power isn't developed through positive thinking alone; it's developed through the daily practice of meditation, where you train your mind and emotions to respond to your direction rather than environmental triggers.

Today, spend 10 minutes in meditation. Sit quietly, close your eyes, and consciously generate feelings of peace, gratitude, or joy without any external reason. Notice how difficult this may feel at first. The mind may want to return to problems, the body may seek familiar emotions. But overcome yourself and be still. This practice is building your capacity to become greater than your circumstances.

February 9

The moment you decide to change is the moment everything changes.

There's a profound difference between wanting to change and deciding to change. Wanting is passive, conditional, contingent. "I want to change... if it's not too hard, if circumstances cooperate, if I feel motivated." Deciding is active, unconditional, and committed. "I have decided to change, period. Circumstances are irrelevant. Feelings are irrelevant. I am doing this."

In the quantum field of possibility, the moment you make a true decision—not a wish, not a hope, but an absolute decision—the universe begins rearranging itself to match your decision. This isn't a mystical theory; it's because a real decision changes your frequency, your perception, your actions, and therefore your results. You begin noticing opportunities you previously overlooked. You take actions you previously avoided. You persist where you previously quit.

The difference between wanting and deciding is commitment—and commitment shows up in action. We often entertain possibilities while maintaining escape routes, calling this a "decision." Real decision means burning the ships, cutting off retreat, committing fully.

Today, identify one area where you've been wanting change but haven't truly decided. What would it look like to actually decide? What would you do differently today if you had genuinely decided? Then do those things. Make the decision real through action. The moment you truly decide, you'll feel a shift—that's the universe responding to your new frequency.

February 10

Your personality creates your personal reality.

Your personality is not your authentic self—it's a constructed identity made up of thoughts you keep thinking, emotions you keep feeling, and behaviors you keep repeating. This personality determines how you perceive the world, how you respond to situations, what you believe is possible, and ultimately what you experience as reality.

If your personality includes chronic worry, you'll create a reality that gives you things to worry about. If your personality includes limiting beliefs about money, you'll create financial limitation. If your personality includes victim consciousness, you'll create situations where you're victimized. This is not punishment—it's creation. Your personality is literally generating your personal reality through its habitual patterns.

The liberating truth is that you can change your personality. It's not fixed at birth or set in stone by your past. Personality is simply a habit, and habits can be changed through conscious effort. To create a new personal reality, you must first create a new personality. This means identifying which thoughts, emotions, and behaviors are generating your current unwanted reality, then consciously replacing them with new patterns that align with your desired reality.

Today, ask yourself: What personality created my current reality? What personality would create my desired reality? Then begin showing up as that new personality, even before your reality has changed. Remember: personality creates personal reality, not the other way around.

February 11

You cannot create a new future by holding on to the emotions of the past.

Every time you recall a memory and feel the emotions associated with it, you're literally living in the past. Your body doesn't know the difference between the actual experience and the memory of it—both create the same chemical response. So when you replay that betrayal, that failure, that hurt, you're not just remembering the past, you're recreating it in your present moment and projecting it into your future.

This is why people who can't let go of past hurts seem to continue to attract similar hurtful situations. They're carrying the emotional signature of the past into every new moment. The future you desire requires a different emotional state than the past you experienced. If your past was characterized by lack, but you continue feeling the emotions of lack, you're creating more lack regardless of your positive affirmations or visualization practices.

The work is to consciously release the emotional charge from past events. This doesn't mean denying that things happened or pretending you weren't affected. It means choosing to no longer be energetically tethered to those events.

Today, identify one past event that still carries emotional charge when you think about it. Then consciously practice overcoming the previous emotion and feeling the elevated emotions of your desired future—peace, joy, abundance, love—without waiting for circumstances to justify these feelings. Each time you do this, you're breaking the energetic bond with the past and creating space for a new future to emerge.

February 12

Changing your state changes your life.

Your state—the combination of your thoughts, emotions, and physiology at any given moment—determines what you can perceive, what actions you'll take, and what results you'll create. When you're in a state of fear, you literally cannot see opportunities; your perception narrows to threats. When you're in a state of confidence, opportunities become visible everywhere. Same circumstances, different state, completely different experience.

People often try to change their circumstances while remaining in the same state that created those circumstances. This is futile. Your state is the cause; circumstances are the effect. Change the state, and circumstances must eventually change to match. The powerful realization is that you can change your state at will, in an instant, through conscious choice. You don't need to wait for circumstances to improve before you can feel better. You can decide right now to shift your physiology (stand differently, breathe differently, move differently), your focus (think about different things), and your emotional chemistry (generate elevated emotions). This isn't positive thinking or denial—it's taking conscious control of your state rather than leaving it at the mercy of circumstances.

Today, practice state management. When you notice yourself in a disempowered state, don't try to think your way out. Instead, change your physiology first—stand up, move, breathe deeply, change your facial expression. Then direct your focus to something empowering. Feel the shift. This is how you reclaim sovereignty over your experience.

February 13

The body is the unconscious mind.

Your body stores every memory, every trauma, every repeated emotional pattern in its cells, tissues, and nervous system. When you can't consciously remember why you react a certain way, your body remembers. It's carrying the emotional signature of past experiences and automatically recreating them through chemical and energetic patterns.

This is why you can have intellectual insights about what you should do differently, yet your body keeps doing the same old thing. Your conscious mind says "I want to be confident," but your body remembers years of feeling insecure and automatically recreates that familiar state. The body literally becomes addicted to certain emotional chemicals and will sabotage your conscious intentions to get its fix.

This is why changing your thinking alone isn't enough—you must also reprogram your body. This happens through two processes: First, consciously interrupt the body's automatic emotional patterns by refusing to indulge in familiar negative feelings. When your body craves anger, anxiety, or sadness, consciously choose different emotions instead. Second, teach your body new emotional states through consistent practice. Generate feelings of gratitude, joy, and abundance daily until your body becomes addicted to these elevated emotions instead.

Today, notice when your body is pulling you toward familiar negative emotions. Feel the physical sensation of that pull—it's real, it's chemical, it's your body wanting its drug. Then consciously generate a different emotion by redirecting your focus to something you're genuinely grateful for—a memory, a person, a simple blessing. Gratitude is the key that unlocks your body from its addiction to negative emotions. This is how you liberate your body from its unconscious programming.

February 14

To change your life you must change your energy.

Everything is energy, vibrating at different frequencies. Your thoughts are energy. Your emotions are energy. Your physical body is energy. The circumstances you experience are energy. When your personal energy—the combination of your thoughts, emotions, and physiology—vibrates at a certain frequency, you attract circumstances that match that frequency. This is not metaphysics; it's physics. Low-frequency energy (fear, anger, shame, victimhood) attracts low-frequency circumstances (drama, conflict, scarcity). High-frequency energy (love, joy, gratitude, creation) attracts high-frequency circumstances (opportunity, connection, abundance).

Often people try to change their circumstances while maintaining the same energy that created those circumstances. They want better relationships while broadcasting the energy of resentment. They want financial abundance while broadcasting the energy of lack. It doesn't work because energy always attracts matching energy. The transformation begins when you realize you have complete control over your energy. You can't always control events, but you can always control how much energy you give to those events, what emotional frequency you choose, and what thoughts you entertain.

Today, become aware of the energy you're broadcasting. Is it the energy of your desired reality or your current reality? If it's not matching what you want, consciously shift it. Change your thoughts, elevate your emotions, adjust your physiology. Your energy is your creative power—use it consciously.

February 15

> *Where you place your attention is where you place your energy.*

Your attention is not passive observation—it's active energy investment. Whatever you give attention to receives your life force, your creative power, and your capacity to affect reality. When you place attention on your problems, you're literally energizing them, feeding them, making them grow stronger and more real in your experience. When you place attention on possibilities or solutions, you're energizing those instead.

People have a tendency to scatter their attention across hundreds of different concerns throughout the day, wondering why nothing substantial manifests. They give little attention to their goals or desires, and far more to their problems, fears, and distractions that serve no purpose. This scattered attention produces scattered results—lots of motion, little creation.

Mastery requires the consolidation of attention. Choose one thing that truly matters—one goal, one vision, one creation—and give it sustained, focused attention. Not occasionally, but daily. Not passively, but with emotional intensity. When you consolidate your attention this way, you're concentrating your creative energy like a laser beam rather than dispersing it like a flashlight.

Today, notice where your attention habitually goes. Are you giving your precious life force to news that upsets you? To social media that drains you? To problems that don't serve you? Consciously redirect your attention to what you want to create, what you want to expand, what you want to experience.

Your attention is your most valuable currency—spend it wisely.

February 16

> *The quantum field responds to who*
> *you are being, not who you want to be.*

You cannot trick the universe. You can say all the right affirmations, do all the right visualizations, and follow all the right techniques, but if your being—your actual state of consciousness—doesn't match your words, nothing will manifest.

As Dr. Joe Dispenza teaches, the quantum field contains all possibilities—every potential future already exists there as information and energy. We bring things to life through the combination of our attention and energy. When we tune into a desired future in the quantum field and intentionally observe that potential with focused attention and elevated emotion, we create an experience now that can manifest in our physical future.

Throughout your day, when you catch yourself in old emotions—anxiety, scarcity, unworthiness—pause and ask: "How would the version of me who already has this feel right now?" Then connect your attention and energy to that reality. Think the thoughts that person would think. Feel the emotions they would feel. Embody their energy in how you stand, speak, and make decisions.

This is not pretending—it's tuning into the version of your future that already exists in the quantum field and making it real through your sustained attention and emotional energy.

Today, practice being the person who already has what you desire throughout your day. Each time you align your being with your desired future, you're collapsing that quantum possibility into physical reality.

February 17

*Your brain doesn't know the difference
between a real experience and an imagined one.*

When you vividly imagine an experience with emotional intensity, your brain creates the same neural patterns as if the experience were actually happening. This is not metaphorical—neuroimaging studies prove that mental rehearsal activates the same brain regions as physical practice.

Athletes use this principle to improve performance by mentally rehearsing their sport. You can use it to reprogram any area of your life. When you mentally rehearse your desired future with rich sensory detail and elevated emotion, you're literally installing the neural hardware for that future. Your brain is building the circuits, creating the connections, and establishing the patterns that will make that future feel familiar when it arrives.

This is why visualization with elevated emotion works—not because of magical thinking, but because you're neurologically preparing yourself for the reality you desire. Most people never practice this. They spend their mental rehearsal time imagining worst-case scenarios and reliving past failures while feeling regret, remorse, or shame, installing neural patterns for more of what they don't want.

Today, spend 10 minutes mentally rehearsing your ideal day from start to finish. See it in detail, feel the emotions, engage all your senses. Don't just visualize—emotionally embody the experience. Your brain is recording this as real, creating the neural pathways that will make this future inevitable. This isn't wishful thinking—this is neurological programming.

February 18

You must become uncomfortable to become unlimited.

Every limitation you experience is paired with a comfort zone. You're limited financially because even though you may want more money, the fear of failure or judgment keeps you from taking bigger risks or putting yourself out there. You're limited in relationships because even though you may want connection, protecting yourself feels safer than being vulnerable. You're limited in health because even though you may want to be healthier, your current routine feels easier than making uncomfortable changes.

The limitation isn't external—it's your addiction to comfort. Growth and comfort cannot coexist. Every expansion requires you to step into discomfort, uncertainty, and unfamiliarity. Your body will resist because the known, even when painful, feels safer than the unknown. Your mind will generate excuses, rationalizations, and fears to keep you in familiar territory. This is not weakness—it's biology.

But transformation requires you to override these survival mechanisms. You must become comfortable being uncomfortable. You must learn to recognize the sensation of discomfort as a sign you're expanding rather than as a warning to retreat.

Today, consciously choose discomfort. Do something your habitual self wouldn't do. Have a conversation you've been avoiding. Take an action that feels uncertain. Each time you choose discomfort over comfort, you expand your capacity. Each time you retreat to comfort, you reinforce your limitations. The choice is always yours—unlimited growth or comfortable limitation. You cannot have both.

February 19

Coherence between your thoughts, feelings, and actions creates manifestation.

When your thoughts, emotions, and actions are aligned and moving in the same direction, you create coherence—a unified signal that powerfully broadcasts into the quantum field. This coherent signal manifests quickly because there's no internal contradiction, no mixed messages, no energetic static.

People often lack this coherence. They think one thing, feel another, and do something else entirely. They think about success, feel unworthy, and take actions based on fear. This incoherence creates a garbled signal that the universe cannot respond to clearly. It's like trying to tune into a radio station but landing between channels—you never get a clear signal, just noise and static.

Creating coherence requires you to align all three levels. Your thoughts must match your desired reality. Your emotions must match those thoughts. Your actions must match those emotions. When all three are synchronized, you become an unstoppable force of creation.

Today, check for coherence in one area of your life. Are your thoughts about this area empowering or limiting? Do your emotions match your thoughts? Do your actions match your emotions? Where you find incoherence, work to align the levels. If you want abundance, ensure your thoughts about money or resources are abundant, your feelings are elevated, and your actions are generous and confident. This alignment creates the coherence that makes manifestation inevitable.

February 20

The present moment is where all power exists.

When you're ruminating about the past, you have no power—the past is unchangeable. When you're anxious about the future, you have no power—the future hasn't happened yet. The only moment where you have complete creative authority is right now.

This present moment is where you can choose a new thought, feel a new emotion, or take a new action. Yet people spend almost no time in the present moment. They're either rehashing yesterday or rehearsing tomorrow, missing the only moment where change is actually possible. This is why presence is so emphasized in transformative teachings—not because the present moment is peaceful (though it often is), but because it's powerful.

When you bring your full awareness into the present moment, you reclaim your creative authority. You can choose right now what to think, regardless of what you thought before. You can choose right now what to feel, regardless of circumstances. You can choose right now what to do, regardless of past patterns.

Today, practice coming back to the present moment repeatedly. When you notice yourself lost in past or future, gently return to now. Feel your body. Notice your breath. Engage your senses. This moment, right now, is where your power resides. The more time you spend fully present, the more creative power you have access to. Your entire life can transform in a single present moment—if you're actually there to experience it.

February 21

Your beliefs are just thoughts you keep thinking.

The beliefs that currently run your life—about money, relationships, success, yourself—are not fundamental truths. They're simply thoughts you've kept thinking until they hardened into beliefs—many adopted from parents, teachers, or culture without ever questioning them. Any belief can be dissolved and replaced with a new one through the same process that created it: repetition.

The challenge is that beliefs feel like truth. When you believe "money is hard to come by," you don't experience it as a belief—you experience it as an accurate observation of reality. But it's not the truth or reality; it's a filter through which you're viewing reality, causing you to notice all evidence that supports the belief while dismissing evidence that contradicts it—effectively creating reality blinders.

To change a belief, you must first recognize it as a belief rather than truth. This creates distance—you shift from "money is hard to come by" (accepted as fact) to "I believe money is hard to come by" (recognized as just a thought, which can be examined and changed). Then you install a new belief through repetition. Choose a new thought that serves you better: "Money flows to me easily." Think this new thought repeatedly, feel it emotionally, look for evidence that supports it. Initially, it will feel false because your old belief is still dominant. But continually persist and eventually, the new thought becomes your new belief, and your reality will shift to match it.

Today, identify one limiting belief. Recognize it as just a thought you've been thinking, not as truth. Then begin thinking a new thought that serves you better.

February 22

You must mentally rehearse your new self before your body believes it.

Your body is living in the past—it's memorized emotions, beliefs, and behaviors from years of conditioning. Even when your mind decides to change, your body wants to remain the person you've always been because that's familiar, safe, and predictable. This is the gap between intention and manifestation that frustrates so many people.

Your mind says "I'm confident" but your body feels insecure, and the body wins because its signals are stronger. The solution is mental rehearsal. Before your body can become your new self, your mind must convince your body that this new self is real, safe, and beneficial. You do this through vivid, emotional mental rehearsal of being your new self. See yourself acting confidently in various situations. Feel the emotions of confidence in your body. Rehearse the physical posture, voice, and movements of confident you. Do this daily, with intensity, until your body begins to recognize this new self as familiar.

Your body will resist at first because change feels threatening to its survival mechanism. But through consistent mental rehearsal, you're teaching your body that this new self is safe, even beneficial. Eventually, your body stops resisting and starts supporting the change.

Today, spend 10 minutes mentally rehearsing being your new self. Make it vivid, emotional, and sensory. This isn't daydreaming—this is actively programming a new reality with your imagination. You're teaching your body who you're becoming so it can support you rather than sabotage your transformation.

February 23

Every time you react the same way, you reinforce the same pattern.

Your brain creates neural pathways through repetition. Every time you react to stress with anxiety, you strengthen the stress-anxiety neural pathway, making that response more automatic in the future. Every time you react to challenge with defeat, you strengthen the challenge-defeat pathway. You're literally training your brain to respond in these ways. For many, this happens unconsciously.

A trigger appears, and they react automatically according to their established neural pathways without ever choosing their response. Then they wonder why they keep experiencing the same patterns, attracting the same problems, feeling the same emotions. The pattern persists because you keep reinforcing it through repetition. Breaking this cycle requires conscious interruption. When a familiar trigger appears, you must pause before reacting. In that pause, you have choice. Will you respond according to your old pattern, strengthening that neural pathway? Or will you observe the choice at hand and choose a different response, beginning to create a new pathway?

The first few times you choose differently, it will feel awkward, forced, and likely unnatural. That's your brain protesting the disruption of its established pathway. But persist. Each time you respond differently, you weaken the old pathway and strengthen a new one.

Today, identify one automatic reaction you want to change. Then commit to pausing before reacting. In that pause, consciously choose a different response. This pause is where your power lives—the power to reprogram yourself through conscious choice rather than automatic repetition.

February 24

Elevated emotions carry elevated information.

When you're in a low emotional state—stress, fear, anger, shame—your perception narrows dramatically. Your brain shifts into survival mode, focused exclusively on threat detection. In this state, you cannot access your higher cognitive functions, your creativity, your intuition, or your connection to infinite intelligence. The information available to you is limited to "how do I survive this moment?"

Conversely, when you're in an elevated emotional state—gratitude, joy, love, inspiration—your perception expands. Your brain opens to possibility, pattern recognition, creative insight, and intuitive knowing. Information that was invisible to you in a low state becomes obvious in an elevated state. This is why your best ideas come when you're relaxed and happy, not when you're stressed and struggling.

The practical application is profound: if you want access to better information, insights, and solutions, you must first elevate your emotional state. You cannot think your way into an elevated state from a low state—you must first change your emotional chemistry through conscious practice. Generate feelings of gratitude, appreciation, or love without needing external reasons. As you elevate your emotions, you'll notice your thinking becomes clearer, solutions appear, and opportunities become visible.

Today, before trying to solve a problem or make a decision, first spend five minutes generating elevated emotions like love, gratitude or joy. Then notice how different your thinking becomes, how much more information is available to you. Elevated emotions aren't luxuries—they're the gateway to elevated information.

February 25

You cannot change what you refuse to acknowledge.

Many people avoid looking honestly at their patterns, behaviors, and beliefs because acknowledgment feels like judgment or failure. So they remain in denial, pretending everything is fine while their lives reflect the very patterns they refuse to see. This denial keeps them stuck because you cannot change what you won't acknowledge.

Acknowledgment is not the same as judgment. To acknowledge means to see clearly: "I have a pattern of self-sabotage. I have beliefs about unworthiness. I react with anger when I feel threatened." This clear seeing doesn't mean you're bad or broken—it means you're aware. And awareness is the first requirement for change. Without acknowledging the current pattern, you'll keep repeating it unconsciously while wondering why nothing improves. The courage to look honestly at yourself, to acknowledge your patterns without defense or justification, is the beginning of transformation.

Today, identify one pattern you've been avoiding acknowledging. Perhaps it's how you respond to criticism, how you handle money, how you behave in relationships. Look at it clearly, without judgment or excuse. Simply acknowledge: "This is what I do. This is the pattern." Once acknowledged, the pattern loses some of its unconscious power over you. You've brought it into the light where it can be examined, understood, and ultimately changed. But this process begins with the willingness to acknowledge what is, not what you wish was or what you pretend is. Truth is the foundation of transformation.

February 26

The gap between where you are and
where you want to be is your personal growth and journey.

Commonly, people view the gap between their current reality and their desired reality as a problem, something to be eliminated as quickly as possible. They want to be "there" without having to traverse the distance between here and there. But this gap is not an obstacle. It's the journey itself, the classroom where you develop the consciousness required to sustain your desired reality.

If you could instantly have everything you want without the growth journey, you'd lack the consciousness to maintain it. This is why lottery winners often return to poverty—they received the result without making the journey that would have prepared them to keep it. The gap is where you develop new skills, new beliefs, new behaviors. It's where you become the person who can not only achieve the goal but maintain it.

Today, reframe how you view the gap. Instead of frustration that you're not there yet, feel appreciation that you're on the journey. Every challenge you face in this gap is developing qualities you'll need in your desired reality. Every setback is teaching you resilience. Every fear you overcome is building courage. The gap is not keeping you from your goal—it's preparing you for it. Embrace the journey. Trust the process. Know that the person you're becoming through traversing this gap is exactly who you need to be to live your desired reality sustainably.

> *Your future is not a continuation*
> *of your past unless you carry your past forward.*

The future is not predetermined. It's not a straight-line projection from your past experiences. Yet for many, the future is remarkably similar to the past because they carry their past forward through their consciousness. They carry forward past traumas as present fears. They carry forward past failures as current limitations. They carry forward past identities as who they are today. This mental baggage ensures the future replicates the past.

But you have a choice: you can travel light into your future. You can leave the past where it belongs—behind you. This doesn't mean denying that events happened or pretending you weren't affected. It means refusing to let those events dictate your future. The betrayal you experienced doesn't have to make you cynical forever. The failure you encountered doesn't have to define your capabilities permanently. The limitations of your childhood don't have to be the limitations of your adulthood. Your future is being created fresh in each moment based on your current consciousness, not your past experiences. If you think thoughts that match your past, you'll recreate your past. If you think thoughts that match your desired future, you'll create that future.

Today, identify what you're carrying forward from your past that doesn't serve your future. What old stories are you repeating? What past-based identities are you clinging to? Then consciously choose to leave them behind. Pack light for your journey forward.

February 28

Transformation is not changing who you are; it's remembering who you really are.

You were not born believing you're limited, unworthy, or incapable. You learned these beliefs. Beneath all the conditioning, beneath all the limiting patterns, beneath all the false identities, there exists your authentic self—unlimited, creative, and powerful.

Personal transformation is not about becoming someone new; it's about removing the layers of conditioning that obscure who you truly are. Think of it as a sculptor removing marble to reveal the form that was always there, or clouds dissipating to reveal the sun that was always shining. Your work is not to create a new self but to uncover your authentic self by releasing what is false.

Every limiting belief you release reveals more of your true nature. Every fear you overcome brings you closer to your authentic power. Every pattern you transform returns you to your original design. This perspective removes pressure. You're not trying to achieve some impossible standard or become someone you're not. You're simply returning to yourself, remembering what you forgot, reclaiming what was always yours.

Today, beneath all your conditioned responses and learned limitations, feel for that authentic self. Who are you when you're not trying to be anyone? What do you know about yourself when you're not listening to others' opinions? This is who you really are. Your transformation journey is simply the path back home to this authentic self. Welcome yourself home.

March

Faith & Mental Equivalents

Building Belief Systems

March 1

Faith is the substance of things hoped for, the evidence of things not seen.

Faith is not passive hoping—it's a state of mind you deliberately develop through repetition and auto-suggestion. Napoleon Hill taught that faith is created by repeatedly passing instructions to your subconscious mind until it accepts them as truth and translates them into physical reality. When you have true faith, your subconscious believes you already possess your desire and begins creating its physical equivalent.

People tend to unknowingly develop faith in limitation through repetition. They repeatedly think "I'm not good enough," "money is hard to earn," or "success is for other people"—and their subconscious mind accepts these as orders and faithfully manifests them. The subconscious doesn't judge whether your repeated thoughts serve you—it simply acts on whatever you give it repeatedly.

Today, begin consciously developing faith through auto-suggestion. State your desire with emotion and conviction, as if you already possess it. Repeat this affirmation to your subconscious mind daily—morning and night. Conduct yourself as you would if you were already in possession of what you desire. This isn't pretending—this is how you instruct your subconscious mind to translate your desire into physical form.

Through repetition and emotional conviction, your subconscious mind will come to believe it. And what your subconscious believes, it creates. Faith is not given to you—it's a state of mind you develop through deliberate, repeated auto-suggestion.

March 2

> *Whatever you can conceive and believe, you can achieve.*

This principle reveals a crucial limitation: you cannot achieve what you cannot first conceive in your mind. If you cannot imagine yourself successful, you will not become successful—not because success is impossible, but because your mind literally cannot navigate toward something it cannot conceive. Your imagination sets the boundaries of your possible reality.

Most people severely limit their conceptions. They imagine slight improvements to their current situation but rarely conceive truly elevated realities because their imagination is constrained by their belief system. This creates a self-fulfilling prophecy: limited beliefs create limited conceptions, which create limited achievements, which reinforce limited beliefs. Breaking this cycle requires you to deliberately expand your conception beyond what you currently believe possible.

Let your imagination run wild. Conceive of extraordinary outcomes, remarkable success, profound transformation. Don't censor these conceptions with "but that's not realistic" or "that's not for people like me." Once you can conceive it, you've taken the first step toward believing it. Belief follows repeated conception—the more often you imagine a reality, the more believable it becomes. And once you truly believe it, achievement becomes inevitable.

Today, give yourself permission to conceive realities far beyond your current circumstances. Let imagination lead, let belief follow, let achievement naturally result. Your imagination is the workshop where your future is designed.

March 3

You must build a mental equivalent
before you can experience the physical manifestation.

A mental equivalent is a clear, detailed, emotionally-charged mental image of what you desire to experience. Before anything can manifest in your physical reality, it must first exist completely formed in your mental reality. The architect creates detailed blueprints before construction begins. The artist sees the finished piece before touching canvas. You must see your desired reality clearly and feel it emotionally before it can materialize.

Many never build proper mental equivalents. They have vague wishes rather than specific visions. They think occasionally about what they want rather than consistently holding the mental image. They imagine their desire intellectually but don't feel it emotionally. This weak mental equivalent produces weak results—or no manifestation at all.

Today, begin building a powerful mental equivalent of your primary desire. See it in specific detail: Where are you? What are you doing? Who is with you? What do you see, hear, feel, smell, touch? Make it so vivid that your mind cannot distinguish it from physical reality. Then charge it with elevated emotion—feel the joy, gratitude, excitement, pride of having achieved this desire. Hold this mental equivalent daily, adding more detail, intensifying the emotion. You're literally constructing the blueprint that physical reality will follow. The more complete and emotionally-charged your mental equivalent, the more inevitable and rapid the physical manifestation.

March 4

Doubt is faith in reverse — faith that it won't work out.

Every time you doubt, you're not lacking faith—you're directing faith toward what you don't want. Doubt is powerful. It has the same creative power as positive faith but directed inversely. When you doubt your ability to succeed, you're creating mental images of failure and feeling the emotions of defeat. This activates the same manifestation process but toward an unwanted outcome.

This faith in reverse often happens unconsciously. Doubt is mistaken for passive uncertainty, when in reality it's active creation toward negative outcomes. Hours are spent worrying about what might go wrong, imagining worst-case scenarios, and feeling the emotions of failure— then wondering why things continue to go wrong.

The solution is not to deny doubt when it arises, but to recognize it quickly and redirect it. When doubt appears, notice it: "I'm experiencing doubt, which means I'm currently directing my faith toward what I don't want." Then consciously redirect your faith: imagine what you do want, feel the emotions of success, and focus on desired outcomes. This isn't suppressing doubt—it's transforming it. You're recognizing doubt as misdirected creative power and consciously redirecting that same power toward what serves you.

Today, catch yourself whenever doubt arises. Don't fight it or judge it. Simply redirect: "I was directing my faith toward failure; now I'm redirecting it toward success." This conscious redirection gradually trains you to direct faith automatically toward desired outcomes.

Act as if it is, and it will be.

One of the most powerful principles of manifestation is to behave as if your desire is already fulfilled. Not pretending for others' benefit, but genuinely embodying the consciousness of someone who has what you want. This works because consciousness creates reality, not the other way around. When you act as if you're prosperous, your thinking aligns with abundance, your emotions shift from lack to sufficiency, and your decisions reflect confidence rather than fear. This consciousness then creates prosperous circumstances to match.

Although, many people do the opposite. They wait for circumstances to change before they'll change how they act. "When I have more money, then I'll feel abundant." But this keeps them trapped because their current consciousness keeps recreating their current circumstances. Acting as if reverses this sequence. You embody the consciousness of your desired reality now, and circumstances then shift to match. This doesn't mean spending money you don't have or being irresponsible. It means carrying yourself with the confidence of success before success arrives. It means thinking with the mindset of abundance before abundance manifests. It means feeling the emotions of your desired reality before you see physical evidence.

Today, identify one area where you want change. Then ask: How would I act if this desire was already fulfilled? How would I think, feel, speak, carry myself? Then begin acting that way now. Your consciousness is creating your reality; change the consciousness, and reality must follow.

March 6

Faith without works is dead.

Faith is essential but not sufficient. You must combine inner faith with outer action. Many people develop strong faith, visualize clearly, feel their desires emotionally, but take no action. They wait for the universe to deliver their desires while they remain passive. This misunderstands how manifestation works.

Faith opens doors, but you must walk through them. Faith creates opportunities, but you must seize them. Faith makes resources available, but you must use them. The universe responds to faith backed by action. When you combine clear mental images with elevated emotions and then take inspired action, you create an unstoppable force of manifestation. The action doesn't have to be perfect or complete—it just has to be in the direction of your desire.

Each action, no matter how small, signals to the universe that you're serious about your intention. It also signals to yourself that you believe what you're visualizing. Action proves faith. Without action, faith remains theoretical, untested, powerless to create physical change.

Today, identify one action you've been avoiding that would move you toward your desire. Then take that action, even if it's imperfect, even if you're afraid, even if you're not sure it will work. Your action activates your faith. Faith provides the vision and energy; action provides the vehicle and direction. Together, they create manifestation. Separately, they remain potential without fulfillment.

March 7

Your beliefs create your reality, but your faith creates your future.

Beliefs are about what you've accepted as true based on past evidence. Faith is about what you know is possible despite current evidence. Your beliefs create your present reality by filtering perception, directing action, and attracting matching circumstances. But faith creates your future reality by opening you to possibilities beyond your current belief system. This distinction is crucial. If you rely only on beliefs, you're trapped in the past. Your beliefs are built from past experiences, past conditioning, and past evidence. They can only recreate variations of what you've already experienced.

Faith transcends this limitation. It allows you to step into possibilities that have no precedent in your past, no evidence in your present. Faith is the bridge between where you are and where you want to be, especially when there's a large gap. When you have faith in a reality you haven't experienced yet, you begin thinking, feeling, and acting in ways that align with that future reality rather than your current reality. Gradually, this shifts your beliefs, which then shifts your reality.

Today, identify the difference between your beliefs and your faith. Your beliefs might say "this is how things are for people like me." Your faith says "but this is how things could be for me." Don't try to force your beliefs to change—that rarely works. Instead, strengthen your faith in new possibilities. As your faith grows stronger through practice, your beliefs will naturally update to match.

March 8

Perfect faith casts out fear.

Fear and faith cannot coexist in the same moment—they are opposing forces. When faith is strong, fear dissolves. When fear is strong, faith wavers. Many people experience wavering between these two states throughout the day. A moment of faith brings clarity and peace. Then fear creeps in bringing doubt and anxiety. They're caught in this oscillation, never establishing firm ground. The solution is to deliberately strengthen faith until it becomes your dominant state.

Perfect faith doesn't mean you'll never feel fear—it means when fear arises, your faith is strong enough that fear cannot maintain its grip. You feel the fear, acknowledge it, and then return to faith. Over time, as faith becomes more established, fear's visits become shorter and less intense. How do you develop perfect faith? Through consistent practice of choosing faith over fear, again and again, in small moments throughout the day.

Each time you face uncertainty and choose to trust rather than worry, you strengthen faith. Each time circumstances look difficult and you choose to believe in positive outcomes, you strengthen faith. Each time you're tempted to give up and you choose to persist with hope, you strengthen faith.

Today, notice when fear arises. Don't fight it or deny it. Simply recognize: "This is fear." Then consciously choose faith: "But I choose to trust that things are working out for my highest good." This conscious choice, repeated consistently, develops the perfect faith that casts out fear.

March 9

Hold the vision, trust the process, let go of the outcome.

This three-part principle balances intention with surrender. Hold the vision means maintaining a clear mental equivalent of your desired outcome—seeing it, feeling it, believing in it daily. Trust the process means having faith that the universe is orchestrating the perfect sequence of events to manifest your vision, even when you can't see how. Let go of the outcome means releasing attachment to specific timelines, methods, or forms that the manifestation must take.

People frequently struggle with this balance. Either they hold the vision but don't trust, constantly worrying about whether it will happen. Or they trust the process but don't hold a clear vision, passively waiting for something to happen. Or they can't let go of the outcome, trying to control every detail and becoming frustrated when things don't unfold according to their exact specifications.

All three elements must be present. Your clear vision gives the universe a target. Your trust allows the universe to work without your interference. Your letting go creates the space for manifestation to occur in ways you couldn't have orchestrated. When you combine all three—clear vision, absolute trust, and relaxed detachment—you become an unstoppable force of manifestation.

Today, practice this balance. Spend time visualizing your desire clearly and emotionally. Then consciously trust that everything is working out for your greatest good, even if current evidence suggests otherwise. Finally, release attachment to how or when it manifests. Your job is the vision and the trust; the universe's job is the manifestation.

March 10

According to your faith, it is done unto you.

This ancient wisdom reveals an uncomfortable truth: you are experiencing exactly the level of reality that matches your level of faith. Not the level you wish you had or the level you project to others, but the actual faith you hold internally. If you have faith that life is hard, you'll experience life as hard. If you have faith that you're not capable, you'll experience incapability. If you have faith that people can't be trusted, you'll attract untrustworthy people.

Your external reality is a mirror of your internal faith. This might feel harsh, especially if you're currently experiencing difficulties. But it's actually empowering because it means you can change your experience by changing your faith. You're not at the mercy of circumstances, other people, or luck—you're responding to the faith you've developed through repeated thought, which you can consciously redirect. The question to ask is not "Why is this happening to me?" but "What faith am I holding that is creating this experience?" When you identify the faith, you can change it.

Today, examine your current reality honestly. What does it reveal about your faith? Not your stated wishes or occasional affirmations, but the beliefs you've been reinforcing through repeated thought. If you're experiencing scarcity, you've likely been thinking scarcity thoughts more often than abundance thoughts—unconsciously building faith in limitation regardless of what you consciously want. If you're experiencing abundance, your habitual thoughts have aligned with abundance—you've developed faith in possibility. Once you see this connection clearly, you can begin consciously developing new faith through repeated thoughts. Faith isn't given to you—it's built by what you think consistently until your subconscious accepts it as truth.

March 11

Faith sees the invisible,
believes the incredible, and achieves the impossible.

Faith operates in a different realm than logic. Logic works with what is visible, proven, already manifested. Faith works with what is invisible, unproven, and not yet manifested. This is why faith is so powerful—it's not limited by current reality. Faith sees possibilities before they become visible.

It looks at an empty plot of land and sees a magnificent building. It looks at a failing business and sees a turnaround. It looks at a broken relationship and sees healing. It looks at poverty and sees prosperity. Faith doesn't deny current reality—it simply refuses to accept current reality as the final word.

To everyone else, certain achievements appear impossible because they're looking at current reality and projecting it forward. But the person with faith is looking from future reality backward, seeing a clear vision from where they are to where they're going, even if that vision isn't visible to others. This capacity to see what others cannot see, believe what others will not believe, and achieve what others deem impossible is what separates those who transform their lives from those who remain stuck.

Today, practice looking beyond what is visible. When you look at your life, your circumstances, your challenges, what invisible possibilities can you see? What incredible outcomes can you believe in despite lack of evidence? What impossible dreams can you commit to achieving? Let your faith expand beyond the boundaries of logic, reason, and current reality. This is where true transformation begins.

March 12

*You must build mental acceptance
before you can experience physical manifestation.*

Mental acceptance means that in your mind and emotions, you have fully accepted your desire as already accomplished. You don't hope it might happen. You don't think it could happen. You accept that it has happened, even while physical evidence is still absent.

This is the crucial step many people miss. They visualize, they affirm, they take action, but deep down they still haven't truly accepted the reality of their desire. There's a part of them that's still waiting, hoping, wondering if it will really happen. This lack of mental acceptance creates resistance that can block manifestation. True mental acceptance feels like relief, like completion. There's no more striving, no more desperate energy, no more checking obsessively for signs. You simply know it's done, the same way you know the sun will rise tomorrow.

Building mental acceptance requires you to live mentally in your desired reality. When you think about your desire, you don't think "I want this" or "I'm trying to create this." You think "I have this." You don't feel yearning; you feel satisfaction. You don't see it as future; you see it as present, simply not yet visible in physical form.

Today, practice mental acceptance. Instead of wanting your desire, accept that you have it. Feel the emotions not of pursuing but of possessing. Think thoughts not of hoping but of knowing. This shift in consciousness from seeking to having is the final step before physical manifestation.

March 13

Faith is the art of holding yourself in receptive attitude.

Many people approach manifestation with a pushing, forcing, desperate energy. They're trying to make things happen through sheer will. But faith operates differently—it's receptive rather than forceful. When you have true faith, you're not pushing for your desire; you're receiving it. The distinction is crucial. Pushing implies it doesn't exist yet and must be created through your effort. Receiving implies it already exists and is simply being delivered to you. This receptive attitude fundamentally changes your energy.

Instead of desperate grasping, you have relaxed confidence. Instead of anxious doing, you have peaceful allowing. Instead of forcing doors open, you're ready when doors open naturally. This doesn't mean you take no action—receptivity is active, not passive. You're actively watching for opportunities, actively responding to intuitive nudges, actively preparing yourself to receive. But the energy is one of expectant receiving rather than desperate pursuing.

Today, practice a receptive attitude. Instead of asking "How can I make this happen?" ask "How can I prepare myself to receive this?" Instead of forcing and pushing, relax and allow. Create space in your consciousness for your desire to flow in. Trust that what you desire is already on its way to you; your job is simply to be ready to receive it when it arrives. This receptive faith is magnetic—it draws to you what forcing would repel.

March 14

Your mental equivalent must be equal to your desire.

Many people wonder why their desires don't manifest despite visualization and affirmation. Often the problem is that their mental equivalent doesn't match their desire. They consciously want one thing, but their subconscious holds a different picture. Someone wants to earn more money, but the mental image that plays automatically—without effort—is themselves anxious about bills, checking their account with dread, feeling the tightness of scarcity. Another person wants partnership, but the picture their mind defaults to shows them alone, because solitude is what they've rehearsed mentally for so long it feels like identity. The mental equivalent is always accurate—it reflects your actual consciousness, not your stated desires. If your mental equivalent doesn't match your desire, the mental equivalent will win every time because it's what your subconscious has been trained to accept as real.

Upgrading your mental equivalent requires honest self-examination. What do you truly see when you imagine your future? What do you truly feel about your goal? What do you truly believe is possible for you? If there's a gap between your desire and your mental equivalent, you must do the work to upgrade the mental equivalent. This means consistently and deliberately visualizing your actual desire with emotion until it feels more familiar than your current mental equivalent. It means catching yourself when you slip back into the old mental equivalent and consciously redirecting to the new one.

Today, examine your primary desire and your mental equivalent for that desire. Close your eyes and imagine your desire—what image actually appears? What do you feel? If you notice yourself automatically picturing limitation instead of your desired outcome, that's your mental equivalent revealing itself. Begin the daily practice of upgrading your mental equivalent until it equals your desire. Remember: you don't get what you want; you get what you consistently hold as real in your consciousness.

March 15

Faith must be fed daily to stay strong.

Faith is not a one-time achievement but a daily practice. Just as your body needs daily food to maintain strength, your faith needs daily nourishment to remain strong. Without this daily feeding, faith weakens and doubt creeps in. How do you feed faith? Through consistent practices that reinforce your vision and elevate your consciousness.

Morning visualization sessions feed faith. Evening gratitude practices feed faith. Reading inspiring materials feeds faith. Associating with positive people feeds faith. Taking action toward your goals feeds faith. Celebrating small wins feeds faith.

People often unknowingly starve their faith while feeding their doubt. They expose themselves to negative news, toxic conversations, and discouraging information, then wonder why their faith feels weak. Meanwhile, they neglect the daily practices that would strengthen faith. Your consciousness is being shaped by whatever you're feeding it most consistently.

Today, commit to feeding your faith daily. Choose one or two practices that resonate with you—perhaps morning visualization and evening gratitude. Do these practices every single day, regardless of your mood or circumstances. Protect your consciousness from influences that weaken faith. Over time, you'll notice that your faith becomes strong and stable, less affected by circumstances, more rooted in inner knowing. This strong faith then makes manifestation not just possible but inevitable.

March 16

What you focus on with faith expands; what you focus on with fear shrinks.

Focus alone is not enough, the quality of consciousness you bring to your focus determines whether things expand or contract. When you focus on your goals with faith—believing they're possible, feeling excited about them, seeing yourself achieving them—that focus expands those goals into your reality. When you focus on your goals with fear—doubting they're possible, feeling anxious about achieving them, seeing obstacles everywhere—that fearful focus shrinks the goals, making them less likely to manifest.

The same principle applies to problems. When you focus on problems with fear, believing they're overwhelming, feeling anxious about them, seeing them getting worse—that focus expands those problems until they dominate your reality. But when you focus on problems with faith—believing solutions exist, feeling confident about resolving them, seeing pathways forward—that faithful focus shrinks the problems, making them easier to solve.

This is why two people can focus on the same thing and get opposite results. One focuses with faith and experiences expansion. The other focuses with fear and experiences contraction. The difference is not what they're focusing on, but the consciousness they're bringing to their focus.

Today, notice what you're focusing on and what consciousness you're bringing to that focus. Are you focusing on goals with faith or fear? Are you focusing on problems with faith or fear? When you catch yourself focusing with fear, consciously shift to focusing with faith. Change the emotion you're bringing to your attention. This shift in the quality of consciousness can dramatically change your results, even when the focus remains the same.

March 17

Your faith must be greater than your circumstances.

It's easy to have faith when everything is going well. The real test of faith comes when circumstances contradict your vision. This is when people tend to abandon their faith and accept their circumstances as reality. But this is precisely when faith is most important.

Your circumstances are the result of your past consciousness. They're showing you where you've been, not where you're going. If you let current circumstances define your faith, you'll only ever experience more of what you're currently experiencing. Your faith must be stronger than your circumstances. When circumstances say "impossible," your faith must say "possible." When circumstances say "you're failing," your faith must say "I'm succeeding." When circumstances say "give up," your faith must say "persist." This isn't denial—you acknowledge circumstances while refusing to let them dictate your faith.

You see what is while maintaining faith in what will be. This is difficult because circumstances feel very real and your faith might feel imaginary. But remember: your circumstances are temporary and changeable; your faith is the creative force that will change them.

Today, if you're facing challenging circumstances, practice keeping your faith stronger than those circumstances. Don't let what you see override what you believe. Don't let temporary conditions weaken your vision of permanent transformation. Your faith, maintained despite contradictory circumstances, is the force that will ultimately transform those circumstances.

March 18

Faith without feeling is just intellectual agreement.

You can intellectually agree that faith is important, that positive thinking works, that you should believe in your goals. But if this agreement doesn't reach the level of feeling, it remains powerless to create change. True faith is felt in your body, in your emotions, in your entire being. It's not just an idea you agree with; it's a state you embody.

Many people's faith is too intellectual. They think about their goals, they say they believe, but they don't feel the reality of their desires. When you truly have faith, you feel the emotions of your desired reality—joy, gratitude, excitement, peace—before you see physical evidence. This feeling-level faith is what creates manifestation because the vibrations of emotions are the language the quantum field of infinite possibilities responds to.

Your thoughts set direction, but your emotions provide the power. Think of it like a rocket: thoughts are the navigation system, emotions are the fuel. Without both, you don't launch.

Today, move your faith from your head to your heart. Instead of just thinking about what you want to create, feel what it would feel like to have already created it. Embody those emotions. Live in those feelings. Let faith become not just a mental concept but an emotional reality. When your faith reaches this feeling level, when you can close your eyes and truly feel your desire as real, manifestation becomes inevitable. You've created the feeling frequency that draws your desire from potential into physical reality.

Your faith will be tested before your manifestation appears.

There's almost always a period between when you commit to faith and when your desire manifests where it seems like nothing is happening or things are getting worse. This is the testing period, and it's where many people abandon their faith. They interpret the lack of immediate results or the appearance of obstacles as proof that their faith isn't working. But this testing period is actually part of the manifestation process. It's where your commitment is proven.

Anyone can have faith when circumstances are supportive. True faith is demonstrated when you maintain your vision despite contradictory evidence, when you keep believing when reason suggests you shouldn't. This period serves a purpose: it strengthens your faith, deepens your commitment, and ensures you're ready for what you're manifesting. If you abandon faith every time things get difficult, you're not ready to sustain success when it arrives. The testing period builds the consciousness required to maintain your manifestation.

Today, if you're in a testing period—if you've committed to faith but don't yet see results—don't interpret this as failure. See it as the strengthening period. Your faith is being tested not to break you but to prove itself, to become unshakeable. Every day you maintain faith despite contrary evidence is a day you're building the consciousness that will sustain your success. Pass the test by refusing to abandon your faith, and you'll discover that manifestation was happening all along, just beneath the surface of visible reality.

March 20

Faith makes the future real in the present.

The power of faith is that it collapses time. Instead of experiencing your desire as something distant in the future, faith makes it real right now. Not physically present yet, but energetically, emotionally, mentally present. When you have true faith, you're not hoping for a future reality; you're experiencing that reality now at the level of consciousness.

This is more than visualization or positive thinking. It's actually living in your desired reality internally while your external reality catches up. You think the thoughts you would think if your desire was already fulfilled. You feel the emotions you would feel. You make decisions you would make. You carry yourself the way you would carry yourself. In every way except physical manifestation, you're already living your desired reality. This present-moment reality of faith is what creates the physical manifestation.

People often keep their desires locked in the future: "One day I'll have that." But faith brings it into the now: "I have this now at the level of consciousness, and the physical manifestation is simply revealing what already exists."

Today, practice making your desired future real in the present. Don't relate to it as something you'll have; relate to it as something you have now, just not yet visible. This shift in consciousness from future to present is the secret to rapid manifestation. When you make it real now through faith, the physical manifestation must follow because physical reality always conforms to consciousness, eventually.

March 21

The size of your faith determines the size of your results.

You will never manifest beyond your faith capacity. If you have faith for small improvements, you'll experience small improvements. If you have faith for dramatic transformation, you'll experience dramatic transformation. Your results are always proportional to your faith.

This is why developing faith is so crucial—it determines your ceiling, your maximum possible achievement. Often, people have what could be called "reasonable faith"—faith that small, logical, probable things will happen. This reasonable faith produces reasonable results. But extraordinary results require extraordinary faith—faith that transcends logic, probability, and reason. The masters throughout history achieved the impossible not because they were more talented or lucky but because they had faith capacity for the impossible. They could hold faith for outcomes that others deemed unrealistic. This expanded their possible reality beyond normal limitations.

Today, examine the size of your faith. What are you capable of believing in? What's beyond your current level of faith? Then consciously begin expanding your faith. Start with achievable goals to build faith, then gradually increase the size of what you're willing to believe in. Each successful manifestation proves faith works and expands your capacity to have faith in something greater. Think of faith like a muscle—it grows stronger through consistent use. As your faith expands, so does your possibility. There is no limit to what you can manifest except the limit of what you can have faith in.

March 22

Faith is knowing without evidence, trusting without proof.

This is what makes faith so challenging for logical minds. Faith asks you to know something is true before you have evidence, to trust in an outcome before you have proof. Every fiber of your logical training resists this. You've been taught to believe only what you can see, prove, or verify. But faith operates beyond the realm of evidence and proof.

Faith is the evidence—it's the substance of things hoped for before they become physical. It's knowing, in your core, that something is true and real even when all external evidence says otherwise. This isn't blind belief or wishful thinking. It's a deeper knowing that comes from beyond the logical mind, from intuition, from connection to source and the quantum field of infinite possibility.

When you truly have faith, you don't need proof because you have inner certainty. You don't need evidence because you have internal validation. This doesn't mean you ignore reality or deny challenges. It means you trust a deeper reality beyond what's currently visible. You know that what exists in consciousness must eventually manifest in physical form.

Today, practice this kind of knowing. Choose something you deeply desire but have no proof it will happen. Then practice knowing it's already done, already real, already manifesting, and give thanks before it ever happens. When doubt arises asking "where's the proof?", respond with "my faith is my proof." This internal knowing, maintained consistently, creates the external proof you seek. Faith doesn't wait for evidence; faith creates evidence.

March 23

What you accept as true becomes true in your experience.

Acceptance is the final stage of manifestation. Before acceptance, you're hoping, wanting, trying, working toward something. After acceptance, you simply know it's done and now can receive. This acceptance is what seals the deal, so to speak. It's your consciousness declaring "this is now my reality" and refusing to entertain any other possibility.

For many, true acceptance never fully arrives. They keep checking—"Is it here yet? Will it really happen? Maybe I should have a backup plan just in case." This uncertainty prevents full acceptance. But when you truly accept something as your reality, you stop checking because there's nothing to check. You wouldn't keep checking whether you have a name or whether the sun will rise—you accept these as givens.

Your desire must reach this same level of acceptance to manifest fully. How do you cultivate acceptance? Through consistent faith practices that make your desire feel increasingly real until one day, you realize you're no longer hoping or believing—you simply accept it as done. There's a shift in your consciousness from "will this happen?" to "this is happening" to "this has happened." That final shift into "this has happened" is acceptance.

Today, practice accepting your desire as already accomplished. Every time you think about it, think from the end—from the place of already having it. Feel the emotions of completion rather than anticipation. Make decisions as if it's already done. And most importantly, give thanks as if it's already yours. This acceptance, maintained consistently, brings the manifestation into physical form.

March 24

Your mental picture must be definite and constant to manifest.

Vague wishes produce vague results or no results at all. The universe responds to clarity, specificity, and consistency. When your mental picture is fuzzy, changing daily, or contradictory, you're sending mixed signals that cancel each other out. One day you imagine success, the next day you dwell on failure. One moment you see abundance, the next moment you focus on lack. This inconsistency prevents manifestation because you're constantly changing your order, so to speak.

For powerful manifestation, your mental picture must be definite— clear, specific, detailed—and constant—held consistently without wavering. This doesn't mean thinking about it every second, but maintaining the same mental picture whenever you do think about it, and redirecting any time a limited or opposing thought enters your mind.

Many people make the mistake of constantly changing their vision. Today they want this, tomorrow they want that. They're like someone planting seeds and then digging them up every few days to plant different seeds. Nothing has time to grow.

Today, create one definite mental picture of your primary desire. Make it detailed and specific. Then commit to holding this exact picture constantly for the next 30 days minimum. Don't change it, don't add to it, don't modify it. Just hold it consistently, adding more detail and emotion but keeping the core picture the same. This definiteness and constancy give the universe a clear, stable target to manifest.

March 25

Faith requires patience — the seed must be planted before the harvest.

One of the greatest challenges of faith is the time lag between planting and harvesting. When a farmer plants seeds, they don't dig them up the next day to check if they're growing. They trust the natural process, water them consistently, protect them from harm, and patiently wait for the harvest.

Yet people practicing manifestation often lack this patience. They visualize for a few days, see no results, and conclude it's not working. They don't understand there's a gestation period, a time when the seed is growing beneath the surface before it becomes visible above ground. During this gestation period, your only job is to maintain faith and continue the daily practices that feed that faith. Not to check obsessively for signs, not to doubt because physical evidence hasn't appeared, not to abandon the vision because it's taking time. Just trust, persist, and wait with active patience. Active patience means you're not passive—you continue taking inspired action—but you're patient about the timeline.

Today, if you're in the waiting period between planting and harvesting, practice patient faith. Trust that things are happening for your greatest good, even when you can't see them. Water your seeds daily with visualization and positive elevated emotion. Protect them from the weeds of doubt and fear. And know with absolute certainty that if you maintain this process, the harvest is inevitable. The universe never fails to produce results that match your faith; it only operates on a different timeline than your urgency might prefer.

March 26

Gratitude is faith for what is, plus faith for what's coming.

Gratitude is one of the most powerful faith practices because it simultaneously acknowledges blessings in your present while holding faith for blessings in your future. When you practice gratitude for what you desire before you receive it, you're demonstrating the highest form of faith. You're giving thanks for what exists only in potential, which signals to the universe that you know it's already done.

This is the practice taught by the masters throughout ages: give thanks for your desire as if you've already received it. Feel genuine gratitude for its fulfillment, even while it's still invisible. This isn't pretending. You're reaching into the field where everything exists in potential, where the life you want has already taken shape—just not yet in physical form. By giving thanks now, you're collapsing the timeline between potential and manifestation.

It's common for people to reserve gratitude for after they receive something. But this limits their manifestation power. Gratitude is the ultimate state of receivership. When you feel genuine gratitude for something before it arrives, you're vibrating at the frequency of already having. You cannot be grateful and lacking simultaneously—gratitude declares completion, fulfillment, and abundance. This is the precise frequency the universe responds to, and giving thanks in advance accelerates manifestation.

Today, practice gratitude for what you're manifesting. Give genuine thanks for its arrival, even though you can't yet see it physically. Feel the emotion of gratitude as if your desire has already been fulfilled. This practice combines faith with elevated emotion—a powerful manifestation formula. Express gratitude morning and evening for your desire's fulfillment. Notice how this practice shifts your energy from yearning to receiving, from hoping to knowing.

March 27

Every thought is a prayer; every emotion is an offering.

You're constantly praying, constantly making offerings to the universe through your thoughts and emotions, whether you realize it or not. Every thought you think is sending out a signal, essentially saying "more of this, please." Every emotion you feel is broadcasting a frequency that attracts matching circumstances. The question isn't whether you're praying but what you're praying for.

Many people unknowingly pray for what they don't want. Through worried thoughts, they're praying for more difficulty. Through fearful emotions, they're praying for more fears to materialize. Through resentful thoughts, they're praying for more reasons to feel resentful. They would never consciously pray for these things, but their unconscious thought-patterns and emotional habits are doing exactly that.

When you understand that every thought is a prayer and every emotion is an offering, you become much more conscious about what you're thinking and feeling. You realize you're in constant communication with the creative force of the universe, and you want that communication to be intentional rather than accidental.

Today, become aware of your unconscious prayers. What are you repeatedly thinking about? What emotions are you habitually feeling? These are your prayers and offerings. Are they aligned with what you want to manifest? If not, consciously redirect them. Choose thoughts that pray for what you desire. Cultivate emotions that offer the frequency of your intended reality. Make every thought a conscious prayer, every emotion a deliberate offering.

March 28

> *Your faith must be bold enough to claim what seems impossible.*

Timid faith produces timid results. If you only have faith for what seems reasonable, logical, and likely, you'll only experience reasonable, logical, likely outcomes. These might be fine, but they'll never be extraordinary. Extraordinary outcomes require bold faith—faith that claims what others would call impossible, unrealistic, or naive. Bold faith says "I don't care that it's never been done. I don't care that others think it's impossible. I don't care that circumstances contradict it. I claim this outcome as mine." This boldness isn't arrogance; it's confidence in the creative power of consciousness.

It's understanding that impossibility is simply a current limitation, not an absolute boundary. Many things considered impossible in the past are commonplace today because someone had bold enough faith to make them real. Your bold faith might seem crazy to others. Let it. Their understanding of possibility is limited by their consciousness, not by true reality. When you claim bold outcomes with unwavering faith, you're accessing possibilities that don't yet exist in the collective consciousness. You're pioneering new territory.

Today, identify what bold outcome you want to claim. Not the reasonable goal that everyone would support, but the outcome that makes you slightly uncomfortable to claim because it seems too big, too unlikely, too extraordinary. Then claim it anyway. Let your faith be bold enough to reach for what seems impossible. This bold faith is the only force powerful enough to make the impossible possible.

March 29

The universe always says yes to your dominate faith.

The universe is not selective about which faith it responds to. It says yes to whatever faith is dominant in your consciousness, whether that faith is positive or negative, empowering or limiting. If your dominant faith is "I'm not good enough," the universe says yes and creates circumstances that make you feel not good enough. If your dominant faith is "I'm becoming more capable every day," the universe says yes and creates circumstances that prove your increasing capability.

The universe doesn't judge, evaluate, or decide which faith deserves manifestation. It simply mirrors back whatever faith is most consistently held. This is why examining your dominant faith is so crucial. Not your stated beliefs or occasional positive thoughts, but the faith that's actually running in the background most of the time.

People tend to have superficial positive faith covering deeper negative faith. They say they believe in abundance, but their dominant faith is in scarcity. They say they believe in their capabilities, but their dominant faith is in limitation. The superficial positive faith doesn't manifest because it's not dominant—it's a hope floating on top of deeper contrary faith.

Today, identify your dominant faith honestly. What do you truly believe most of the time when you're not consciously trying to think positively? This dominant faith is what's creating your reality. Once you see it clearly, you can begin the work of making your desired faith dominant through consistent practice, until it becomes your automatic, unconscious operating system.

March 30

Doubt delays, but faith delivers.

Every moment you spend in doubt adds time to your manifestation journey. Doubt creates resistance, static in the signal, obstacles in the path. Faith removes these barriers, creating a clear channel for manifestation to flow through. It's not that doubt prevents manifestation entirely, it delays it, complicates it, makes it harder than necessary.

Faith, on the other hand, accelerates and simplifies manifestation. Things fall into place more easily, opportunities appear more quickly, obstacles dissolve more readily. The person with strong faith experiences what others call luck but is actually just the natural flow when consciousness is aligned. This doesn't mean you'll never experience doubt; doubt is natural when you're reaching for something beyond your current experience. The key is how quickly you recognize doubt and return to faith. Doubt appears, you acknowledge it, then you consciously choose faith again. Over time, the returns to faith become faster, the periods of doubt become shorter, until faith becomes your dominant state.

Today, notice how much time you spend in doubt versus faith. When doubt appears, don't condemn yourself for it. Simply recognize: "I'm in doubt, which is delaying my desired outcome." Then consciously shift back to faith: "I choose to trust that this is working out." Each time you make this shift, you're training yourself to spend more time in the state of faith that delivers rather than the state of doubt that delays.

March 31

Faith is the master key that unlocks all doors.

Throughout this month, we've explored faith from many angles—its nature, its power, its practice. As we close this month, understand that faith is not just one tool among many; it's the master key that unlocks every door, solves every problem, creates every possibility. Without faith, all other techniques and strategies have limited power. You can take massive action without faith and still struggle. You can think positively without faith and still fail. But with faith, even small actions produce remarkable results. Even simple visualizations create powerful manifestations.

Faith is the multiplier that amplifies everything else. It's the secret ingredient that transforms ordinary effort into extraordinary outcomes. As you move forward, carry this understanding: cultivating unwavering faith is the single most important work you can do. Everything flows from it. Every other principle and practice works better when built on a foundation of faith. Invest time daily in strengthening your faith. Through visualization, through affirmation, through gratitude, through mental rehearsal, through whatever practices resonate with you. Make faith your priority, and watch as doors begin opening that you didn't even know existed.

Your faith in the source of all creation, in yourself, in your vision, in the benevolent universe that supports your highest good—this faith is your most powerful tool. Use it consciously, strengthen it daily, and let it unlock every door between where you are and where you want to be.

April

Personal Responsibility

Taking Ownership of Your Life

April 1

You are 100% responsible for your life.

This principle is both liberating and terrifying. It means you cannot blame circumstances, other people, your past, your genes, the economy, or bad luck for where you are. Most the conditions in your life are the result of choices you've made or responses you've had to situations. This doesn't mean everything that happens to you is your fault—you cannot control external events. But you are 100% responsible for how you respond to those events and what you make them mean.

Two people can experience the same difficulty: one uses it as an excuse for failure, the other uses it as fuel for growth. The difference is in taking responsibility. When you accept complete responsibility, you reclaim complete power. You're no longer waiting for circumstances to change, people to behave differently, or luck to smile on you. You recognize that your life is created by you, through your choices, your attitudes, and your actions.

Today, practice radical responsibility. When something goes wrong, resist the urge to blame. Instead ask: What's my responsibility here? What choice led to this? What can I do about it now? This practice transforms you from victim to creator, from powerless to powerful. Total responsibility equals total power.

April 2

Blame is the surrender of power.

Every time you blame someone or something for your circumstances, you give away your power to change those circumstances. Blame says: "I am powerless. They have the power. Until they change, I can't change." This keeps you trapped in victimhood, waiting for external forces to grant you permission to succeed. The truth is, blame might feel temporarily satisfying—it absolves you of responsibility and gives you someone to be angry at. But this satisfaction comes at an enormous cost: your power.

When you blame your parents for your issues, you're saying they control your life—that their past actions determine your present reality more than your current choices do. When you blame the economy for your finances, you're saying external conditions control your prosperity—that market forces matter more than your mindset, decisions, and actions. When you blame your partner for your unhappiness, you're saying someone else controls your emotional state— that their behavior determines your internal experience. All of these blame statements surrender your creative authority. They make you dependent on things outside yourself changing before you can change. They place your wellbeing, success, and happiness in someone else's hands. This is the definition of powerlessness.

Today, notice whenever you blame. Catch yourself saying or thinking things like "because of them, I can't..." or "if only they would..." or "it's their fault that..." Each of these statements is a power leak. Instead, reclaim your power by asking: Regardless of what they did, what can I do? Regardless of circumstances, how can I respond powerfully? This shifts you from blaming to creating, from victim to victor. Your power returns the moment you stop blaming.

April 3

Your life is the sum of your choices.

Look at your life honestly. Your current health is the sum of your food choices, exercise choices, and lifestyle choices. Your current finances are the sum of your spending choices, earning choices, and investment choices. Your current relationships are the sum of your communication choices, boundary choices, and partner choices.

Every area reflects accumulated choices made over days, months, and years. This is empowering because it means you can change any area by changing your choices, starting now. You're not stuck with the results of past choices—you're always one choice away from a different path. But many resist this truth because it requires acknowledging that their current dissatisfaction is largely self-created through their choices. It's easier to believe you're a victim of circumstances than to admit you created your circumstances through thousands of small choices.

Today, examine one area of your life you want to change. Trace it back to the choices that created it. Be honest but not harsh with yourself. Then ask: What different choices can I begin making today? You don't need to change everything at once. One different choice, repeated consistently, compounds over time into dramatically different results. Your future will be the sum of the choices you make starting now. Choose consciously.

April 4

Build solutions, not excuses.

Every excuse you make is building a monument to your limitations rather than building a path to your goals. Excuses feel necessary—they protect your ego from the discomfort of acknowledging that you could do better but aren't. They create a story where you're not responsible for your lack of results. But excuses exact a heavy price: they keep you exactly where you are.

The person with excuses for why they can't succeed will never succeed because their excuses prevent them from taking the actions that would lead to success. Meanwhile, the person who refuses to make excuses finds ways around obstacles, learns from failures, and persists until they succeed. Look at any highly successful person, and you'll find someone who had plenty of reasons to make excuses but refused to do so. They had disadvantages, faced obstacles, experienced setbacks—but they didn't let these become excuses. They took responsibility and found solutions.

Today, identify your most common excuses—the ones you tell yourself and others about why you can't do what you know you should do. Write them down. Look at them honestly. Then ask: What would I do if this excuse wasn't available to me? What action would I take if I couldn't hide behind this excuse? Then take that action. Each time you act despite an excuse, you weaken its power over you. Eventually, you become someone who creates results instead of excuses.

April 5

You cannot control what happens, but you always control your response.

Life is 10% what happens to you and 90% how you respond to what happens. This might seem like an exaggeration, but it's not. The events themselves matter far less than your interpretation of and response to those events.

You cannot control whether you lose your job, but you control whether you see it as devastating or as an opportunity for something greater. You cannot control whether someone betrays you, but you control whether you become bitter or use the experience to develop better judgment. You cannot control whether you face financial setbacks, but you control how you respond and what actions you take to recover. Your response is always within your control, and your response determines your experience and your outcome.

Much attention is placed on trying to control events, which is largely futile and exhausting. Far less attention is given to developing the ability to respond powerfully, even though this is entirely within one's control and infinitely valuable.

Today, when something happens that you don't like, pause before reacting. Remind yourself: I cannot control this event, but I can control my response. Then consciously choose a response that serves you. Choose the interpretation that empowers rather than defeats. Choose the action that moves forward rather than retreats. This conscious response-ability is your greatest power and can transform any event from obstacle to opportunity.

April 6

Success is never owned; it's rented, and the rent is due every day.

You cannot achieve success once and then coast. Success requires daily maintenance through daily choices and actions. The business owner who built a successful company cannot stop leading, innovating, and serving customers. The athlete who achieved peak fitness cannot stop training and expect to maintain that fitness. The person who created a fulfilling relationship cannot stop investing attention and care into that relationship.

Success in any area requires continuous effort—not backbreaking labor every single day, but consistent daily deposits into that area. This is where personal responsibility becomes crucial. You must take responsibility not just for achieving success but for maintaining it. Many people taste success and then slack off, believing they've "arrived." But success is not a destination; it's a daily practice.

Today, identify areas where you achieved some success but have been coasting. Perhaps you got in shape but stopped exercising. Perhaps you built savings but stopped contributing. Perhaps you improved a relationship but stopped nurturing it. Success begins to erode the moment maintenance stops. Recommit to paying the daily rent through consistent action. The person who understands that success requires daily renewal takes nothing for granted and maintains their achievements through unwavering daily discipline. This is the responsibility that comes with success—and the price of sustaining it.

April 7

If it is to be, it is up to me.

This simple rhyme contains profound truth. Whatever you want to create, achieve, or experience in your life—if it's going to manifest, you must do your part. No one can hold your vision for you. No one can change your consciousness for you. No one can take the actions that are yours to take. You are the primary creator of your reality through your thoughts, your faith, and your inspired action.

This is not about forcing outcomes or doing everything alone—it's about taking responsibility for both your internal state and your external steps. You must hold the vision, develop the faith, feel it as real, and then act on the opportunities and impulses that arise from that aligned state. The universe responds to consciousness backed by action. Faith without works is dead, but works without faith is futile.

Many people wait passively for life to happen to them—for opportunities to appear, for circumstances to improve, for someone to rescue them. They abandon responsibility to fate, luck, or external forces. But transformation requires you to meet the universe halfway: align your consciousness with your desire, then take the actions that feel aligned. The internal work creates the possibility; the external action allows it to materialize.

Today, take full ownership of both your internal state and your external response. Hold your vision with faith, feel your desire as already accomplished, and then act on the inspired impulses that emerge. Stop waiting for perfect circumstances or someone else's permission. Declare: If it is to be, it is up to me—to align my consciousness, to maintain my faith, and to take aligned action. This integration of internal work and external movement is how desires become reality.

April 8

Taking responsibility means giving up all excuses.

You cannot simultaneously take responsibility and make excuses—they're mutually exclusive. Either you're responsible for your results, or you have excuses for why you didn't get results. You cannot have both. This is a hard truth that many people resist because excuses are comforting. They protect our ego, explain away our failures, and absolve us of having to do difficult things. But this comfort keeps us trapped in mediocrity.

The moment you truly take responsibility, all excuses must be abandoned. No more "I didn't have time." You have the same 24 hours as everyone else; it's about priorities. No more "I didn't have the resources." Plenty of people have achieved more with less. No more "I didn't have support." Many successful people started alone. Every excuse can be countered with examples of people who succeeded despite facing that same excuse. The person who takes full responsibility stops making these excuses and starts making progress.

Today, make a declaration: I give up my excuses. I take full responsibility for my results. Write down your most common excuses, then ceremonially release them. From this day forward, when you're tempted to make an excuse, stop yourself and ask instead: What action can I take? This shift from excuse-making to action-taking is the hallmark of personal responsibility and the foundation of achievement.

April 9

Your circumstances do not define you; your response to them does.

You may have been born into poverty, but poverty doesn't define you unless you accept it as your identity. You may have experienced trauma, but trauma doesn't define you unless you let it become your story. You may have faced discrimination, but discrimination doesn't define you unless you surrender to victimhood.

Circumstances are external; your essence is internal. Who you become is determined not by what happens to you but by how you respond to what happens. History is full of people who faced terrible circumstances but refused to be defined by them. They used adversity as fuel for growth rather than accepting it as an excuse for failure. They took responsibility for their response, even when the circumstances weren't their responsibility. This is the key distinction: you're not responsible for all circumstances, but you are responsible for your response to all circumstances.

Today, if you've been letting circumstances define you, reclaim your identity. You are not your circumstances—you are how you respond to circumstances. You are not where you came from—you are where you're going. You are not what happened to you—you are what you're doing about it. This shift from circumstance-defined to response-defined identity is liberating. It means your past doesn't control your future, your circumstances don't limit your potential, and your current situation doesn't determine your ultimate destination.

April 10

> *Accountability is the bridge between goals and accomplishment.*

Many people set goals but never achieve them because they lack accountability. They make declarations about what they'll do but don't create mechanisms to ensure they follow through. Without accountability, goals remain wishful thinking.

Accountability means you answer to someone—yourself or others—for whether you're doing what you said you'd do. It creates consequences for inaction and rewards for progress. It makes your commitments real rather than just ideas. Self-accountability requires brutal honesty. At the end of each day, you must honestly assess: Did I do what I committed to? If not, why not? What will I do differently tomorrow?

In many cases, people aren't honest with themselves—they rationalize, justify, make excuses, or simply avoid the assessment. External accountability—sharing your goals with someone who will check on your progress—can be powerful because it's harder to lie to others than to yourself.

Today, create an accountability system. If you're disciplined, commit to daily self-accountability through journaling. If you need external support, find an accountability partner—someone who will ask weekly if you did what you said you'd do. The discomfort of admitting you didn't follow through is powerful motivation to actually follow through with your commitments. Remember: goals without accountability are just wishes. Accountability transforms intentions into actions and actions into accomplishments.

April 11

The quality of your life is determined by the quality of your decisions.

Your life, right now, is the cumulative result of thousands of decisions—some major, most minor. The decision to exercise or not. To save or spend. To learn or coast. To speak up or stay silent. To persist or quit. Each decision, in isolation, seems insignificant. But decisions compound over time, creating trajectories that lead to vastly different destinations.

Good decision-making is not about perfection—you'll make some poor decisions inevitably. It's about improving your batting average. If you make slightly better decisions consistently, your life improves dramatically over time. Poor decision-making often stems from short-term thinking. You choose immediate pleasure over long-term benefit, immediate relief over long-term growth, immediate ease over long-term success. Good decision-making requires you to consider future consequences, not just present desires.

Today, before making any significant decision, pause and ask: What are the likely consequences of this decision in one week? One month? One year? Five years? This simple practice of projecting forward improves decision quality dramatically. Also ask: Is this decision aligned with my values and goals? Many poor decisions happen when we act in ways that contradict what we claim to value. Taking responsibility means recognizing that you are the decision-maker of your life, and the quality of your decisions determines the quality of your experience.

April 12

Discipline is choosing what you want most over what you want now.

People frequently lack discipline not because they're weak but because they never clearly defined what they want most. They have vague desires but no compelling vision that's stronger than immediate temptations. When you know what you want most—and why it matters deeply— discipline becomes natural. You're not forcing yourself to resist temptation; you're choosing your greater desire over a lesser one.

The person who wants long-term health more than immediate pleasure finds it easy to choose the salad over the pizza. The person who wants financial freedom more than momentary satisfaction finds it easy to save rather than splurge. The person who wants mastery more than comfort finds it easy to practice rather than procrastinate. Discipline looks different depending on clarity of vision. Without clear priorities, every choice is difficult because you're torn between competing desires of equal strength. With clear priorities, choices become obvious because you know what matters most.

Today, get crystal clear on what you want most in one key area of your life. Why do you want it? How will achieving it change your life? Make this vision so vivid and compelling that the daily disciplines required to achieve it no longer feel like sacrifice—they feel like obvious choices. When temptation arises, remind yourself of what you want most. This isn't about willpower. It's about clarity. Discipline is easy when you know what you want most and remember it in moments of decision.

April 13

You teach people how to treat you by what you tolerate.

If you tolerate disrespect, you're teaching people that disrespecting you is acceptable. If you tolerate broken commitments, you're teaching people that keeping their word to you is optional. If you tolerate poor treatment, you're teaching people that you don't value yourself highly. People will treat you exactly as well or as poorly as you require them to.

This is hard to accept because it means that mistreatment you've experienced is partly due to boundaries you failed to establish or enforce. But accepting this responsibility empowers you to change your experience. You cannot control how people initially treat you, but you absolutely control what you tolerate. When someone crosses a boundary, you can address it immediately or let it slide. Letting it slide teaches them that behavior is acceptable with you. Addressing it teaches them where your boundaries are.

People commonly avoid setting boundaries because they fear conflict or rejection. But the cost of not setting boundaries is much higher: resentment, disrespect, and relationships that don't serve you.

Today, examine your relationships. Where are you tolerating behavior that doesn't align with your values? Identify one boundary you need to establish or reinforce. Then communicate it clearly and calmly: "I'm not comfortable with X. I need Y instead." Taking responsibility means recognizing that the treatment you receive is largely a reflection of the treatment you accept. Raise your standards, and watch how people's behavior changes to meet them.

April 14

The difference between who you are
and who you want to be is what you do.

There's often a gap between your current self and your ideal self. This gap isn't closed through wishes, intentions, or self-help book reading. It's closed through action—specifically, through doing the things your ideal self would do. If you want to be healthy, do what healthy people do. If you want to be successful, do what successful people do. If you want to be confident, do what confident people do.

Your identity follows your actions, not the other way around. It's common for people to try to wait to feel like their ideal self before acting like them. But this is backwards. You become through doing. Each time you take an action aligned with your desired identity, you're proving to yourself that you are that person. Over time, these consistent actions reshape your self-concept until the gap closes. The procrastinator who wants to be productive doesn't become productive by wishing—they become productive by consistently taking productive action, even when they don't feel like it, until productivity becomes their identity.

Today, identify one action your ideal self would take that your current self hasn't been taking. Then take that action, regardless of whether you feel like it or whether it feels authentic. Do the action first; the feeling of authenticity will follow. This is taking responsibility for who you become by consciously taking the actions that create that identity. You are not stuck being who you've been—you can become anyone through consistent action.

April 15

Your life reflects your priorities, not your intentions.

Many people say health is important, but they don't exercise, eat well, or sleep enough. They say relationships matter, but they don't invest quality time, communicate meaningfully, or show appreciation. They say growth is important, but they don't read, learn new skills, or seek challenges. The gap between stated values and actual behavior reveals true priorities.

There's often a massive gap between stated priorities and actual priorities. Your actual priorities are revealed not by what you say but by how you spend your time and energy. If you want to know what you truly prioritize, look at your calendar and your credit card statement. These show where your resources actually go, which reveals your real priorities.

This isn't about judging yourself harshly. But it is about rigorous self-honesty. If you claim family is your top priority but spend more time on social media than with your family, family isn't actually your priority. If you say financial freedom matters but spend impulsively rather than budgeting and investing wisely, financial freedom isn't actually your priority. If you declare self-work or connection to source is essential but don't meditate or practice daily communion, that inner work isn't actually your priority.

Today, do an honest priority audit. Look at how you actually spent the last week. What does your time allocation reveal about your real priorities? Do they match your stated priorities? If not, you have two choices: change your stated priorities to match your behavior (be honest about what you truly value), or change your behavior to match your stated priorities (align your actions with your values). Taking responsibility means closing the gap between what you say matters and how you actually live. Your life will always reflect your true priorities—make sure they're priorities worth reflecting.

April 16

Everything you want is on the other side of responsibility.

Freedom, success, fulfillment, peace, love—everything you desire exists on the other side of taking full responsibility for your life. Why? Because responsibility is power, and power is what creates results. When you take responsibility for your health, you gain the power to improve it. When you take responsibility for your finances, you gain the power to transform them. When you take responsibility for your relationships, you gain the power to enhance them.

As long as you avoid responsibility—blaming, making excuses, playing the victim—you remain powerless to change your circumstances. You're waiting for external forces to change things for you, which rarely happens. The irony is that people avoid responsibility because they think it means more burden, more stress, or more pressure. But the opposite is true. Avoiding responsibility creates burden because you're carrying resentment, helplessness, and frustration. Taking responsibility is liberating because it returns your power to create change.

Today, identify something you want but haven't achieved. Be honest: Where have you avoided responsibility in this area? Have you blamed circumstances? Made excuses? Waited for someone else to solve it? Now declare: I take full responsibility for creating what I want in this area. Then identify one action you can take today, however small, that moves you toward what you want. Everything you desire is available to you the moment you stop avoiding responsibility and start embracing it.

April 17

Small daily improvements compound into massive success.

People often overestimate what they can achieve in a day and underestimate what they can achieve in a year through daily consistency. They want immediate transformation, so they take massive action for a few days, burn out, and quit. Then they're back where they started, frustrated and convinced change is impossible. But the secret to transformation isn't massive action all at once, it's consistent small action over time.

If you improve by just 1% each day, you're 37 times better after a year due to compounding. If you read 10 pages daily, you'll read 3,650 pages per year, about 12 books. If you save $10 daily, you'll have $3,650 plus interest after a year. If you exercise 15 minutes daily, you'll have completed over 90 hours of exercise in a year.

These small actions seem insignificant on any given day, which is why it's easy to dismiss them. But over time, they compound into extraordinary results.

Today, identify one small daily improvement in an important area. Make it so easy that you cannot fail to do it. Not "exercise for an hour", that's too big. Instead, "do 5 or 10 pushups" or "walk for 10 minutes." Not "save $100", instead, "save $5." The size of the action matters less than the consistency. Take responsibility for making this one small improvement every single day. Track it. Celebrate it. Over time, this tiny daily discipline will compound into massive transformation, proving that success isn't about doing extraordinary things, it's about doing ordinary things extraordinarily consistently.

April 18

Comfort is the enemy of growth.

Everything you want lies outside your comfort zone. If it was comfortable, you'd already have it. The very definition of growth is expanding beyond current limits, which is inherently uncomfortable. Yet most people organize their entire lives around maximizing comfort and minimizing discomfort. They avoid difficult conversations, challenging situations, unfamiliar experiences, anything that creates discomfort. This comfort-seeking keeps them trapped in a life smaller than their potential.

Taking responsibility means accepting that discomfort is not just inevitable but necessary for growth. You must intentionally put yourself in uncomfortable situations—not recklessly, but strategically. The shy person must have uncomfortable conversations to develop social confidence. The unhealthy person must embrace uncomfortable exercise to build physical fitness. The financially struggling person must make uncomfortable sacrifices to build wealth. Each time you choose discomfort over comfort, you expand. Each time you choose comfort over growth, you contract.

Today, identify one thing you've been avoiding because it's uncomfortable. Maybe it's a difficult conversation, a challenging task, or an uncertain situation. Then do it anyway. Feel the discomfort, acknowledge it, and move through it. Notice that the anticipation of discomfort is usually worse than the discomfort itself. Build your discomfort tolerance by deliberately choosing uncomfortable actions. This is how you become comfortable being uncomfortable, which is the foundation of unlimited growth.

April 19

You are the author of your life story.

Many people live as if their life story is being written by someone else—fate, circumstances, or other people. They see themselves as characters in a story they don't control. But this is a disempowering illusion. You are not a character in someone else's story; you are the author of your own story.

True, you didn't choose all the circumstances—the opening chapters were written by others. But from the moment you gained awareness, you became the co-author, and as you mature, you become the primary author. Every day, you're writing new pages through your choices, your thoughts, your actions, and your responses. The question is: What story are you writing? Is it a victim story—poor me, everything happens to me, I have no power? Or is it a hero story—challenges arise, I overcome them, I grow stronger? The events might be similar, but the story you tell about them determines whether you remain stuck or move forward.

Today, think about the story you've been telling about your life. Is it empowering or disempowering? Does it position you as victim or victor? Then consciously rewrite any disempowering narratives. You're not "someone who always struggles with money"—you're "someone who is learning to create financial abundance." You're not "unlucky in love"— you're "becoming clear about what you want in a partner." This isn't denial—it's authorship. Take responsibility for the story you tell, because that story shapes your identity and your future.

April 20

Responsibility without self-compassion becomes self-punishment.

As you embrace responsibility, there's a danger: becoming overly harsh with yourself. If every problem is your responsibility, you might conclude that you're failing at everything. This self-judgment can become paralyzing and counterproductive. Healthy responsibility includes self-compassion. Yes, you're responsible for your results, but that doesn't mean you should berate yourself for imperfect results. You're human, learning, growing. You'll make mistakes, have setbacks, sometimes fail. This is part of the process, not evidence that you're inadequate.

The balance is, take responsibility without taking on shame. "I'm responsible for this outcome, and I can learn from it, take the lesson, and do better next time" is very different from "I'm responsible for this outcome, which means something is wrong with me." One is empowering; the other is destructive.

Today, practice responsible self-compassion. When you notice an area where you haven't gotten desired results, acknowledge your responsibility: "I created this through my choices." But immediately add compassion: "I'm doing my best with the awareness I have. I'm learning and growing." This balance allows you to take responsibility for change without drowning in self-judgment. You can be accountable and kind to yourself simultaneously. In fact, self-compassion often accelerates growth because you're not wasting energy on self-punishment. Take responsibility, but do it with the same compassion you'd show a friend who's trying their best and sometimes falling short.

April 21

The foundation of self-trust.

Every time you make and keep a commitment, you strengthen your relationship with yourself. Every time you make and break a commitment, you weaken it. Many are careful about commitments to others but careless about commitments to themselves. "I'll exercise tomorrow"—then the alarm goes off and you hit snooze. "I'll start saving next month"—then the money gets spent elsewhere. "I'll work on my goals this weekend"— then the weekend disappears to scrolling or binge-watching the new show.

Each broken self-commitment teaches your subconscious that your word doesn't matter, that you can't be trusted, that your intentions are meaningless. Over time, you stop believing yourself when you say you'll do something because your history proves you won't follow through. This makes any change exponentially harder. Conversely, keeping commitments to yourself—especially small ones—builds self-trust and self-respect. When you say you'll do something and you do it, you prove to yourself that you're reliable, trustworthy, and capable.

Today, make one small commitment to yourself and keep it, no matter what. Not a huge goal—something simple like "I'll drink eight glasses of water" or "I'll read for 10 minutes." Then honor that commitment as if it were a promise to your most important client. Because it is—you are your most important client. Each kept commitment builds the foundation of self-trust that makes all transformation possible. When your word to yourself becomes unbreakable, you've discovered true power—the power to direct your life through conscious choice and follow-through.

April 22

> *The price of discipline is always less than the price of regret.*

Discipline requires effort, discomfort, and sacrifice in the short term. You must wake up early, resist temptation, and do hard things. This has a price. But regret—the pain of looking back at what could have been if only you'd been more disciplined—has a much higher price. It's the permanent ache of unrealized potential, the what-ifs that haunt you, the knowledge that you could have done better but didn't.

People commonly calculate the immediate cost of discipline and decide it's too high. They don't calculate the long-term cost of indiscipline, which is always higher. The cost of exercising is 30 minutes of discomfort. The cost of not exercising is years of poor health, low energy, and medical issues. The cost of saving money is delayed gratification. The cost of not saving is decades of financial stress and limited freedom. The cost of learning a skill is time and effort. The cost of not learning is stagnation and missed opportunities.

Today, identify an area where you've been avoiding discipline because it feels difficult. Then honestly calculate the long-term cost of continuing to avoid it. What will this avoidance cost you in one year? Five years? At the end of your life? When you see the true cost of indiscipline, the price of discipline suddenly seems reasonable. Take responsibility by choosing the temporary discomfort of discipline over the permanent pain of regret. Your future self will thank you.

April 23

You can't have a million-dollar dream with a minimum wage work ethic.

Many people have big dreams but refuse to do the work those dreams require. They want extraordinary results from ordinary effort. They want to be exceptional while doing what everyone else does. This disconnect between aspiration and action is why most dreams die. The size of your dreams must match the size of your effort.

If you want results that 5% of people achieve, you must do what 95% of people won't do. This doesn't necessarily mean working more hours—it means working with more focus, more intensity, and more consistency. It means doing difficult things most people avoid.

The minimum-wage work ethic—doing just enough to get by, avoiding discomfort, seeking the easy path—produces minimum-wage results. The million-dollar work ethic—going above and beyond, embracing challenges, pursuing excellence—produces million-dollar results.

Today, honestly assess the gap between your dreams and your work ethic. If you want exceptional health, are you exercising exceptionally? If you want exceptional wealth, are you working and learning exceptionally? If you want exceptional relationships, are you communicating and connecting exceptionally? Taking responsibility means acknowledging that your current work ethic is producing your current results. If you want different results, you need a different work ethic. Upgrade your effort to match your aspirations, or downgrade your aspirations to match your effort. But you cannot keep them mismatched and expect satisfaction.

April 24

Stop waiting for perfect conditions; take action with what you have.

Perfectionism is often disguised procrastination. People say they're waiting for the perfect time, the perfect conditions, the perfect preparation. But perfect never comes. There's always a reason to wait— not enough money, not enough time, not enough knowledge, not enough support. Meanwhile, years pass and dreams remain unrealized.

The truth is, you'll never feel completely ready. You'll never have all the resources. Conditions will never be perfect. Successful people don't wait for perfect conditions—they create progress with imperfect conditions. They start before they're ready. They learn as they go. They adjust based on feedback. Taking responsibility means accepting that you have everything you need to begin, right now. Not to finish—to begin. You don't need to see the entire staircase; you just need to take the first step. You don't need perfect conditions; you need committed action.

Today, identify something you've been postponing until conditions are better. Then take one small action on it today, with current conditions, imperfect as they are. Maybe you can't launch the full business, but you can register the domain. Maybe you can't run a marathon, but you can walk around the block. Maybe you can't write the entire book, but you can write the first page. Stop using imperfect conditions as an excuse for inaction. Your responsibility is not to have perfect conditions but to make progress with the conditions you have. Perfect conditions are a myth; progress is a choice.

April 25

The gap between knowing and doing is where dreams die.

Most people already know what they should do. They know they should exercise, save money, pursue their goals, and nurture relationships. Knowledge isn't the problem. Action is. There's a massive gap between knowing and doing, and this gap is where many dreams die.

Tony Robbins expressed this clearly in *Awaken the Giant Within* when he said, "Every book you read, seminar you attend, or audio you listen to is worthless until you make the decision to use it." Information alone does not change lives. Decisions followed by action do.

You can read every book, attend every seminar, watch every video, but if you don't implement what you learn, nothing changes. Knowledge without action is merely entertainment. It may inspire you temporarily, but it produces no lasting transformation. Taking responsibility means closing the gap between what you know and what you do. Stop consuming more information and start implementing what you already know. You don't need to know more; you need to do more with what you know.

The person who knows little but does everything they know will achieve far more than the person who knows everything but does nothing.

Today, identify one thing you know you should do but haven't been doing. Not something you need to research or learn. Something you already know and understand. Then do it today. Don't wait for more information, more preparation, more motivation. Take action now.

Each time you close that gap, you build momentum and prove to yourself that you're someone who acts on their knowledge. This transforms you from perpetual learner to an actual achiever. Knowledge is potential. Action is realization.

April 26

No one is coming to save you. You must save yourself.

This might sound harsh, but it's liberating: you are your own rescue. No parent, partner, boss, or government is going to swoop in and fix your life. No lottery win is coming. No perfect opportunity will magically appear. Waiting for external salvation keeps you stuck because you've given away your power away to forces you cannot control.

Many people live their entire lives waiting—waiting for recognition, waiting for permission, waiting for someone to believe in them, waiting for lucky breaks. Meanwhile, others are taking responsibility and creating the life they want through their own efforts. They're not waiting to be saved; they're saving themselves. This doesn't mean refusing all help or going it completely alone. It means recognizing that you are the primary agent of your life. Help, support, and opportunities are available, but you must seek them, ask for them, position yourself to receive them. Even accepting help requires you to take action.

Today, stop waiting for someone or something to save you from your current situation. Whatever needs to change in your life, you must change it. Whatever dreams you have, you must pursue them. Whatever growth you desire, you must do the work. You have within you everything necessary to create a better life. Stop waiting for external salvation and start creating internal transformation. You are both the problem and the solution, the obstacle and the opportunity, the reason you're stuck and the way forward.

April 27

When you change, everything changes.

People often try to change their circumstances while remaining the same person. They want different results without different inputs. But the universe doesn't work that way. Your external world is a reflection of your internal world. When you change—your thinking, your beliefs, your habits, your standards—your circumstances must change to match your new internal state.

This is why personal development is not self-indulgent or superficial—it's the most practical strategy for improving your life. When you become more disciplined, your results improve. When you become more confident, opportunities appear. When you become more grateful, abundance flows. The change must happen within you first, then it manifests externally. Waiting for external changes while remaining internally the same is futile.

Today, instead of trying to fix circumstances, focus on changing yourself. Identify one internal shift you need to make—a belief, a habit, an attitude. Then commit to making that shift. As you change, watch how circumstances begin shifting to match your new internal state. You are the cause; circumstances are the effect. Change the cause, and effects must follow. Taking responsibility means recognizing that you are the common denominator in all your life circumstances. When you change, everything changes, because you're the source point from which your entire experience flows.

April 28

You get what you tolerate, not what you deserve.

Many people believe they deserve better—better treatment, better opportunities, better circumstances. And they might be right. But the universe doesn't operate on deserve; it operates on tolerance. You don't get what you deserve; you get what you tolerate. If you tolerate mediocrity in your work, you'll experience mediocrity in your results. If you tolerate toxic relationships, you'll be surrounded by toxicity. If you tolerate financial chaos, you'll experience financial struggle.

Your tolerance level sets your experience level. Raising your standards means lowering your tolerance for what doesn't serve you. It means saying "this is no longer acceptable" to behaviors, situations, and standards that fall below what you want.

But, people tend to have incredibly low standards for themselves and their lives because they've tolerated substandard conditions for so long that it feels normal. But normal doesn't mean acceptable.

Today, identify what you've been tolerating that you need to stop tolerating. Maybe it's your own procrastination. Maybe it's others' disrespect. Maybe it's poor health or financial disorganization. Then declare: I no longer tolerate this. Set a new standard and enforce it through your actions. Stop accepting what you've been accepting. Taking responsibility means raising your standards and refusing to tolerate anything less. You might deserve better, but you'll only get better when you stop tolerating less.

April 29

Your legacy is being written by your daily choices.

Legacy is often thought of as something to consider later in life, near the end. But legacy isn't created in the final years—it's created daily, through the accumulation of choices, actions, and impacts over a lifetime.

Every day, you're writing your legacy. Not through grand gestures but through small choices: how you treat people, what values you demonstrate, what example you set, what contributions you make. The parent who is present with their children is writing a legacy. The professional who does excellent work and goes above and beyond is writing a legacy. The person who uplifts others is writing a legacy.

These daily actions compound into the mark you leave on the world. When you take responsibility for your legacy, you stop living reactively and start living intentionally. You ask: What do I want to be remembered for? Then you align your daily actions with that answer. You don't wait until you're "successful enough" to start making an impact—you make an impact today, from where you are, with what you have.

Today, reflect on the legacy you're currently writing through your daily choices. Is it the legacy you want to leave? If not, what needs to change? How do you need to show up differently? What values need to be more prominent in your actions? Your legacy is not some distant future consideration—it's being written right now, in this moment, through the choice you're about to make. Choose consciously.

April 30

> *Taking responsibility is not a burden; it is your liberation.*

As we close this month on personal responsibility, embrace this final truth: responsibility is not the heavy burden most people imagine. Yes, it requires you to stop blaming, stop making excuses, and stop playing the victim. Yes, it requires you to acknowledge your role in creating your current circumstances. But this acknowledgment is not a burden—it's the liberation that sets you free.

When you take responsibility, you reclaim your power. You're no longer at the mercy of circumstances, other people, or luck. You recognize that you are the primary creative force in your life. This is true freedom. The burden is actually in avoiding responsibility—carrying resentment, feeling helpless, waiting for change that never comes. Taking responsibility releases this burden and replaces it with action, possibility, and hope.

Today, make peace with responsibility. Stop resisting it, fearing it, or seeing it as punishment. Instead, embrace it as your pathway to freedom. Everything you want becomes possible the moment you take full responsibility for creating it. You are powerful beyond measure, and that power is activated through responsibility. As you move forward, carry this month's lessons with you. Remember that you are 100% responsible for your life, and that this responsibility is not a burden but a blessing. It's the key that unlocks every door, the foundation upon which all success is built. Take responsibility and take control of your destiny.

May

Reality Transurfing & Intention

Conscious Creation Principles

May 1

You choose your reality by choosing your intention.

Reality is not a fixed, singular thing that happens to you. It's a field of infinite possibilities, and your intention determines which possibility you experience. In every moment, countless potential realities exist simultaneously. Your intention acts as a tuning fork, selecting which frequency you vibrate at, which in turn determines which reality manifests in your experience.

People often live with unconscious, scattered, or contradictory intentions. They want success but intend to play it safe. They want love but intend to avoid being vulnerable. These mixed intentions create mixed results or no results at all. Clear, focused intention is like a laser beam cutting through the fog of possibility, illuminating one specific path.

When you set clear intention, knowing exactly what you want and committing fully to it, you align your energy with that reality. The universe then starts to reorganize itself around that intention, not through magic but through the focusing of your attention, energy, and actions toward that specific outcome.

Today, examine your intentions. Are they clear or confused? Focused or scattered? Single-minded or contradictory? Choose one primary intention for an important area of your life. Make it specific, compelling, and emotionally resonant. Then commit to holding this intention consistently, letting it guide your choices, actions, and focus. Your intention is your creative power—use it consciously.

May 2

Excess potential creates balancing forces.

One of the most important principles of reality creation is understanding excess potential. Whenever you create excessive importance around something—wanting it desperately, fearing its loss, overvaluing its significance—you create an energetic imbalance. The universe then seeks equilibrium.

When you create excess potential through excessive importance, balancing forces arise to restore equilibrium, often in ways that work against your desires. For example, desperately needing a relationship creates excess potential that repels relationships. Obsessing over money creates resistance that blocks money. Fearing failure creates the very failure you fear. The balancing forces manifest as obstacles, setbacks, and opposite outcomes. The solution is to reduce importance. Want things, pursue goals, but don't make them excessively important. Hold your desires lightly rather than desperately. Be committed but not attached. This doesn't mean you don't care—it means you care without creating energetic distortion through excessive significance.

Today, notice where you've created excess potential through excessive importance. What are you desperate for? What are you terrified of losing? What have you made overly significant? Then consciously reduce the importance. Remind yourself: "This matters, but it's not life or death. I want this, but I'm complete without it or if it doesn't go my way." This reduction of importance eliminates the balancing forces and allows your intention to manifest smoothly.

May 3

Your thoughts choose the reality you experience from infinite possibilities.

Imagine reality as a vast supermarket with infinite aisles, each containing a different possible version of your life. Your thoughts determine which aisle you walk down, which products you see, which reality you experience.

Every thought is a choice point, directing you toward one possibility or another. Positive, empowering thoughts direct you toward positive realities. Negative, limiting thoughts direct you toward negative realities. The realities already exist as potentials; your thoughts simply determine which one you actualize.

Most people don't understand this, so they think randomly, jumping from positive to negative, from empowering to limiting. This mental chaos creates an incoherent signal that attracts chaotic, unpredictable results. Consistency in thought creates consistency in reality. When you consistently think thoughts aligned with your desired reality, you consistently walk the aisles that contain that reality. Eventually, you find yourself living it.

Today, become aware of your thought patterns. Are you consistently thinking thoughts that align with your desired reality? Or are you bouncing between hopeful and fearful thoughts? Choose one desired reality and commit to thinking only thoughts that align with it for the entire day. Every time a contradictory thought arises, gently redirect: "That's not the reality I'm choosing." This conscious thought selection is how you navigate the infinite field of possibility toward your intended destination.

May 4

Let go of the outcome; hold the intention.

This is one of the most challenging but essential practices in reality creation: hold your intention clearly and strongly, while simultaneously releasing attachment to the specific outcome. Your intention is the "what" you desire. The outcome is the "how" and "when" it manifests. You must be clear and committed about the what, but flexible and detached about the how and when.

It's common for people to do the opposite. They're clear about what they want while being rigidly attached to exactly how and when it must happen. They insist it must come through this specific job, this particular person, or this exact timeline. This creates resistance because they're trying to control the manifestation process, which operates according to principles beyond their conscious management. When you hold intention while releasing attachment to outcome, you're stating clearly what you want while having faith and trusting the universe to deliver it in the perfect way and perfect timing for your highest good. You're not attached to the specific path or method—you're focused on the end result and open to however it arrives. This trust eliminates the excess potential created by desperate attachment.

Today, clarify your intention for something important. State it clearly: "This is what I intend." Then practice releasing attachment to how it manifests: "I trust this will come to be in the perfect way and perfect timing for my highest good. I don't need to control how or when." Notice the relief this brings—the burden of control lifts, and trust takes its place. This combination of clear intention and detached allowing is the optimal state for manifestation.

May 5

Your inner state creates your outer reality.

The external world is a mirror reflecting your internal world. When you're in a state of lack internally, you perceive and create lack externally. When you're in a state of abundance internally, you perceive and create abundance externally. This is not a metaphorical theory—it's the mechanism of reality creation.

Your inner state—your thoughts, emotions, beliefs, and energy—broadcasts a signal. This signal interacts with the quantum field of infinite possibility, collapsing potential into actual experience that matches your broadcast.

People often try to change their outer reality while maintaining the same inner state. They want external abundance while feeling internal scarcity, lack, or fear. They want external success while feeling internal inadequacy. But the outer cannot change without the inner changing first.

Today, instead of trying to fix external circumstances, focus on cultivating your ideal internal state. If you want abundance externally, cultivate feelings of abundance internally—gratitude for what you have, appreciation of life's richness, generosity towards others. If you want success externally, cultivate feelings of success internally—confidence, capability, seeing the achievement of your goal already complete.

Create the inner state first, regardless of current external conditions. This is counterintuitive and requires faith because you're feeling abundant before seeing abundance, successful before seeing success. But this is precisely how you design a new reality. Change the inner broadcast, and the outer reflection must eventually change to match.

May 6

Intention without action is just wishful thinking.

Clear intention is essential, but it's not sufficient alone. You cannot simply set an intention and passively wait for the universe to deliver. Intention must be coupled with inspired action. The universe provides opportunities, synchronicities, and guidance, but you must act on them. Think of intention as setting your destination in a GPS. The GPS can show you the route, but you must drive the car. The route may change based on conditions, and you must adjust, but you must keep moving.

Many people set intentions but take limited or no action, waiting for their desires to appear on their own. Or they take action but without clear intention, moving frantically without direction. Both approaches fail. The optimal approach combines clear intention with consistent, inspired action. Set your intention clearly. Then take action in alignment with that intention. Not forced action driven by desperation, but natural action inspired by clarity.

When clear intention guides your actions, you magnetize opportunities. When you set intentions and then remain alert and responsive to guidance, the universe orchestrates circumstances to support your intention.

Today, identify one clear intention. Then ask: What action can I take today that aligns with this intention? Then take that action. This combination of clear intention and aligned action creates unstoppable momentum toward manifestation.

May 7

You are not separate from creative power; you are an expression of it.

One of the biggest illusions is the sense of separation—that you are here and the universe is there, that you request and the universe grants or denies. But this is false. You are not separate from the creative force of the universe; you are an expression of it. The same intelligence that grows flowers, orbits planets, and beats your heart is the intelligence creating through you.

When you set an intention, it's not you asking the universe for something. It's the universe intending through you. Your desires are not random wants; they're the universe pulling you toward experiences that serve your evolution. When you understand this, everything changes. You stop feeling like you're begging an external force for favors and start recognizing yourself as a creative force. You stop wondering if the universe will help you and start knowing that the universe is expressing through you. This doesn't make you arrogant—it makes you humble before the magnificence of what you are.

Today, shift from seeing yourself as separate from creative power to recognizing yourself as an expression of creative power. When you set intentions, feel into this truth: this is not me wanting something from the universe; this is the universe intending through me. This shift eliminates the energy of lack and need, replacing it with the energy of creative power expressing itself.

May 8

The alternatives space creates all possible realities.

In Reality Transurfing, Vadim Zeland introduces the concept of the alternatives space—a field containing all possible past, present, and future realities. Everything that could ever happen already exists as a possibility in this space. Your current reality is just one version, one possibility that has been actualized. But infinite other versions exist simultaneously.

The life where you're healthy and wealthy exists. The life where you're fulfilled and joyful exists. They're not future possibilities you must create; they're present possibilities you must tune into. The question isn't "Can I create this reality?" but "Can I tune into the frequency of this reality that already exists?"

This is profoundly liberating. You're not building something from nothing. You're selecting from what already exists in potential form. How do you select? Through your intention, your beliefs, your emotions, your actions—all of which determine your frequency, which determines which reality you experience. One of the most powerful tools for this is what Zeland calls a "slide"—a vivid mental image of your desired end result. When you imagine your desired reality as if it's already accomplished, feeling the emotions of that accomplishment, you create a slide that pulls you toward that life line in the alternatives space.

Today, contemplate this: the reality you desire already exists in the alternatives space. You don't need to create it; you need to align with it. Create a slide—a clear, vivid mental image of your desired reality as already accomplished. See it in detail. Feel the emotions of living it. Experience it as real. What frequency does that reality vibrate at? Match that frequency through your thoughts, emotions, and actions. When you repeatedly visualize your slide, you tune into that frequency and begin moving toward that life line. Trust that as you shift your frequency, you're automatically shifting into a different version of reality that already exists, waiting for you to discover it.

May 9

Go with the flow.

Life has a natural flow, a current moving in a certain direction. You can feel this flow—sometimes things unfold easily, doors open naturally, circumstances align. Other times, you're pushing against resistance, forcing doors, struggling to make things happen. The difference is whether you're moving with the flow or against it.

When you're aligned with your true path, life flows. This alignment happens when your heart and mind are unified—when what you desire (heart) matches what you think and do (mind). Your heart relates to the alternatives space where all possibilities exist, while your mind interprets the material world. The heart knows the goal and how to realize it through intuition—that quiet inner voice, the rustle of the morning stars beneath the mental noise. The mind analyzes, judges, and often overrides what the heart already knows.

When your mind says yes but your heart says no, you create inner tension and outer resistance. This misalignment produces struggle. When you're pursuing what you think you should want rather than what you truly want, you create resistance. When you're attached to specific outcomes rather than trusting the process, you create resistance. When you're acting from fear or ego rather than inspiration, you create resistance.

What you were meant for knows no inner discomfort. If tension persists despite your efforts, it's a signal of misalignment—you may be forcing something that isn't yours to have.

Today, pay attention to the difference between flow and force. Where do things feel easy and natural? Where do you feel persistent inner tension? Notice the difference between the resistance of growth (challenging but right, no inner discomfort) and the resistance of misalignment (exhausting and wrong, constant tension). When you feel the latter, pause and tune into your heart's knowing. Then align your mind's actions with that truth and move with the natural flow.

May 10

Your goal is not to control reality but to consciously choose it.

Many people approach manifestation as an attempt to control reality—to force outcomes, manipulate circumstances, make things happen through willpower. But this creates tremendous resistance and exhaustion because you're relying purely on inner intention when outer intention is what actually shapes reality.

Reality creation is not about control; it's about conscious choice. You don't force reality to bend to your will—that's inner intention trying to reposition yourself relative to the alternatives space. Instead, you choose which reality you prefer from the infinite alternatives that already exist, then align yourself with that choice through the unity of heart and mind. When your heart desires it and your mind believes it's possible, you create coherence that tunes you into that sector of the alternatives space—and that reality begins manifesting naturally.

The difference is subtle but profound. Control creates excess potential—inflated importance that summons balanced forces to work against you. Choice simply tunes into a sector of the alternatives space that's already there, following the path of least resistance. When you try to control, you push. When you consciously choose and allow, you receive.

You're not forcing anything into existence; you're selecting from what already exists and allowing it to materialize. Relax the need to control, reduce importance, and strengthen your ability to choose clearly.

Today, notice where you're trying to control outcomes. Feel the tension, the grip, the forcing energy—these are signs of excess potential. Then shift to choice: "I release control and choose to align with the reality where this outcome exists naturally." Select your goal with your heart, release attachment with your mind, and trust the alternatives flow to deliver it. This is the art of Reality Transurfing.

May 11

Your attitude determines your altitude in life.

Two people can face identical circumstances and have completely different experiences based solely on their attitude. One sees opportunity; the other sees an obstacle. One feels empowered; the other feels victimized. One expects success; the other expects failure. The circumstances are the same; the attitude creates the difference.

Your attitude is your habitual way of interpreting reality. It's the lens through which you view everything that happens. A positive attitude doesn't mean denying difficulties—it means approaching them as temporary and solvable rather than permanent and insurmountable.

Your attitude broadcasts a frequency that attracts matching circumstances. A defeatist attitude attracts defeating circumstances. An optimistic attitude attracts opportunistic circumstances. Not because the universe is judging you, but because your attitude determines what you perceive, how you respond, and what actions you take.

Today, audit your attitude. When things go wrong, do you tend toward catastrophizing or problem-solving? When opportunities appear, do you doubt or embrace them? When people challenge you, do you become defensive or curious?

Your predominant attitude is creating your predominant reality. If you want to change your altitude in life—how high you rise, how far you go—start by changing your attitude. Choose to interpret circumstances in ways that empower rather than defeat you. This choice creates a completely different reality from the same raw material.

May 12

The path appears when you start walking.

One of the biggest obstacles to manifestation is waiting for the complete path to be visible before taking the first step. People want to see the entire route mapped out, all obstacles identified, all solutions known.

But reality doesn't work this way. The path reveals itself step by step. You must take the first step before the second step becomes visible. You must take the second step before the third appears. This is walking by faith, not by sight. It's moving forward with your intention clear but the method uncertain.

Many stay frozen at the starting line, waiting for certainty that never comes. Meanwhile, those who achieve their goals are the ones who started walking despite uncertainty. Each step they took revealed the next step. Opportunities appeared because they were in motion. Doors opened because they approached them.

Today, if you've been waiting for the complete path to be clear, stop waiting. You won't see the whole path. You'll see the next step. And that's enough. Trust that if you keep moving in the direction of your intention, the path will continue appearing before you. Set your intention clearly. Take the first step that's visible. Then wait for the next step to reveal itself.

This is how reality navigation works—one revealed step at a time, not a complete visible roadmap. Start walking and watch the path appear.

May 13

Pendulums feed on your emotional energy.

In Reality Transurfing, pendulums are energy structures created by groups thinking in the same direction. Political movements, ideologies, consumer trends, social causes, even sports teams—any collective belief system becomes a pendulum when enough people contribute thought energy to it.

A pendulum's purpose is survival through consuming your energy. It provokes strong emotions—anger, fear, guilt, outrage, devotion. The more emotionally you react, the more energy you give, the stronger it becomes.

Pendulums don't distinguish between positive and negative energy—love and hate both feed them equally. Fighting a pendulum feeds it as much as supporting it. Political polarization, social media outrage—both sides feed the same pendulum.

Pendulums create disbalance to hook you. They make you feel guilty, angry, fearful, obsessed, or inferior. Once hooked, you can't stop thinking about the issue. Your attention becomes captured, and what you fear seems to chase you everywhere. Your energy gets diverted to feeding collective structures while your own intentions remain unfulfilled.

Today, notice what pendulums have captured your attention. What movements or dramas consume your thoughts and provoke intense emotions? You cannot avoid pendulums, but you can refuse to feed them. Don't fight them—that strengthens them. Become an observer without emotional reaction. When a pendulum tries to hook you through guilt, fear, or outrage, acknowledge it without engaging emotionally. Care about issues without fanatical attachment. You defeat pendulums by refusing to play their game. Protect your energy for your own intentions. This is not apathy; it's energetic sovereignty.

May 14

Outer intention works through you, not for you.

There are two types of intention: inner and outer. Inner intention is your will to act in the material world—taking direct action to achieve goals through your own effort. Outer intention is your will to have, aligned with the alternatives space—accessing reality where your goal already exists.

People tend to rely exclusively on inner intention, exhausting themselves trying to force outcomes. But inner intention alone is limited and creates excess potential when contaminated with the combination of importance and desire. Outer intention taps into the infinite alternatives space where all possibilities already exist.

Outer intention is achieved through the unity of heart and mind. Your heart must know what it wants (will to have), and your mind must trust that knowing without doubt (will to act). When these are unified, circumstances orchestrate themselves in your favor, opportunities appear synchronistically, and the alternatives space delivers through the path of least resistance.

How do you access outer intention? By reducing importance, releasing attachment to specific outcomes, unifying the heart and mind, and having faith your desire will manifest. This doesn't mean taking no action—it means taking inspired action that flows from alignment rather than forced action that comes from desperation or fear.

Today, shift from forcing outcomes to choosing and receiving them. Set your intention clearly with your heart, release doubt with your mind, and trust the alternatives space to deliver. Reduce importance by accepting: "however it works out is how it should be." Watch for signs and synchronicities. Take action when inspired, rest when guided. This is Reality Transurfing—moving with outer intention rather than forcing with inner intention alone.

May 15

> *Your intention must align with your authentic self; not your ego.*

Not all intentions serve you equally. Some intentions arise from your authentic self—your true desires, values, and soul's calling. Others arise from your ego—the need to prove something, to compensate for insecurity, to gain others' approval. Ego-driven intentions create internal conflict because your authentic self resists manifesting what the ego wants.

You might consciously want the impressive career that brings status, but if that's an ego desire rather than an authentic desire, you'll sabotage your own success. Your authentic self will create resistance to protect you from a path that doesn't truly serve you. The key is to distinguish authentic intentions from ego intentions. Authentic intentions feel aligned, energizing, right, and without discomfort in the heart—even when challenging. Ego intentions feel like "shoulds," pressures, or attempts to fill an inner void.

Today, examine your primary intentions. For each one, ask: Is this what I authentically want, or what I think I should want? Is this desire arising from my true self, or from my ego's need for validation? If you discover ego-driven intentions, don't judge them—just notice them. Then connect with your authentic desires. What does your soul truly call you toward? What would you pursue even without external validation? Align your intentions with authentic desires, and watch resistance dissolve. Your authentic self will support what's genuinely right for you.

May 16

The slide technique creates a bridge to your desired reality.

In Reality Transurfing, a "slide" is a positive mental image that directs your thought energy toward your desired reality. A slide contains the image of your ideal life line—the reality you want to manifest. Unlike negative slides (distorted self-perceptions that limit you), positive slides control outer intention by focusing your consciousness on what you want to create.

There are three levels of visualization: the dream (observing without control), the film (observing with control), and the actor (playing a role in the experience). The most powerful slides occur at the actor level— you don't just watch yourself living your desired reality, you experience being in it. Feel the emotions, sense the environment, embody the version of you who already has this life.

Create your slide with these elements: See and feel yourself living your desired reality. Include specific sensory details and emphasize the feeling of already having it—fulfillment, joy, gratitude. The emotional tone of already possessing your goal matters more than specific details. This is not wanting or hoping; it's knowing and experiencing.

View your slide daily with positive emotion, but without attachment or importance. Don't strain or force—the absence of importance grants freedom. Over time, as you run this slide systematically, your thought energy gradually shapes the reflection in the mirror. Your reality will shift to match the image you've been holding, but only if it's truly your slide, aligned with your heart's authentic desire.

Today, create your slide. Make it vivid, emotionally resonant, and yours alone. Then view it daily from the actor level—experience it as already real. Live inside the slide you want to realize.

May 17

Excess importance creates the problems you're trying to avoid.

When you make something overly important, you create excess potential—and you also coordinate your entire behavior around protecting that importance. This coordination creates rigid, fear-based patterns that generate the very problems you're trying to avoid.

There are two types of importance: inner importance (inflating your own significance) and outer importance (inflating the significance of external circumstances). Both create excess potential that summons balanced forces to restore equilibrium—and balanced forces always work against you.

For example, if you make money overly important, you coordinate all your behavior around not losing it. This creates stinginess, fear-based decisions, and missed opportunities. If you make others' opinions overly important, you coordinate all behavior around avoiding criticism. This creates inauthenticity and people-pleasing. The coordination of importance is exhausting and generates exactly what you fear. When money is overly important, financial problems increase. When approval is overly important, criticism increases.

The solution is reducing importance across the board. Care about things, but don't inflate their importance. Value things, but don't make them the center of your existence. Release the idea that you can control external circumstances through worry and vigilance.

Today, identify what you've made overly important. Notice how you've coordinated your life around protecting this importance. Then consciously reduce it: "This matters, but it's not everything. I care about this, but I'm not defined by it." As importance reduces, coordination relaxes. As coordination relaxes, balanced forces cease working against you, and problems dissolve. You're freed to pursue your goals from relaxed confidence rather than rigid fear.

May 18

Your energy determines what you attract and repel.

Everything in the universe operates on energy and frequency. You are constantly broadcasting an energetic signature based on your thoughts, emotions, beliefs, and state of being. This signature attracts experiences, circumstances, and people that match its frequency, while repelling those that don't.

When your energy is contracted—fear, worry, lack, negativity—you attract contracted circumstances. When your energy is expanded—love, gratitude, abundance, positivity—you attract expanded circumstances. This is not mysticism; it's the law of resonance.

People often try to attract what they want while maintaining the energy of its opposite. They want abundance while broadcasting scarcity energy. They want love while broadcasting unworthiness energy. This doesn't work because their energy repels what they're trying to attract.

Today, pay attention to your energetic state. Throughout the day, check in: What frequency am I broadcasting right now? Is it the frequency of my desired reality or my current reality? Become aware. If you notice low-frequency energy (fear, lack, negativity), consciously shift to high-frequency energy (gratitude, abundance, positivity). This might feel fake at first, but energy is malleable, you can choose to shift it. Elevate your energy, and you automatically become magnetic to higher experiences. Your energy is your most important tool for reality creation.

May 19

Desperation creates what you're trying to avoid.

Desperation—thrashing about frantically trying to force something to happen—creates massive excess potential. It comes from fear and inflated importance, signaling to the universe that you don't believe your goal is achievable. When you act from desperation, you create inner and outer importance, summoning balanced forces that work against you. You try to control every detail, micromanage every aspect, force outcomes through sheer willpower. This resistance usually produces the opposite of what you want.

Calm confidence is the energy of outer intention. You know what you want (heart), you trust it will manifest (mind), and you take action without attachment to specific outcomes. You remain alert but not controlling. You stay committed but release importance. The difference in energy is profound. Desperation feels tight, frantic, exhausting—it's excess potential broadcasting. Confidence feels clear, calm, energizing—it's unity of heart and mind.

Today, notice where desperation has crept into your life. Where are you frantically forcing, controlling, pushing? Feel the exhaustion this creates—it's the weight of excess potential. Then shift to calm confidence: state clearly what you want, reduce its importance by accepting "however it works out is how it should be," and take inspired action without desperation. Practice saying: "I know this is mine. I release the need to control when and how. I act with confidence, not desperation." This shift from desperation to confidence is like unclenching a fist—immediate relief as excess potential dissolves, followed by energy returning, followed by the alternatives space delivering through the path of least resistance.

May 20

The journey is the destination.

People often believe that achieving the goal will bring happiness, fulfillment, or peace. But when they achieve the goal, they discover these feelings are temporary. Soon they're pursuing the next goal, always believing that the next achievement will finally deliver lasting satisfaction. This is the endless pursuit—constantly chasing but never arriving.

In Reality Transurfing, intention is realized in the process, not the goal. The goal gives you direction, but your power lies in taking action—placing one foot in front of the other without attachment to when or how the goal manifests. When you fixate on the outcome, you create importance and excess potential. When you focus on the process, you activate outer intention and move with the flow.

The goal is the destination, but the journey transforms you. You don't feel lasting fulfillment from achievement—you feel fulfillment from having become someone capable of achieving it. The qualities you develop, the growth that occurs, the person you become—this is where true satisfaction lives.

This realization changes everything. You stop postponing happiness until you've achieved the goal and start enjoying the journey itself. You stop seeing obstacles as problems delaying your happiness and start seeing them as opportunities to develop the qualities needed for your goal.

Today, reflect on a goal you're pursuing. What kind of person must you become to achieve this goal? Then realize: your power lies in the process of becoming that person, not in obsessing over the outcome. Move toward your goal without thinking of failure or success. Place one foot in front of the other with confidence. Fall in love with the journey. The goal will manifest when you focus on the process, not when you fixate on the result.

May 21

When the goal is truly yours.

It's common for people to choose goals based on what they think they should want rather than what their heart truly desires. They struggle toward destinations that don't resonate. Even if they arrive, they feel empty—because the goal wasn't truly theirs.

Your heart knows what you're meant for. When you think about your true goal, your heart should sing. You should feel comfort, not tension. If you need to convince yourself, it's a false goal. A true goal feels right without justification, and the path toward it feels alive, not draining.

When your heart and mind are aligned around a true goal, resistance dissolves. You stop needing guarantees, timelines, or validation. Doubt quiets because you are no longer trying to convince yourself. Action flows naturally, without force, because the goal itself is pulling you forward. This is how you know the goal is truly yours. It hardly requires discipline to sustain it. It generates its own momentum.

Today, examine your goals. Does your heart sing when you think about them? Does the journey feel energizing or exhausting? If exhausting, you may be pursuing a false goal imposed by your mind or pendulums that conflict with your heart. Release it. Find what your heart truly wants. Then focus on the process. Place one foot in front of the other. When the goal is truly yours, the journey becomes the reward.

May 22

Clear intention without importance.

This might sound contradictory: know exactly what you want while simultaneously not making it overly important. But this paradox contains the secret of outer intention. When your heart and mind are unified—you know what you want (heart) and trust it will manifest (mind)—you create focused direction. When you reduce importance—you want it but don't inflate its significance—you eliminate excess potential and balanced forces working against you.

These two elements together create perfect conditions for reality to arrange itself. Clear intention without reduced importance creates desperate forcing and excess potential. Reduced importance without clear intention creates aimless drifting with formless energy. But combine them—unified heart-mind direction plus absence of importance—and the alternatives space delivers through the path of least resistance.

Why does this work? Because heart-mind unity activates outer intention, directing your energy toward a specific sector of the alternatives space. Reduced importance eliminates the excess potential that summons balanced forces. You're moving toward your goal with confidence while accepting "however it works out is how it should be." You're committed to the direction, not attached to controlling the outcome.

Today, notice where you're gripping too tightly, making outcomes overly important. Feel the tension—it's excess potential summoning balanced forces against you. Then reduce importance while maintaining direction. Say: "I choose this goal with certainty. I release the timeline and the how. I move forward with confidence, not desperation." Hold your goal lightly but firmly—like water in cupped hands. Grip too tight and it spills. Hold too loosely and it drains. Find the balance: clear direction, minimal importance. This is how outer intention delivers.

May 23

Your reality reflects your dominate frequency.

Everything vibrates at a certain frequency—thoughts, emotions, objects, situations. Your dominant frequency—the frequency you maintain most consistently—determines what you attract and experience. Fear aligns you with fearful circumstances. Love aligns you with loving experiences. Abundance aligns you with abundant outcomes.

For many people, this dominant frequency is set unconsciously through conditioning, circumstances, and habitual thought patterns. They experience whatever reality matches that frequency and assume it is simply "how life is." But once you understand this principle, you regain choice. You can consciously elevate from lower frequencies such as fear, anger, and shame into higher frequencies like love, joy, and gratitude. As your frequency shifts, your reality reorganizes to reflect it.

Today, identify your current dominant frequency. What emotion or state do you spend most time in? Is it worry? Contentment? Frustration? Hope? Be honest. This frequency is creating your present reality. Then choose the frequency that matches the reality you desire. Abundance aligns with gratitude and sufficiency. Love aligns with connection and openness.

Throughout the day, practice maintaining this chosen frequency. When you notice yourself slipping, gently return to it. This is not about suppressing emotion, but about choosing where you predominantly reside. Your dominant frequency becomes your dominant reality.

May 24

Act from your desired reality, now towards it.

There is a subtle but decisive shift that changes how reality responds to you: instead of acting toward your desired reality, act from it. Acting toward something places you in a position of lack. It reinforces the idea that what you want exists somewhere else, in another time. Acting from it means you mentally step into the reality where it already exists and move as the version of yourself who lives there.

In Reality Transurfing, you are not creating a new reality, you are choosing a sector of the alternatives space. When you act from your desired reality, you align your behavior, decisions, and energy with that sector. You stop signaling "I don't have this yet" and begin signaling calm certainty. Reality responds to certainty, not striving.

Do not act toward confidence. Act from confidence.
Do not act toward success. Act from success.
Do not act toward abundance. Act from abundance.

Ask yourself: How would I think, speak, and act if this were already my normal life? Then behave accordingly, without tension or importance.

Today, choose one desired reality. Then move through the day as the person who already lives there. Make decisions calmly. Take action naturally. Hold conversations without proving or convincing. You are not trying to make something happen. You are allowing reality to deliver what you have already chosen.

May 25

Signs and synchronicities confirm you're on the right path.

When you set clear intention and align with it, the universe responds with signs and synchronicities—meaningful coincidences that confirm you're on the right track. You think of someone and they call. You need information and it appears. You face an obstacle and a solution presents itself. These are not random—they're communication from the universe, feedback that you're aligned with your intention.

Many people miss these signs because they're looking for dramatic miracles rather than subtle guidance. But most signs are quiet—a book that falls open to the perfect page, a conversation overheard that provides insight, a "random" encounter that opens a door. When you're alert to signs, you realize the universe is constantly communicating, constantly orchestrating support for your intentions.

Today, become aware of signs and synchronicities. Don't dismiss coincidences as random. When something meaningful aligns perfectly with your needs or intentions, recognize it as confirmation. Express gratitude for these signs—this strengthens your connection to universal guidance. Also, trust your intuition. Often signs come as inner knowing, gut feelings, or sudden certainties. When you feel drawn to take a certain action or avoid a certain path, pay attention. This is outer intention communicating through you. The more you acknowledge and act on signs, the more clearly and frequently they appear. You're learning the language the universe uses to guide you toward your intentions.

May 26

Thoughts today are reality tomorrow.

There's always a time lag between thought and manifestation. The thoughts you hold today shape the circumstances you'll experience tomorrow, next week, and next month. Likewise, what you're experiencing today are the results of thoughts you were thinking weeks or months ago.

This lag can be frustrating because people expect instant results. They think positively for a day and look for immediate change. When nothing appears to happen, they decide it doesn't work and return to old patterns. What they fail to understand is the lag. Past thinking is still unfolding as present experience. New thinking is creating future conditions, but it has not yet had time to appear. This is why consistency matters. You must maintain aligned thoughts long enough for old patterns to complete and new ones to take their place.

Today, accept that what you're experiencing now is the result of past thinking. Don't let current circumstances discourage you—they're temporary, the tail end of old patterns. Focus instead on what you're thinking today, because these thoughts are building tomorrow's reality. Think consistently aligned thoughts for 30, 60, 90 days, and watch as your reality gradually shifts to match. The lag doesn't mean it's not working—it means you must be patient and persistent. Your thoughts today are powerful; you just won't see their full effects until tomorrow.

May 27

Let go of how; focus on what and why.

One of the biggest obstacles to manifestation is fixating on the "how." People know what they want but become paralyzed trying to figure out how to make it happen. They need to see the complete plan before taking the first step. But this is backwards and relies purely on inner intention.

Your job is to define the "what"—what you want with your heart—and trust that outer intention will reveal the path. When you try to control the how, you create excess potential through importance and worry. You limit possibilities to what your conscious mind can imagine. But the alternatives space contains infinite pathways beyond your imagination.

The heart knows the goal. The mind acts on what's in front of it. When you fixate on the entire path, you're trying to control reality rather than choose it. When you release the how and focus on placing one foot in front of the other, the alternatives space delivers the next step naturally.

Today, clarify what your heart truly wants. Be crystal clear on this. Then consciously release the need to see the entire path. Every time your mind tries to figure out how it will all happen, gently redirect: "Not my job right now. My job is to know what I want and take the next step with confidence." Reduce the importance of needing to know. Trust that as you move forward with unified heart and mind, the path reveals itself step by step. This is how outer intention works—not by showing you the entire map, but by lighting the next step as you walk.

May 28

Your relationship with reality determines your experience with reality.

Do you relate to reality as hostile or friendly? As abundant or scarce? As supportive or indifferent? Your relationship with reality—your fundamental beliefs about how the dual mirror works—determines your entire experience.

In Transurfing, the world is like a dual mirror reflecting your relationship to it. If you view reality as hostile, you emit that energy, and the mirror reflects hostility back. If you view reality as supportive, you emit trust, and the mirror reflects support. Reality doesn't exist independently of your perception—it responds to the image you project, not the reflection you see.

This is why battling with reality never works. When you fight against circumstances, you're trying to change the reflection in the mirror instead of changing the image you're projecting. The reflection cannot change until the image changes.

People tend to focus on the reflection—what's happening to them—and react with fear, scarcity, or resistance. This keeps them trapped inside the mirror, living by external rules. But when you shift your focus to the image—your inner state, your relationship to reality—you step outside the mirror and gain control.

Today, examine your relationship with reality. What do you fundamentally believe about how life works? Are you focused on the reflection (what's happening) or the image (how you're relating)? Be honest. Then consciously choose a new relationship. Declare: "I choose to relate to reality as fundamentally friendly. I accept that the mirror reflects my inner state. I shift my image, and the reflection will follow." This shift in relationship transforms everything, because the dual mirror must eventually reflect your new image back to you.

May 29

You're always choosing, even when you think you're not.

Many people feel like victims of circumstance, as if life is happening to them without their choice. But this is an illusion often reinforced by pendulums—external forces that want you to believe you have no choice so they can control your energy and direction.

You are always choosing. Not choosing is a choice. Staying in a bad situation is a choice. Accepting mediocrity is a choice. Following someone else's path is a choice. Most "non-choices" are actually choices made unconsciously or by surrendering to pendulums. You're still choosing; you're just not choosing consciously.

In Transurfing, freedom comes from recognizing: "I have the right to choose." This is your birthright. Not the right to change external circumstances, but the right to choose your response, your direction, your relationship to what's happening. When you recognize you're always choosing, you reclaim your power from pendulums.

You might not like your options—sometimes all choices feel difficult. But you still have choice, even if it's choosing how to respond to unchangeable circumstances. The power is not in always having easy options; the power is in recognizing you're the one choosing and choosing consciously based on your heart's desires, not external demands.

Today, notice where you've been pretending you have no choice. Where have you surrendered your right to choose to a pendulum—a job, a relationship, or societal expectations? This isn't about blame, it's about empowerment. When you acknowledge "I am choosing this," even if you choose to stay for now, you shift from victim to maker. You reclaim your freedom. Then ask: Is this choice aligned with my heart? If not, what different choice will I make? You are always choosing your reality. Choose consciously, from your heart, not from pendulums.

May 30

Trust the process, not the timeline.

After you set a clear intention, there's often a delay before it appears in physical reality. This is not evidence that your intention isn't working—it's simply how the dual mirror operates. There is always a delay in the reflection of the mirror.

When you project a new image through your intention and energy, the reflection takes time to adjust. The mirror doesn't respond instantly. Many people abandon their intention during this delay period, interpreting the lag as failure. They return to old thoughts, old emotions, and old inner images, and the mirror faithfully reflects those familiar patterns instead.

This is where doubt disrupts manifestation. Doubt broadcasts the frequency of the failure life line rather than the success life line. It breaks the unity between heart and mind, weakening the state that activates outer intention.

The alternatives space contains both the life line where your goal is realized and the life line where it is not. Your sustained thought energy determines which one you align with. When you maintain an elevated emotional state, continue living within your slide, and trust that "however it works out is how it should be," you remain aligned with the success life line.

Today, if you're in a delay period—you've set clear intentions but nothing appears to be happening yet—don't interpret this as failure. Recognize it as the natural operation of the dual mirror. The reflection is forming, but it requires time. Maintain your image: keep visualizing from already having, keep directing thought energy toward your goal, keep reducing importance. Show the alternatives space you're committed to this frequency. Refuse to let doubt create misalignment. The delay is temporary; your knowing needs to be permanent. Trust the mirror's delay without abandoning your image.

May 31

You are a maker, not a victim.

As we close this month on Reality Transurfing and intention, integrate this fundamental truth: you are not a passive recipient of reality. You are a maker—someone who asserts their right to choose and consciously create their layer of reality. The alternatives space contains infinite possibilities. Your consciousness—through the unity of your heart and mind, your thought energy, and outer intention—selects which sector becomes your material reality.

For many, life is lived as a guest experience, accepting whatever reality presents. They react to circumstances, follow pendulums, create excess potential through importance, and wonder why life feels like struggle. They're trapped inside the mirror, trying to control the reflection.

You can choose differently. You can live as a maker—choosing intentions from your heart, maintaining heart-mind unity, reducing importance to eliminate balanced forces, directing thought energy through slides, and moving with the alternatives flow. Instead of being trapped inside the mirror, you stand before it, consciously creating the image that will be reflected.

This month you've learned that heart-mind unity activates outer intention, reducing importance eliminates excess potential, living inside your slide directs thought energy, trusting the mirror's delay allows reality to reorganize, and accepting "however it works out" releases attachment.

Today, commit to being a maker. Assert your right to choose. No more surrendering to pendulums. No more inflating importance. No more doubt breaking heart-mind unity. You are the creator of your layer of reality. The alternatives space is infinite. Your unified consciousness selects which possibility manifests. Choose from your heart, act with your mind, reduce importance, and trust the alternatives flow. The reality you desire already exists. Your consciousness brings it into material form. Use that power consciously from this day forward.

June

Visualization & Future Self

Mental Rehearsal Techniques

June 1

Your imagination is the preview of your life's coming attractions.

Einstein said that imagination is more important than knowledge, and he was right. Your imagination is not mere fantasy or escapism—it's the workshop where your future is designed and constructed.

Everything that exists in physical reality first existed in someone's imagination. The chair you're sitting on, the paper or device you're reading this on, the building you're in—all of these were imagined before they were created. Your life works the same way. What you consistently imagine becomes the blueprint for what you create. If you imagine struggle, you're previewing and creating struggle. If you imagine success, you're previewing and creating success.

People often use their imagination unconsciously, replaying past failures or imagining worst-case scenarios. This creates a preview of more problems. But when you consciously direct your imagination toward your desired future, you're literally previewing coming attractions. Your brain doesn't distinguish between vividly imagined experiences and real ones, so each time you imagine your desired future, you're creating the neural pathways, emotional states, and behavioral patterns that will make that future real.

Today, take control of your imagination. Stop letting it run wild with worries and what-ifs. Instead, deliberately imagine your ideal future in vivid detail. See it, feel it, experience it in your mind. This mental rehearsal is not daydreaming—it's reality creation. Your imagination is showing you the preview. Make sure it's a movie you want to watch.

June 2

Visualization is mental rehearsal for physical manifestation.

Athletes use visualization to improve performance—they mentally rehearse their sport, seeing themselves executing perfectly. Studies show this mental practice produces measurable improvements, sometimes nearly as much as physical practice. Why? Because the brain creates the same neural patterns during vivid visualization as during actual performance. You can use this same principle to rehearse your ideal life.

When you visualize your desired outcomes with clarity and an elevated emotion like gratitude or joy, you're training your brain and nervous system to recognize and respond to opportunities that align with those outcomes. You're creating familiarity with success so it doesn't feel foreign when it arrives. You're programming automatic behaviors that support your goals.

Most people never mentally rehearse their desired life. They mentally rehearse their fears, their past failures, and their worries instead. Then they wonder why these patterns keep repeating.

Today, commit to daily visualization practice. Spend 5-10 minutes in a quiet space, eyes closed, vividly imagining your ideal. See yourself waking up in your ideal circumstances, moving through your day successfully, interacting confidently, achieving your goals, feeling fulfilled. Make it sensory-rich—what do you see, hear, feel, smell? Add emotion—feel the joy, pride, gratitude of living this life. This daily mental rehearsal programs your entire being for success. You're not wishing; you're training.

June 3

> *Your future self already exists; you just need to become them.*

In the quantum field, all versions of you exist simultaneously—past versions, present version, and future versions. The you who has achieved your goals already exists as a possibility. Your work is not to create this future self but to become them by aligning with their frequency.

Think of your future self—the version of you who has everything you could imagine. How do they think? How do they feel? How do they act? What beliefs do they hold? What habits do they have? Your future self is not fundamentally different from your current self—they simply have different patterns. When you identify these patterns and begin adopting them now, you accelerate your journey to becoming that future self. You don't wait to achieve the goal before thinking and acting like your future self. You think and act like your future self now, and the achievement follows naturally.

Today, connect with your future self. Close your eyes and imagine the you who has achieved your primary goal. Ask them: What advice do you have for me? What should I stop doing? What should I start doing? What do I need to know? Listen for answers—they might come as thoughts, feelings, or intuitions. Then begin embodying your future self today. Think their thoughts, feel their feelings, take their actions. You're not pretending to be someone you're not; you're becoming who you're meant to be.

June 4

What you focus on expands; what you visualize materializes.

Focus and visualization are powerful creative forces. Your sustained attention on anything causes it to grow in your experience. When you focus on problems while visualizing worst-case scenarios, problems expand and worst cases materialize. When you focus on possibilities while visualizing best-case scenarios, possibilities expand and best cases materialize.

The mechanism is both psychological and energetic. Psychologically, focus directs your perception—you notice evidence of whatever you're focused on while filtering out contradictory evidence. Energetically, focus directs your creative power—like sunlight through a magnifying glass, concentrated attention ignites manifestation.

For many, attention is scattered across hundreds of concerns, worries, and distractions. This diffused focus produces diffused results—lots of activity, little intentional creation. To create powerfully, you must concentrate your focus on your desired outcome while visualizing it clearly and consistently.

Today, notice where your attention habitually goes. Are you focused on what you want or what you don't want? Are you visualizing success or failure? Make a conscious decision to redirect your focus entirely toward your ideal outcomes. Whenever you notice attention drifting to problems or fears, gently redirect to possibilities and ideals. Focus on what you want to expand. Visualize what you want to materialize. This disciplined direction of attention and imagination is how you consciously create your reality.

June 5

Create in your mind first, then reality will follow.

All creation is dual: first you create mentally, then physically. The mental creation must precede the physical creation. An architect doesn't start building without blueprints. A chef doesn't start cooking without a recipe. You shouldn't start building your life without a clear mental image of what you're building.

The mental creation is not less important than the physical creation—it's more important because it determines what the physical creation will be. When you skip the mental creation stage, you end up creating haphazardly, building a life by default rather than by design.

In many cases, people's lives are unintentional creations. The result of reacting to circumstances, following conditioning, and accepting whatever comes. But intentional creators know the secret: create exhaustively in your mind first. See every detail. Feel every emotion. Experience it completely in imagination. Then physical creation becomes almost effortless because you're simply bringing into form what already exists completely in consciousness.

Today, choose one goal and complete its mental creation. Don't think about how to achieve it physically yet. Just create it fully in your mind. See yourself living it. Feel yourself experiencing it. Make it so real in your imagination that it feels more real than your current circumstances. This mental creation is the essential first step. Once mental creation is complete and vivid, physical creation flows naturally.

June 6

Your vision must be so compelling it pulls you forward.

Many people set goals but never achieve them because the vision isn't compelling enough. It's not pulling them forward with magnetic force; it's sitting there as a nice idea they hope to get to someday. A truly compelling vision is different. It excites you. It energizes you. When you think about it, you feel alive. You're willing to sacrifice short-term comforts because this vision is so much more attractive. It's not that you're forcing yourself toward your goal—you're being pulled by desire.

This is the difference between willpower-based achievement and vision-based achievement. Willpower is exhausting and unsustainable. Vision is energizing and natural. Willpower says: "I should do this even though I don't want to." Vision says: "I'm doing this because I want the outcome more than I want to stay comfortable." Your vision must be so clear, so detailed, so emotionally charged that it has gravitational pull. You're attracted to it, drawn toward it, magnetized by it.

Today, evaluate your primary goal. Is your vision of achieving it truly compelling? When you imagine it, do you feel genuine excitement? If not, you may need to amplify your vision. Add more sensory detail—what will you see, hear, feel when you achieve it? Add more emotional depth—how will it feel to have accomplished this? Make your vision so compelling that your current reality feels bland by comparison. When the vision is strong enough, action becomes natural.

June 7

Visualization without emotion is just pictures; emotions makes it real.

Many people visualize correctly in terms of imagery but miss a crucial component: emotion. They form mental pictures of desired outcomes, yet feel little connection to them. Without emotion, visualization lacks impact. Emotion gives meaning to images. It conditions belief and signals importance to the subconscious. While the conscious mind works with words and pictures, the subconscious responds more strongly to feeling and familiarity. What you feel consistently shapes how you think, act, and perceive opportunities. When visualization is paired with emotion, it becomes embodied rather than imagined.

When you visualize with strong, positive emotion—joy, gratitude, excitement, love—you're sending a powerful signal that says "this is important, this is real, this is who I am." Your subconscious accepts it as true and begins to reorganize your behaviors accordingly. The quantum field resonates with this frequency and attracts matching circumstances. Without emotion, visualization remains mental imagery. With emotion, it becomes embodied experience.

Today, when you visualize your desired outcomes, don't just see the images—feel the feelings. How would you feel if you achieved this goal right now? Would you feel relieved? Proud? Joyful? Grateful? Generate those feelings now, during visualization. Don't wait for achievement to feel them; feel them now as if achievement has already occurred. This emotional visualization is what makes your mental images real enough to manifest physically. Images provide direction; emotion gives them force.

June 8

See yourself as already being the person who has what you want.

Most visualization focuses on having—I have the money, the relationship, the success. But more powerful is visualization focused on being—I am wealthy, loved, successful. When you visualize from the being state rather than the having state, you're creating identity-level change rather than just circumstantial change.

Identity is more fundamental than circumstances. Your identity determines what circumstances feel natural. If your identity is that of a struggling person, you will unconsciously recreate struggle even when circumstances briefly improve. If your identity is that of a successful person, successful circumstances tend to follow naturally. When you visualize yourself being the person who has what you want, not just possessing things but embodying the identity, you begin reshaping yourself at the deepest level. You're no longer imagining temporary outcomes. You're imagining a lasting transformation.

Today, shift your visualization from having to being. Don't just visualize having wealth; visualize being a wealthy person. How does a wealthy person carry themselves? How do they think? How do they make decisions? Don't just visualize having a great relationship; visualize being a person that is deeply loved. How does a person who is deeply loved feel? How do they interact? Don't visualize having success; visualize being successful. This identity-level visualization creates permanent change rather than temporary circumstances.

June 9

Your future self is grateful to your present self for the vision you hold.

Imagine meeting your future self five years from now. They've achieved everything you're currently working toward. They're living the life you're visualizing. When they look back at your current self, they feel profound gratitude. Why? Because they know that the vision you're holding now is what made their success possible.

Every moment you spend visualizing, you're building the foundation for your future self's reality. Every time you imagine your desired outcome, you're programming your subconscious, creating neural pathways, and shifting your frequency. Your future self exists because your present self held the vision. This perspective makes daily visualization practice feel meaningful rather than tedious. You're not just daydreaming—you're building someone's (your future self's) reality. You're giving them the life they deserve by holding the vision that makes it possible.

Today, visualize as an act of service to your future self. Imagine them five years from now, grateful that you didn't give up on the vision. Feel their appreciation for your persistence. Let this gratitude flow both directions—from your future self thanking your present self, and from your present self honored to be building your future self's reality. This connection between your present and future self creates powerful motivation to maintain your visualization practice consistently.

June 10

Mental practice is as powerful as physical practice.

Research with athletes proves that mental practice produces nearly the same performance improvements as physical practice. Basketball players who mentally rehearse free throws improve almost as much as those who physically practice. Pianists who mentally practice improve nearly as much as those who physically practice. This is because the brain creates similar neural patterns whether you're actually doing something or vividly imagining doing it.

You can leverage this for any area of life. Want to become more confident? Mentally practice confident interactions. Want to become more successful? Mentally practice successful behaviors. Want to become more peaceful? Mentally practice peaceful responses to stress. The key is vividness and repetition. The mental practice must be detailed and realistic, not vague or generic. And it must be repeated consistently, just like physical practice. Five minutes of vivid mental practice daily creates measurable change within weeks.

Today, identify one skill or quality you want to develop. Then design a mental practice routine. Each day, spend 5-10 minutes vividly imagining yourself demonstrating this skill or quality in various situations. See yourself acting confidently, deciding wisely, responding peacefully—whatever you're practicing. Make it detailed and realistic. Feel the emotions of successfully demonstrating this quality. This daily mental practice will create the same neural changes as physical practice, preparing you to naturally demonstrate these qualities in real life.

June 11

You cannot outperform your self image.

Your self-image—how you see yourself—creates an invisible boundary around your performance. You might temporarily exceed your self-image through unusual effort or circumstances, but you'll always return to levels consistent with your self-image. This is why people who suddenly acquire wealth often lose it—their self-image is still rooted in lack, and they unconsciously recreate familiar financial patterns. The same principle applies to weight loss. Many people regain weight because their self-image has not shifted, and they return to what feels normal to them.

The solution is not trying harder at the external level but changing your self-image through consistent visualization. When you regularly visualize yourself as successful, capable, and worthy, you gradually reshape your self-image. At first, there's dissonance—visualizing success while still identifying as unsuccessful. But with persistence, the visualized self begins to replace the old self-image. Once your self-image changes, external performance naturally rises to match it, without force or strain.

Today, examine your self-image honestly. How do you truly see yourself? Not how you wish you were seen or how you present yourself to others, but how you see yourself in private moments. Then begin consciously reshaping this self-image through visualization. See yourself differently. Create a new self-image that matches your desired reality. Visualize this new self-image daily until it becomes your actual self-image. When your self-image changes, your performance will rise effortlessly to match it.

June 12

The more detailed your visualization, the more powerful the manifestation.

Vague visualization produces vague results. If you visualize "being successful" without any specific details, your subconscious doesn't know what to create. But when you visualize with precise detail—the specific work you're doing, the exact environment you're in, the particular people around you, the precise feelings you're experiencing—you give your subconscious clear instructions.

Detailed visualization works better for several reasons. First, detail makes it feel more real to your brain, which creates stronger neural patterns. Second, detail eliminates ambiguity about what you're creating. Third, detail helps you recognize opportunities when they appear because you know exactly what you're looking for.

People often keep their visualizations vague because specific details feel scary—making them real, creating pressure. But vague visualizations don't manifest powerfully. You must be willing to get specific, even if it feels vulnerable.

Today, take your primary goal and create an extremely detailed visualization. Not just "I want financial abundance" but specific: What's your exact income? What's your daily routine? Where do you live—what does your home look like, down to the furniture? What do you wear? How do you spend your time? Who are you with? Get so specific that you could write a detailed story of a day in this desired reality. Then practice visualizing this detailed scene daily. The specificity might feel uncomfortable at first, but it dramatically increases manifestation power.

Visualize the process, not just the outcome.

While outcome visualization is powerful, process visualization is equally important. Outcome visualization shows you celebrating the achievement. Process visualization shows you taking the actions that lead to achievement. Both are necessary for complete manifestation. If you only visualize outcomes, you might not recognize or take the necessary steps when they appear. If you only visualize process, you might lose sight of why you're doing it. Together, they create complete preparation.

Visualize yourself successfully navigating challenges, making good decisions, persisting through difficulties, learning from setbacks, and gradually progressing toward your goal. This prepares your nervous system for the actual journey. When similar situations arise in reality, you've already practiced handling them in your mind. You respond automatically with the successful patterns you've visualized. Athletes do this constantly—they don't just visualize winning; they visualize each move, each decision, each challenge they might face during competition. When the day comes, they've mentally practiced hundreds of times.

Today, add process visualization to your practice. Visualize not just having achieved your goal, but also visualizing yourself taking the actions, making the decisions, and demonstrating the qualities that lead to achievement. See yourself overcoming obstacles successfully. See yourself staying committed when it's difficult. This prepares you psychologically and neurologically for the actual journey.

June 14

Your visualizations are instructions to your subconscious mind.

Your subconscious mind is incredibly powerful, but not discerning. It accepts whatever you consistently present to it as instructions for creating reality. When you regularly visualize success, your subconscious receives a clear directive: "Create success." It then works continuously to influence behavior, recognize opportunities, and align circumstances in support of that outcome.

When you unconsciously visualize failure or struggle, the same process occurs. Your subconscious accepts those images as instructions as well: "Create failure and struggle." It applies the same effort, consistency, and responsiveness to producing those results. The power is neutral. The direction comes from what you repeatedly imagine and emotionally reinforce.

Your subconscious doesn't judge whether the instructions are good or bad—it simply follows them. This is why controlling your mental imagery is crucial. Every vivid image you hold is an instruction you're giving to the most powerful part of your mind. Often, people give their subconscious chaotic, contradictory instructions through scattered, unfocused mental imagery. Then they wonder why their lives feel chaotic and unfocused.

Today, recognize that your visualizations are instructions. Before visualizing anything, ask: Is this an instruction I want to give my subconscious? Am I instructing it to create what I want or what I fear? Then take control of your mental imagery. Consciously visualize only what you want to create. Give clear, consistent instructions. Your subconscious is waiting for guidance—make sure the guidance you give leads where you want to go.

June 15

*First person visualization creates
identity; third person visualization creates objectivity.*

There are two perspectives for visualization: first-person (seeing from your own eyes) and third-person (seeing yourself as if watching a movie). Both are valuable for different purposes.

First-person visualization is more immersive. When you visualize from your own perspective—seeing what you would see, hearing what you would hear—your brain treats it more like actual experience. This is powerful for creating identity-level change and emotional conditioning. Use first-person when you want to embody a new way of being.

Third-person visualization creates more objectivity. When you see yourself from outside, as if watching yourself in a movie, it's easier to maintain emotional balance and see the bigger picture. Use third-person when you want to review your desired life without getting lost in details, or when you're working with challenging scenarios where too much immersion might create anxiety.

Today, experiment with both perspectives. Spend time visualizing from first-person—see your desired reality from your own eyes, feel it from inside your body. Then switch to third-person—watch yourself living your desired reality as if watching a movie. Notice which perspective feels more natural for you. Use first-person for identity and emotion work. Use third-person for clarity and objectivity. Many practitioners find value in combining both perspectives in the same visualization session.

June 16

Visualization is not escape from reality; it's creation of reality.

Some people criticize visualization as escapism—avoiding reality by retreating into fantasy. But this misunderstands what visualization is. Properly practiced, visualization is not an escape from reality; it's a conscious creation of future reality. You're not hiding from current circumstances in pleasant daydreams. You're deliberately programming your mind and emotions to create different circumstances.

The difference between escapist fantasy and creative visualization is intent and consistency. Escapist fantasy is passive, random, and used to avoid taking action. Creative visualization is active, deliberate, and coupled with inspired action. Fantasy says: "I wish things were different, so I'll imagine they are and ignore my actual life." Visualization says: "I'm programming my subconscious and emotional state to create what I desire, and I'm taking aligned action toward it." One is avoidance; the other is creation.

Today, ensure your visualization practice is creative rather than escapist. After visualizing, ask yourself: What action can I take today that aligns with this vision? What small step moves me toward this reality? If you're only visualizing without ever taking action, you're engaged in fantasy. But when visualization is coupled with action—using the mental programming to guide your decisions and efforts—you're engaged in conscious creation. This is not escape; this is the most practical form of reality engineering.

June 17

Your future self is a choice, not a prediction.

Many people think of their future self as something that will happen to them—a natural evolution based on their current trajectory. But this is passive and limiting. Your future self is not predetermined; it's chosen. You get to decide who you become. Right now, you're choosing your future self through your daily thoughts, actions, and visualizations. Are you choosing consciously or by default?

Often, people choose by default—they become a slightly older version of their current self, carrying forward the same patterns, habits, and limitations. But you can choose differently. You can consciously design who you want to become and then become that person through consistent visualization and aligned action.

Think of it this way: five years from now, you'll definitely be different than you are today. The question is not whether you'll change but who you'll change into. Will you change by default, becoming whoever circumstances and conditioning make you? Or will you change by design, becoming whoever you consciously choose to become?

Today, make a clear choice about your future self. Who do you choose to become? What qualities do you choose to develop? What kind of person do you choose to be? Write it down. Then begin visualizing this chosen future self daily. You're not predicting your future; you're choosing it. Your future self is a conscious decision, not an inevitable outcome.

June 18

Consistency in visualization is more important than intensity.

Many people have intense visualization sessions occasionally—spending an hour creating detailed mental images when they're motivated. But then they go days or weeks without visualizing at all. This inconsistent practice produces minimal results. What matters more than intensity is consistency. Five minutes of visualization every single day is more powerful than an hour-long session once per month. Why? Because you're training your nervous system and programming your subconscious. This requires repetition, like learning any skill.

One intense session doesn't create lasting neural change. But consistent daily practice, even if brief, gradually rewires your brain. Think of it like physical exercise. One marathon workout followed by weeks of inactivity doesn't build fitness. But 15 minutes of exercise daily consistently builds significant fitness over time. Mental and emotional conditioning works the same way.

Today, commit to daily visualization practice, even if it's just five minutes. Make it non-negotiable, like brushing your teeth. Don't wait for motivation or large blocks of time. Just spend five minutes each morning or evening visualizing your desired reality. The consistency will create compounding results. Five minutes daily for 30 days equals 150 minutes of neural programming. Five minutes daily for a year equals over 30 hours. This consistent practice will transform your self-image, emotional state, and ultimately, your reality.

June 19

What you imagine with belief becomes your reality.

Imagination alone is not enough. You can imagine building a successful business, but without belief, it remains fantasy. The combination of imagination and belief is what creates a purposefully designed reality.

Imagination provides the blueprint—the detailed picture of what you want. Belief provides the power—the conviction that it's possible and attainable for you. Together, they're unstoppable.

People often imagine better lives but don't believe they're possible. This imagination without belief creates yearning rather than manifestation. Others believe change is possible but never imagine specifically what they want. This belief without imagination produces unfocused effort and aimless motivation. Belief without imagination produces unfocused effort and aimless motivation. Both are necessary: clear imagination of what you want, paired with genuine belief that it is attainable.

How do you develop belief if you don't currently have it? Through small successes. Start with visualizing outcomes you can almost believe in. Achieve those first. Each success builds evidence that visualization works, and evidence strengthens belief. Over time, gradually expand the scale of what you visualize and believe is possible.

Today, assess whether you have both imagination and belief for your goals. Can you imagine your desired reality clearly? Do you genuinely believe you can achieve it? If imagination is weak, make your visualizations more detailed. If belief is weak, start with more believable goals and build from there. The sweet spot is imagining what you deeply desire while genuinely believing it's achievable. This combination is creative magic.

June 20

Your dominant mental images become your physical reality.

Whatever mental images you hold most consistently and emotionally will eventually materialize in your physical reality. This is not mysticism—it's how your brain works. Your dominant mental images program your reticular activating system (the part of your brain that determines what you notice), shape your beliefs about what's possible, influence your decisions and actions, and determine your emotional state. All of these factors directly create your external circumstances.

If your dominant mental images are of struggle, limitation, and failure, your brain will notice opportunities for struggle, believe limitation is real, make decisions that maintain failure, and create emotional states that repel success.

If your dominant mental images are of ease, possibility, and success, your brain does the opposite—noticing opportunities, believing in possibility, making successful decisions, and creating emotional states that attract success.

The key word is dominant. Occasional positive visualizations don't override dominant negative images. What matters is what you imagine most consistently.

Today, audit your dominant mental images. What do you spend most of your time imagining? Your fears or your desires? Problems or solutions? Lack or abundance? Be honest about your dominant images, not your occasional ones. Then commit to shifting your dominant images. Every time you notice yourself imagining what you don't want, redirect to imagining what you do want. Over time, your dominant mental images will shift, and your physical reality will shift to match.

June 21

> *Visualization is the language your subconscious understands best.*

Your conscious mind processes language and logic. But your subconscious mind—which controls 95% of your behavior, beliefs, and automatic responses—processes images and emotions. You can tell yourself logically "I am confident" all day, but if the images your subconscious holds are of you failing and embarrassing yourself, logic won't override those images. Your behavior will reflect the images, not the logic.

This is why visualization is so powerful—it speaks the native language of your subconscious. When you create vivid, emotional images of yourself succeeding, your subconscious accepts these as real and adjusts your automatic behaviors accordingly. You become confident not because you logically understand confidence but because your subconscious holds images of you being confident. Changing your subconscious programming through logic alone is slow and difficult. Changing it through visualization is faster and more natural because you're using the right language.

Today, recognize that telling yourself things rationally has limited power to change deep patterns. But showing yourself things through visualization has tremendous power. Want to change a belief? Don't just think different thoughts; visualize experiences that would create that belief. Want to change a habit? Don't just resolve to change; visualize yourself successfully demonstrating the new habit. Speak to your subconscious in its language—images and emotions—and watch how quickly it responds.

June 22

Your vision must be bigger than your current circumstances.

If your vision perfectly matches your current circumstances, you're not really visualizing—you're just observing. True visualization requires you to imagine realities beyond what currently exists in your life. This feels uncomfortable because it creates dissonance: "I'm imagining abundance but experiencing scarcity. I'm imagining success but experiencing struggle." This dissonance is necessary. It's the tension that pulls you forward.

Your current circumstances are the result of your past thinking and actions. They're already created; they're done. Your vision is the blueprint for your future circumstances. They're not yet created; they're potential. The gap between current circumstances and vision is the creative tension that motivates action, inspires solutions, and attracts resources. Without this gap, there's no reason to change, grow, or act.

Today, ensure your vision is genuinely bigger than your current circumstances. If you're playing it safe by visualizing only slightly improved versions of what you already have, you're limiting yourself. Dream bigger. Imagine realities that feel almost impossible. Let yourself vision what you truly desire, not just what seems reasonable. Yes, this creates dissonance. Yes, this feels uncomfortable. But this creative tension is what pulls you forward into expanded reality. Don't let current circumstances limit your vision. Let your vision expand your circumstances.

Each visualization lays another plank in the bridge.

Between your current reality and your desired reality exists a gap. This gap can feel overwhelming—so much distance to travel, so many changes needed. But visualization builds a bridge across this gap. Each time you visualize, you're laying another plank in that bridge. Initially, the gap seems uncrossable. But with consistent visualization, you begin to feel familiar with your desired reality.

It starts to feel like somewhere you've been before, somewhere you know. This familiarity reduces fear and resistance. When opportunities appear that align with your vision, you recognize and take them because you've practiced them mentally. When challenges arise, you handle them confidently because you've rehearsed them in your mind. The gap shrinks not because you've physically traveled the distance but because you've mentally traversed it so many times that it no longer feels foreign.

Today, see your visualization practice as bridge-building. You're not just daydreaming—you're constructing a mental and emotional pathway from where you are to where you want to be. Each visualization session adds another section to this bridge. Be patient with the process. Bridges take time to build. But every visualization session is progress. You're making your desired reality more familiar, more accessible, more inevitable. Keep building the bridge through consistent visualization, and one day you'll discover you've crossed the gap.

June 24

See yourself succeeding before anyone else believes you can.

When you're pursuing big goals, most people around you won't believe you can achieve them. They're not being malicious—they simply can't see beyond their own limitations and project those limitations onto you. If you wait for others' belief before visualizing success, you'll never start.

You must see yourself succeeding before anyone else does. Your visualization must be so strong that external doubt doesn't shake it. This requires courage because you're believing in something no one else believes in. You're seeing something no one else sees. You're holding a vision that others think is delusional. But every great achievement in history began with someone seeing success before others believed it possible. The Wright brothers saw themselves flying when everyone knew humans couldn't fly. Walt Disney saw Disneyland when everyone thought it was financial suicide. Every innovator, creator, and breakthrough achiever held a vision that others couldn't see.

Today, give yourself permission to see success that others doubt. Your visualization doesn't need others' validation. In fact, it's better if you keep your most precious visions private, protecting them from skeptics who would diminish them. See yourself succeeding with such clarity and conviction that others' disbelief becomes irrelevant. Your vision is for you, not for them. When success arrives, they'll believe. Until then, your belief is enough.

June 25

*Your mental imagery determines
your emotional state, which determines your frequency.*

There's a clear cause-and-effect chain: the images you hold in your mind shape how you feel, and those feelings influence the internal state you consistently project.

That internal state guides the kinds of circumstances you experience. Images rooted in fear or lack generate anxiety and scarcity, reinforcing those conditions. Images centered on love, abundance, or success evoke confidence and gratitude, aligning you with experiences that reflect those qualities.

It's common to try to change frequency directly by attempting to feel better without changing mental imagery. This approach is backward. Change the images, and emotions shift naturally. As emotions change, frequency adjusts. As frequency adjusts, circumstances begin to follow. The true leverage point is mental imagery. When that changes, everything else follows.

Today, treat your mental imagery as your primary tool for emotional and energetic alignment. When you notice low emotional states, pause and check what you were imagining. Redirect your focus to images that empower and uplift you, and allow your emotions to recalibrate on their own. You don't need to force positive feelings. Change the imagery, and the emotional state will follow naturally. This is one of the most efficient ways to influence your internal state and the experiences that arise from it.

June 26

Rehearse success so often that success becomes your new normal.

Your brain has a concept of "normal," what feels familiar, safe, and expected. For many, their current circumstances have become that baseline, even if those circumstances are limiting. Anything significantly better can feel abnormal, uncomfortable, or even threatening. This is why self-sabotage often appears when success approaches. When improvement feels unfamiliar, the brain attempts to restore what it recognizes as normal, pulling you back toward old patterns.

The solution is to rehearse success so consistently in your mind that success becomes familiar. When you visualize yourself succeeding daily for weeks and months, success starts to feel normal. Your brain begins to expect success instead of resisting it. When real opportunities appear, they feel natural rather than foreign, so you move toward them instead of pulling away.

This is the difference between those who achieve success briefly and those who maintain it. The maintainers have rehearsed success so thoroughly that it no longer surprises them. They're comfortable with success because it feels like home.

Today, commit to rehearsing success often enough that it becomes your new normal. Visualize successful outcomes daily until they feel as familiar as your current circumstances. When success feels normal in your mind, it can become normal in your life. Until success feels normal, you will unconsciously resist it even while consciously pursuing it. Make success feel normal through consistent mental rehearsal.

June 27

*Your future self already knows
the path; visualization helps you hear their guidance.*

Your future self, the version of you who has achieved your goals, exists in potential form. They have already walked the path you are about to walk. They know what worked, what didn't, what to avoid, and what to embrace. When you visualize connecting with your future self, you are not just imagining. You are accessing insight from a version of you who has already succeeded.

This may sound mystical, but there is growing understanding that information is not limited to linear time. Your future success can inform your present actions. During visualization, imagine meeting your future self. Ask questions. What should I focus on right now? What should I stop doing? What matters most in this moment? Then listen. The answers may arrive as words, feelings, images, or a quiet sense of knowing. Trust what comes through.

Today, practice connecting with your future self through visualization. See them clearly, successful, fulfilled, and calm. Feel their presence. Ask for guidance and listen for the response. Then act on what you receive. You are tuning into your own potential path. Your future self benefits from the choices you make now, and that connection is always available to you. Listen closely and let that wisdom guide your actions today.

June 28

*Visualization without action
is fantasy; action without vision is chaos.*

You need both visualization and action. Visualization without action becomes fantasy, pleasant mental imagery with no real-world effect. Action without visualization becomes busy movement without direction, effort spent with little return.

The optimal approach combines both: visualize clearly to program your mind and emotions, then take inspired action aligned with your vision. Visualization provides the target and the motivation. Action provides the vehicle and the result. Each strengthens the other.

Visualization makes your actions more effective because you're working toward a clear target with confident expectation. Actions make your visualizations more real because you're proving to yourself through behavior that you're serious about your vision.

Today, make sure you're balancing visualization and action. The balance matters. Spend time visualizing daily to program your subconscious and maintain motivation. Then take action daily to prove your commitment and build momentum. Visualization plants the seed. Action nurtures its growth. Both are necessary. Don't get stuck visualizing without acting. Don't get stuck acting without vision. When you combine the two, progress accelerates naturally.

June 29

The quality of your vision determines the quality of your life.

In many cases, people's visions are too small, too vague, or too influenced by what they believe is realistic rather than what they truly desire. They settle for modest improvements rather than genuine transformation. They visualize what others expect of them rather than what their soul calls them toward. A small, compromised vision produces a life that never fully expands.

But when you dare to hold a larger vision—to see yourself living the life you truly desire, not the life that seems acceptable—you activate different creative forces. You inspire yourself to unprecedented action. You attract resources and opportunities that would never appear for small visions. You become someone different than who you've been. The size and quality of your vision literally determines the size and quality of your life. Small vision, small life. Grand vision, grand life. Compromised vision, compromised life. Authentic vision, authentic life.

Today, audit your vision. Is it truly what you desire, or what you think you should desire? Is it big enough to excite you, or so modest it leaves you bored? Is it authentic to who you are, or designed to please others? Upgrade your vision to match your true desires, not your fears or others' expectations. Give yourself permission to vision the most extraordinary life you can imagine. An upgraded vision creates an upgraded life. The quality of your vision determines everything.

June 30

You are the artist,
and your life is the canvas. Visualize the masterpiece.

As we close this month on visualization and future self, embrace this truth: your life is not something that happens to you—it's something you create. You are the artist. Your consciousness is the brush. Your imagination provides the vision. Your emotions provide the color. Your actions apply the paint. Every day, you're painting your life, stroke by stroke, choice by choice. The question is: Are you painting intentionally or randomly? Are you creating a masterpiece or accepting whatever appears?

People frequently never pick up the brush consciously. They let circumstances, other people, and unconscious patterns do the painting. Then they look at the canvas and wonder why it doesn't match what they wanted. But you now understand the power of visualization—it's the preliminary sketch that guides your painting. Before an artist puts paint to canvas, they visualize what they want to create. They see it in their mind's eye first. Then they bring that vision to life through skillful application.

You can do the same with your life. Visualize the masterpiece—the life that would make your soul sing. See it clearly, feel it deeply, believe it completely. Then pick up your brush and start painting through conscious daily choices and actions. This is your canvas. This is your one life. Make it a masterpiece. The vision is yours to create, and the masterpiece is yours to paint.

July

Creating Abundance

From Scarcity to Prosperity

July 1

Abundance is your natural state, scarcity is learned.

You were not born believing in scarcity. As a child, you didn't worry about whether there was enough love, joy, or possibility in the universe. Scarcity is a learned belief, most often absorbed from parents, culture, and experiences of limitation. But learned beliefs can be unlearned.

Abundance is actually the natural state of the universe—look at nature's abundance, the endless growth, the countless stars, the inexhaustible creativity of life. Scarcity only exists in human consciousness, created by fear and maintained by belief. When you recognize that scarcity is just a belief system rather than reality, you can choose to adopt a mindset of abundance instead.

This doesn't mean denying practical realities or spending irresponsibly. It means shifting from a mindset of "there's never enough" to "there's always enough, often more than enough." This shift changes everything—how you perceive opportunities, how you make decisions, how you feel about money and resources.

Today, begin dismantling your scarcity beliefs by examining their origin. Where did you learn that there's not enough? Who taught you to worry about scarcity? Recognize these as learned patterns, not truth. Then consciously choose abundance: "The universe is abundant. Resources flow to me easily. There is always enough." This is not denial. It's a return to your natural state of abundance that existed before scarcity beliefs were imposed.

July 2

What you appreciate, appreciates.

This principle works in two ways. First, what you appreciate grows in value to you. You notice it more, enjoy it more, and benefit from it more. Second, what you appreciate tends to increase in your life, both in quality and in quantity.

When you appreciate the money you have, you open yourself to greater financial resources. When you appreciate your relationships, they deepen and new supportive connections appear. When you appreciate opportunities, additional opportunities arise. Appreciation carries a consciousness of abundance. When you value what you already have, you signal that there's enough. In turn, the universe responds by giving you more to value.

When attention is placed on what's missing, through complaint or dissatisfaction, a consciousness of scarcity is reinforced. Focusing on lack tends to create more experiences that confirm it.

It's common to postpone appreciation until circumstances improve. People tell themselves they'll be grateful when they have more money, a better job, or a nicer home. But this approach is backwards. Appreciation comes first. Expansion follows.

Today, practice genuine appreciation for what is already present. Appreciate the money in your account, even if it feels modest. Appreciate the food in your pantry, the roof over your head, the opportunities already present. Feel genuine gratitude for these things. As you appreciate what is, you create space for what can be. What you appreciate, appreciates.

July 3

Abundance flows to those who feel abundant, not to those who need it most.

This seems unfair but it's how energy works. The person who feels abundant—even before having much—attracts abundance because they're broadcasting an abundant frequency. The person who feels needy—even if they objectively need resources—repels abundance because they're broadcasting a frequency of lack.

The universe doesn't respond to your objective needs; it responds to your energetic frequency. When you feel needy, desperate, or lacking, you're in a scarcity mindset. This contracts your energy, clouds your perception, and creates desperate actions that push opportunities away.

When you feel abundant, grateful, and sufficient, you're in a mindset of abundance. This expands your energy, clarifies your perception, and creates confident actions that attract opportunities. This is why the rich often get richer—not just because they have more resources, but because having resources makes it easier to feel abundant, which attracts more resources.

But you can break this cycle. You don't need to have abundance to feel abundant. You can choose to feel abundant now, regardless of current circumstances, by focusing on what you have rather than what you lack, by trusting rather than fearing, by giving rather than hoarding.

Today, practice feeling abundant even if your circumstances seem scarce. Find evidence of abundance around you—the air you breathe freely, the sun that shines without charge, the opportunities available to you. Cultivate the feeling of abundance, and watch as abundance begins flowing to match your frequency.

July 4

Your beliefs about money determine your experience with money.

Money is neutral energy—it's simply a tool for transferring value and facilitating exchange. But your beliefs about money are charged with emotion and meaning. These beliefs determine how freely this energy flows to you and through you.

If you believe money is hard to earn, you restrict the flow and experience difficulty. If you believe you're not worthy of wealth, you'll unconsciously repel opportunities. If you believe there's never enough, you'll hoard and create blockages in the flow.

Understanding money as energy changes everything. Energy flows. Energy multiplies. Energy transforms. When you hoard it in fear, you stop the flow and the energy stagnates. When you use it, invest it, and circulate it with confidence, the energy multiplies and returns to you amplified. Money wants to move—it's currency, from the word "current." Like electricity, it flows through circuits. When you believe it's scarce and grip it tightly, you break the circuit. When you believe it's abundant and let it flow, you complete the circuit and more flows back.

Most money beliefs were formed in childhood by watching their parents' relationship with money and hearing their statements about it. These beliefs operate unconsciously, treating money as a limited physical object rather than unlimited flowing energy. This creates patterns that feel like facts but are actually just inherited programming about energy.

Today, examine your beliefs in regards to money. Complete these sentences: Money is... Rich people are... I can't have money because... When you identify limiting beliefs, challenge them—are they true or just inherited programming? Then install empowering beliefs: Money is energy that flows to me easily. Energy circulates—when I give, I receive. Change your beliefs, and the energy flow must change to match.

July 5

Give freely and you will receive abundantly.

The law of circulation states that what you give flows back to you multiplied. When you give freely—money, time, knowledge, support— you're declaring to the universe "I have abundance to share." This broadcasts an abundance mindset and attracts more abundance to you. When you hoard and withhold, you're declaring "I don't have enough; I must protect what little I have." This broadcasts a mindset of scarcity and repels abundance.

Giving is not about depleting yourself or giving beyond your means. It's about giving from overflow, from joy, from the recognition that giving creates receiving.

Many people resist giving because they're in a mindset of scarcity. They think "If I give this away, I'll have less." But universal laws work differently: giving creates a vacuum that the universe rushes to fill. The more you give, the more you receive—not from the same source you gave to, but from the universal flow.

Today, practice giving something—money, time, knowledge, appreciation, support. Give without expectation of return, but with the knowing that giving creates receiving. If you have little money, give what you can—even small amounts given with the right mindset create abundance. If you have time, give it generously. If you have knowledge, share it freely.

Watch what happens when you give from a mindset of abundance rather than scarcity. You'll discover that giving doesn't deplete—it multiplies.

July 6

Act as if you are already wealthy, and wealth will follow.

This doesn't mean spending money you don't have or pretending to be rich. It means adopting the mindset, attitudes, and behaviors of a wealthy person now, before the money arrives.

How does a wealthy person think about money? They think abundantly. There's always more where that came from. They think generously. They tip well, donate freely, and help others. They think confidently. They trust their ability to create more. They think gratefully. They appreciate what they have. How does a wealthy person act? They act with worthiness and self-respect. They dress well within their means. They invest in themselves and their growth. They make decisions based on value, not just price. They carry themselves with quiet confidence.

When you adopt these wealthy attitudes and behaviors now, you program your subconscious for wealth. You also signal to the universe that you're ready for wealth. You create a self-fulfilling prophecy. Acting wealthy makes you feel wealthy. Feeling wealthy changes how you think and decide. Those decisions open the door to wealth-building opportunities, and opportunities lead to real results.

Today, identify one way you can act as if you're already wealthy. Maybe it's how you tip, how you dress, how you carry yourself, how you make decisions. This is not about spending more money—it's about embodying a wealthy mindset. Act from abundance rather than scarcity, from generosity rather than fear, from confidence rather than worry. This shift in how you act creates a shift in what you attract.

July 7

Wealth is attracted to those who appreciate it and repelled by those who resent it.

People tend to claim they want wealth while simultaneously resenting wealthy people. They criticize the rich, assume wealth comes from exploitation, or believe that wanting wealth is selfish. This creates internal contradiction—conscious desire for wealth coupled with subconscious rejection of it. Your subconscious won't create something you secretly despise.

If you resent wealth or wealthy people, you're energetically repelling the very thing you claim to want. To attract wealth, you must appreciate it—in yourself when you have it, and in others who have it. This doesn't mean endorsing unethical behavior or worshipping money. It means recognizing that wealth itself is neutral and can be used for tremendous good. When you see wealthy people, instead of resentment, practice appreciation: "I appreciate that they created that. Good for them. I can create wealth too." When you encounter displays of wealth, instead of judgment, practice openness: "Abundance is available to everyone, including me."

Today, examine your relationship with wealth and wealthy people. Do you secretly resent or judge them? If so, recognize this is repelling wealth from your life. Consciously shift to appreciation. When you see someone successful, silently appreciate their achievement and affirm that success is available to you too. When you encounter wealth, appreciate it rather than resent it. This shift from resentment to appreciation removes a major block to your own wealth creation.

July 8

Your income can only grow to the extent that you do.

There's a direct correlation between your personal development and your income. As Jim Rohn said, "To have more, you must become more." You cannot out-earn your self-image, your skills, your value to the marketplace, or your consciousness.

If you want to increase your income, you must increase yourself. This means developing valuable skills that the marketplace rewards. It means expanding your consciousness to hold a larger vision of what's possible. It means growing your confidence to negotiate better deals, pursue bigger opportunities, and handle greater responsibility. It means becoming someone capable of managing and multiplying money rather than someone who earns and loses it.

It's common for people to focus exclusively on trying to make more money without developing themselves. But this approach has limited effectiveness. You might temporarily earn more through extra effort, but without corresponding personal growth, you'll plateau or even regress.

Today, shift focus from "how can I make more money?" to "how can I become more valuable?" What skills can you develop? What knowledge can you acquire? What limiting beliefs can you transcend? What capabilities can you expand? As you grow in value, skill, consciousness, and capability, your income will naturally grow to match.

Don't just work hard for money; work deliberately on yourself. Your income is a reflection of you—grow yourself, and your income will follow.

July 9

To those who have, more will be given.

Your dominant thought patterns about resources—money, opportunities, love, time—directly create your experience of those resources. When you think from scarcity, you operate from fear and protection. You hoard what you have, afraid to use it or share it. You see opportunities as limited and competition as threatening. This contracted energy repels the very abundance you're trying to create or protect.

When you think from abundance, you operate from confidence and expansion. You use what you have, knowing more will come. You see opportunities as plentiful and others' success as evidence of possibility. This expansive energy attracts more abundance.

This principle appears in the Parable of Talents: "For whoever has, to him more will be given, and he will have abundance; but whoever does not have, even what he has will be taken away from him." The servants who believed they could multiply their talents invested them and received more. The servant who feared losing his talent buried it to protect it— and lost even that. He operated from scarcity and created scarcity. The law is this: whatever you focus on expands. Abundance attracts abundance. Scarcity attracts scarcity.

Today, examine your dominant thinking pattern. When you receive money, do you think about only protecting it or using it to create more? When you see opportunity, do you think "there's not enough" or "abundance is everywhere"? When someone succeeds, do you feel threatened or inspired?

If you discover scarcity in your thinking, consciously shift to abundance. Practice: "I have enough. The universe is abundant. I can use what I have to create more." Act from abundance even when circumstances suggest scarcity. Use your talents, share your resources, invest your energy. To those who think and act from abundance, more abundance will be given.

July 10

The universe rewards those who take action.

An abundance mindset is essential, but it must be paired with action. You can't sit on your couch visualizing wealth while taking no steps towards creating it and expect money to appear. Support shows up for those who move, who take action, who demonstrate through behavior that they're serious about their intentions.

Think of it this way. An abundance mindset sets the destination, but action hoists the sails. You can know exactly where you want to go, but without raising the sails and making the proper adjustments, the wind can't move you in your desired direction. Action allows you to catch the wind, respond to changing conditions, and keep making forward progress.

Action demonstrates commitment. When you take action toward your goals, you're telling the universe "I'm serious about this. I'm willing to work for it. I'm ready to receive it." The universe responds to this commitment by opening doors, creating opportunities, and orchestrating circumstances in your favor. But these opportunities only appear for those already in motion.

Today, identify one action you've been avoiding that would move you toward greater abundance. Maybe it's applying for a better position, learning a new skill, starting a side business, investing in your education, improving your health, or strengthening your discipline. Take that action today. Don't wait for perfect circumstances or complete confidence.

Action creates momentum, momentum creates opportunities, and opportunities create abundance. Pair an abundant mindset with consistent action, and meaningful change accelerates.

July 11

Money is energy; let it flow through you.

Money is a form of energy that's meant to flow—coming in and going out in continuous circulation. When money flows freely through you, more comes in. When you grip it tightly out of fear, the flow stops and money stagnates.

Think of money like water. If you're by a river, water flows constantly past you—abundant and endless. But if you try to dam the river to hoard water, the flow stops, and what you've captured becomes stagnant. Money works the same way. Let it flow. Receive it gladly when it comes. Release it confidently when it goes for worthy purposes. Trust that more is always flowing toward you.

This doesn't mean spending irresponsibly. It means releasing the grip of fear that makes you hoard, worry obsessively, or make decisions from scarcity. It means understanding that money's value comes from circulation, not accumulation. Money sitting unused creates nothing. Money flowing through the economy creates value, opportunities, and more money.

Today, practice letting money flow. Pay your bills with gratitude rather than resentment—you're circulating energy. Tip generously—you're enabling the flow. Donate to causes you support—you're participating in the circulation of abundance by supporting what you value. Invest in yourself—you're directing energy toward growth.

Each time money leaves, bless it and trust that more is flowing in. This shift from hoarding to flowing transforms your relationship with money from fear-based to trust-based, from scarcity to abundance.

July 12

Value yourself highly, and others will value you too.

Your external compensation reflects your internal valuation of yourself. If you don't value yourself highly, neither will others. If you believe you're worth minimum wage, that's probably what you'll earn. If you believe you're worth six figures, you'll find ways to earn that.

This isn't arrogance—it's acknowledging your inherent worth and the value you provide. People commonly undervalue themselves out of false humility or low self-esteem. They charge less than they're worth, accept poor treatment, and settle for inadequate compensation. This under-valuation creates under-compensation.

The universe and the marketplace will value you exactly as you value yourself. When you value yourself highly, you communicate this through your pricing, your negotiations, your standards, and your boundaries. You don't apologize for your worth. You don't work for less than you're worth. You don't tolerate being undervalued. This isn't about being difficult or demanding—it's about knowing your value and expecting others to recognize it too.

Today, examine how you're valuing yourself. Are you charging what you're worth? Are you accepting treatment that honors your value? Are you negotiating for appropriate compensation? If you're undervaluing yourself, consciously upgrade. Decide what you're worth and begin communicating that worth through your actions, your standards, and your expectations.

As you value yourself more highly, others will naturally follow suit, and your compensation will rise to match your elevated self-valuation.

July 13

Focus on creating value, and money will follow.

Money is not the goal—it's the byproduct. The actual goal is creating value for others. When you focus on creating exceptional value—solving problems, meeting needs, serving people—money naturally flows as a reward for that value. But when you focus only on money without caring about value, you struggle because you're trying to extract without contributing.

The marketplace rewards value creation. The more value you create, the more money you can earn. The more people you serve, the more wealth you can accumulate. This is the abundance equation: massive value creation equals massive wealth creation.

Today, shift your focus from "how can I make more money?" to "how can I create more value?" What problems can you solve? What needs can you meet? What can you offer that would genuinely help people? When you make this shift, everything changes. You're no longer taking from the marketplace; you're contributing to it. You're not worried about getting yours; you're focused on giving value.

Paradoxically, this shift from taking to giving accelerates the flow of money. When you create genuine value and serve authentically, money chases you rather than you chasing money. You attract abundance because you're being abundant—giving value freely, serving generously, contributing meaningfully. Focus on creating value, and money becomes a natural consequence of your contribution rather than a desperate pursuit.

July 14

Gratitude for what you have attracts more to be grateful for.

Gratitude is the fastest way to shift from a mindset of scarcity to a mindset of abundance. When you're grateful, you're acknowledging that you have enough, that good things are already present, that life is working. This acknowledgment creates a high-frequency emotional state that attracts more good things.

Conversely, when you focus on what you lack—complaining, worrying, feeling deprived—you're in low-frequency emotional state that attracts more lack. The universe doesn't respond to what you need; it responds to what you feel. Feel grateful, and the universe provides more to be grateful for. Feel lacking, and the universe provides more experiences of lack.

This isn't just positive thinking—it's quantum physics. Your emotional frequency determines what you attract. Gratitude is one of the highest frequencies, attracting abundance naturally.

Today, practice radical gratitude. Instead of focusing on what you want but don't have, focus intensely on what you already have. Be grateful for the money in your account, even if it's less than you want. Be grateful for your skills and abilities. Be grateful for opportunities available to you. Be grateful for your health, your relationships, your experiences.

Write a gratitude list of at least 10 things. Feel genuine appreciation for each item. This practice shifts your frequency from lack to abundance, and as your frequency shifts, circumstances begin shifting to match. Gratitude is magnetic—it attracts more abundance to appreciate.

July 15

Your dominant thoughts about money determine your financial reality.

What do you think about most often when it comes to money? Do thoughts like "I never have enough" come up automatically? Do you worry about bills or feel anxious about your financial future? These dominant thoughts are shaping your financial reality. Your subconscious doesn't judge thoughts as good or bad. It simply responds to what you think about most consistently.

When dominant money thoughts are fearful or scarcity-based, the subconscious is guided toward struggle. When dominant money thoughts are confident and abundance-based, the subconscious more easily supports success. For many people, these thoughts operate unconsciously. They are inherited from parents, culture, and early experiences. Money is often viewed through fear simply because that is how it was modeled.

Today, bring awareness to your dominant money thoughts. As money comes to mind throughout the day, notice what arises automatically. Are those thoughts empowering or limiting? Once you identify them, begin to redirect them consciously.

Each time a limiting thought appears, replace it with a more supportive one. "I never have enough" becomes "Money flows to me with ease." "I'm always broke" becomes "I'm building wealth consistently." "I can't afford it" becomes "I'm finding creative ways to afford what I want." Over time, this redirection shifts your dominant thinking. As your thinking changes, your subconscious programming changes, and your financial experience begins to reflect that shift.

Your money thoughts are shaping your money reality—make sure they're aligned with what you want to create.

July 16

Prosperity is not about having more money; it's about having more life.

True prosperity isn't measured by bank account balances alone. It's measured by quality of life—rich relationships, meaningful work, vibrant health, personal growth, joyful experiences, and freedom to live authentically. Many financially wealthy people are poor in prosperity because their lives lack richness in these other dimensions. Many modestly wealthy people are rich in prosperity because their lives overflow with meaningful connections, purposeful work, and authentic joy.

The goal isn't just accumulating money—it's creating a prosperously rich life where money serves your well-being rather than consuming it. This perspective shift is crucial. When prosperity becomes only about money, you sacrifice everything else to get it—health, relationships, experiences, authenticity. You might achieve financial wealth while becoming poor in life. When prosperity is defined more holistically, you pursue money as one component of a rich life, not as a substitute for living.

Today, expand your definition of prosperity beyond money. What makes your life rich? Is it meaningful work? Deep relationships? Creative expression? Adventure? Service? Health? Define prosperity in your own terms, including but not limited to money. Then pursue prosperity in all dimensions simultaneously.

Build wealth while also building rich relationships. Increase income while also increasing health. Accumulate resources while also accumulating experiences. This holistic prosperity is sustainable, fulfilling, and truly abundant—not just financially rich, but life-rich.

July 17

The amount of money you can receive is limited only by your capacity to receive it.

In many cases, people have a receiving problem, not an earning problem. Opportunities for money and growth exist all around them, but they struggle to receive because their capacity is limited by unworthiness, guilt, fear, or ingrained beliefs. Your ability to receive is shaped by your sense of self-worth, your beliefs about deserving, your comfort with having more than others, and your willingness to handle the responsibility that comes with greater resources.

If you believe you're unworthy of wealth, you'll unconsciously undermine opportunities. If you feel guilty about having more than your parents or peers, you'll limit yourself. If you're uncomfortable with the visibility or responsibility that wealth brings, you'll avoid expansion. Increasing your receiving capacity requires inner work. You strengthen worthiness by recognizing your inherent value. You release guilt by understanding that your prosperity doesn't diminish others. You grow into responsibility by seeing wealth as an opportunity to contribute more.

Today, examine your receiving capacity with honesty. When money or opportunities come, do you receive them comfortably or deflect them? Do you feel deserving of abundance or guilty about having it? Do you embrace financial responsibility or fear it? Where you notice limitations in your capacity to receive, work on expanding them.

Practice receiving compliments gracefully. Allow people to give to you without immediately reciprocating. Say yes to opportunities that stretch your comfort zone. As your capacity to receive expands, what you receive will expand to match it. The universe can only give you as much as you're willing and able to receive.

July 18

Invest in yourself first, always.

Your greatest asset is yourself—your skills, knowledge, capabilities, health, and consciousness. Any investment in developing these pays the highest returns. When you invest in self-education, you increase your earning potential. When you invest in health, you increase your energy and longevity. When you invest in skills, you increase your value to the marketplace. When you invest in consciousness, you increase your ability to create wealth.

Yet many people are stingy with self-investment. They'll spend freely on entertainment or material goods but hesitate to invest in courses, coaching, books, or experiences that would develop them. This is short-sighted. Material goods depreciate; self-investment appreciates. A nice car loses value the moment you buy it. Knowledge, skills, and consciousness gained through self-investment compound in value over your lifetime.

Today, commit to consistent self-investment. Allocate a percentage of your income to personal development—books, courses, coaching, seminars, experiences that expand you. Don't see this as expense; see it as investment with guaranteed returns. The more you invest in becoming more capable, knowledgeable, skilled, and conscious, the more valuable you become, and the more money you can command.

Many successful people spend 10-20% of income on self-investment. This might seem like a lot, but the returns dwarf the investment. Invest in yourself first, always. Your development is your best investment.

July 19

Good stewardship attracts abundance.

Financial abundance requires financial stewardship. You cannot manage what you don't track. People frequently remain financially stuck not because they don't earn enough but because they don't know where their money goes. Without a budget, money disappears on impulse purchases, forgotten subscriptions, and unconscious habits.

Creating a simple budget reveals the truth. When you track every dollar for one month, you'll discover you're spending far more than you realized in certain areas. This awareness alone creates change. A budget isn't restrictive—it's liberating. It shows exactly where your money is going so you can redirect it toward what matters.

The universal law of stewardship is clear: if you cannot manage what you have, you will not be given more. As the Proverb teaches: "The borrower is slave to the lender." Living beyond your means through debt creates bondage. Living within your means through conscious management creates freedom.

Being a good steward means respecting money as energy that flows through your life. When you waste it carelessly, the flow diminishes. When you manage it wisely, the flow increases. Abundance flows to those who demonstrate they can handle it responsibly.

Today, commit to basic financial stewardship. Create a simple budget tracking your income and expenses for 30 days. Use a free budgeting app or write down every dollar coming in and going out. No judgment, just awareness. Ask yourself: Am I spending more than I make? Where is my money going? Am I being a responsible steward?

Once you see the truth, make adjustments. Cut wasteful spending. Live within your means. Pay off debt to free yourself from slavery to lenders. The universe rewards good stewardship with increased abundance. Prove you can manage what you have, and you'll receive more to manage.

July 20

Success loves speed; procrastination loves poverty.

When opportunity appears, successful people act quickly while unsuccessful people hesitate, overthink, and delay. By the time they finally decide to act, the opportunity has passed. This pattern repeats throughout life, creating vastly different outcomes.

Why does success love speed? Because quick action demonstrates commitment, builds momentum, and seizes opportunities before they disappear. Quick action also triggers the universe's support—when you move decisively, doors open, resources appear, and circumstances align. Why does procrastination love poverty? Because delay is often fear in disguise. Fear of failure, fear of looking foolish, fear of the unknown.

This fear-based hesitation causes you to miss opportunity after opportunity, leaving you with whatever circumstances provide by default rather than what you could create through decisive action. This doesn't mean reckless action without thought. It means once you've evaluated an opportunity and decided it's aligned with your goals, act quickly rather than endlessly preparing, seeking more information, or waiting for perfect circumstances.

Today, notice where you've been procrastinating on an opportunity. What action have you been delaying? Why? Is the delay legitimate caution or disguised fear? If it's fear, feel the fear and act anyway. Take the step you've been avoiding. Send the email. Make the call. Submit the application. Launch the project. Speed of implementation separates successful people from unsuccessful people. Success rewards those who act quickly while opportunity is present.

July 21

Your money story determines your reality.

Everyone has a money story—a narrative about money shaped by their experiences, beliefs, and personal interpretation. Some money stories are empowering: "Money comes easily to me. I always find opportunities. Wealth is my natural state." These stories create positive financial realities.

Other money stories are limiting: "Money is always a struggle. I never have enough. Rich people are greedy." These stories create difficult financial realities. Your money story is not an objective truth—it's a subjective narrative you've constructed and reinforced through selective attention.

You notice evidence that confirms your story while dismissing evidence that contradicts it. If your money story is "I always struggle with money," you'll notice every financial challenge as proof while overlooking every financial success as a fluke. In this way, your money story becomes a self-fulfilling prophecy.

Today, identify your money story. What narrative have you been repeating about money and your relationship with it? Write it out. Then evaluate: Is this story serving you? Is it creating the financial reality you want? If not, consciously rewrite your money story. Create a new narrative grounded in abundance. Then begin living from this new story. Look for evidence that supports it and repeat it until it replaces the old one.

Your money story is powerful—it's shaping your financial reality. Make sure it's a story that supports growth and possibility rather than one that keeps you tied to struggle.

July 22

Multiple streams of income create financial security and abundance.

Relying on a single income source—typically a job—is financially risky. If that source disappears, an immediate crisis can follow. But when you develop multiple streams of income, you create resilience and accelerated wealth building. If one stream slows, others continue flowing. When all streams flow simultaneously, abundance multiplies.

Multiple income streams can include: employment, freelancing, consulting, a small side business, investments, rental assets, digital products, or online selling. Not everyone needs seven streams, but having 2-3 provides meaningful security and accelerates wealth building. The key is to start developing additional streams while your primary income is secure. Don't wait for crisis to diversify. Start small with a side project, an investment account, a rental property, or a digital product. Over time, these additional streams grow and compound.

Today, consider what additional income streams you could develop. What skills could you monetize beyond your primary job? What forms of passive income could you create? What investments could you begin? Start small, but start now. Even an additional $500 per month from a side project adds up to $6,000 per year, and that's just the beginning. As you develop the habit of creating multiple streams, you'll discover that wealth building accelerates dramatically.

Financial security and abundance come not from earning more at one source but from developing multiple sources that flow simultaneously.

July 23

Don't wish it was easier, wish you were better.

Everyone faces financial challenges. What separates those who emerge stronger from those who remain stuck is not their circumstances but their response. As Jim Rohn taught, "Don't wish it was easier, wish you were better. Don't wish for less problems, wish for more skills."

When facing financial difficulty, you have two focus options. You can focus on the problem—dwelling on lack, worrying about bills, feeling victimized, complaining about unfairness. This keeps you trapped in the problem. Or you can focus on solutions—becoming more valuable, developing new skills, taking action, learning from the situation. This shifts you into the solution.

Rohn's mentor taught him: "To have more, you simply have to become more." Financial challenges are signals that you need to develop new skills or increase your value to the marketplace. The problem isn't that life is hard—it's that you haven't yet developed the skills to handle this level of challenge.

Instead of wishing your financial situation was easier, focus on becoming the person who can handle financial challenges with skill and confidence. Work harder on yourself than you worry about your circumstances.

Today, if you're facing financial difficulty, consciously choose to focus on the solution. Ask: What can I learn from this? What skills do I need to develop? How can I become more valuable? What opportunities exist? This isn't just positive thinking—this is personal development. You're using difficulty as feedback for where you need to grow. Choose to become better, and watch how your improved skills create improved results. Financial difficulties are temporary unless you make them permanent through complaint and stagnation.

July 24

Work harder on yourself than you do your job.

Most people work hard at their jobs. They come in early, stay late, put in effort, and take pride in their work. Yet many struggle financially. Why? Because they're working hard on the wrong thing.

As Jim Rohn taught: "If you work hard on your job, you'll make a living. If you work hard on yourself, you can make a fortune." This distinction changed his life at age 25, and it can change yours too.

Working hard on your job means showing up, completing tasks, and fulfilling responsibilities. This earns you a paycheck—a living. But it doesn't make you more valuable. You're trading time for money, and there are only so many hours in a day. Working hard on yourself means developing skills, expanding knowledge, and increasing your value to the marketplace. This multiplies your worth and opens opportunities.

You don't get paid for time—you get paid for value. Two people can work the same hours, but one earns far more because they've become more valuable. The marketplace rewards value, not effort alone. Most people spend 40-60 hours per week working on their job and zero hours working on themselves. Then they wonder why their income stays flat.

Today, commit to reversing this. Dedicate time every day to personal development. Read 10-30 minutes of books that expand your thinking. Learn skills that increase your value. Study successful people. Invest in yourself relentlessly.

Your job pays your bills today, but investing in yourself pays your bills for life. Personal development is the path to financial freedom.

July 25

Success is nothing more
than a few simple disciplines, practiced every day.

Presented with the same circumstances, successful people and unsuccessful people see completely different realities. Where successful people see opportunities, unsuccessful people see obstacles and reasons why something won't work. As Jim Rohn taught, the difference isn't in their circumstances—it's in their daily disciplines.

Rohn said: "Success is nothing more than a few simple disciplines, practiced every day. Failure is simply a few errors in judgment, repeated every day." The discipline of seeing opportunities instead of obstacles, practiced daily, creates wealth. The error of seeing obstacles instead of opportunities, repeated daily, creates poverty.

Successful people don't avoid obstacles—they've disciplined themselves to focus on the opportunity beyond the obstacle. They've made it a daily practice to ask "How can I make this work?" People tend to naturally default to obstacle-thinking, but opportunity-thinking must be practiced.

The accumulative weight of your daily disciplines determines your future. Practice seeing opportunities every day, and you build a wealth mindset. Practice seeing obstacles every day, and you build a poverty mindset. Small disciplines or small errors—repeated daily, compound into your destiny.

Today, examine your habitual perception. When presented with new ideas, do you immediately see opportunities or obstacles? If you tend toward obstacle-focus, consciously practice opportunity-focus. Make it a discipline: every time you catch yourself thinking why something won't work, force yourself to find three reasons it could work.

This perceptual shift isn't a one-time decision. It's a simple discipline you must practice every single day until it becomes automatic.

July 26

Celebrate others' success, it proves success is possible.

When you see others succeed—earning more money, achieving goals, living abundantly—you have two choices: celebrate or resent. Resentment says "They have what I want, which means I can't have it." This scarcity-based response creates bitterness and blocks your own success. Celebration says "If they can do it, so can I. Their success proves it's possible." This abundance-based response creates inspiration and opens pathways to your own success.

Others' success is not your limitation—it's your proof of possibility. Every successful person demonstrates that success is achievable, that the path exists, that it can be done. When you celebrate rather than resent others' success, you're affirming that success is available, which programs your subconscious for success. You're also creating positive energy that attracts success to you. When you resent others' success, you're reinforcing the belief of scarcity and repelling success.

Today, practice celebrating others' success genuinely. When you see someone thriving, feel happy for them rather than jealous. Say silently: "Their success proves success is possible. If they can achieve it, so can I." When you hear about someone's big win, congratulate them sincerely. When you encounter displays of wealth, appreciate rather than resent them.

This shift from resentment to celebration removes a major block to abundance and aligns you with the frequency of success. Others' success is not your obstacle—it's your evidence that success is possible for you too.

July 27

> *You're the average of the five people you spend the most time with.*

Jim Rohn taught that you're the average of the five people you spend the most time with. This is especially true financially. If you associate primarily with people who complain about money, think small, and stay stuck, you'll tend toward those patterns. If you associate with people who think abundantly, pursue goals, and create wealth, you'll tend toward those patterns instead.

Your associations shape your beliefs about what's normal, what's possible, and what's acceptable. If everyone around you accepts financial mediocrity, you probably will too. If everyone around you pursues financial excellence, you probably will too. You unconsciously adopt the standards, attitudes, and behaviors of your peer group.

This doesn't mean abandoning old friends. It means consciously expanding your network to include people who are where you want to be financially. Spend time with people whose financial thinking elevates rather than diminishes yours.

Today, audit your associations. Who do you spend the most time with? What financial attitudes do they hold? Are these the attitudes you want to adopt? Then strategically expand your associations. Join groups where successful people gather. Attend events where wealthy-minded people network. Find mentors who've achieved what you want to achieve. Read books by people who think bigger than you do. Listen to podcasts by wealth builders.

As your associations shift toward more successful people, your own success will naturally rise to match. You cannot consistently outperform your peer group—so choose a peer group that lifts you up.

July 28

Wealth comes from solving problems, not avoiding them.

Every significant amount of money ever earned came from solving problems for people. The bigger the problem you solve, the more money you can earn. The more people you solve it for, the wealthier you become. Yet many people try to build wealth while avoiding problems, seeking easy paths with no challenges. This approach leads nowhere because problems are where value creation happens.

If there's no problem to solve, there's no reason for people to pay you. Wealthy people understand this. They don't avoid problems—they seek them out. They ask: What problems exist that I could solve? What do people struggle with that I could help them overcome? What inefficiencies exist that I could improve? They see problems as opportunities rather than obstacles.

Today, shift your perspective on problems. Stop avoiding them and start seeking them. What problems do you notice in your industry, community, or life? What are people complaining about? What inefficiencies frustrate people? Where is there unmet need? These problems are opportunities for wealth creation.

Choose a problem that matters to you and that you have the skills or desire to solve. Then focus on solving it so well that people will pay you for the solution. The more valuable the solution, the more money you can earn. Wealth is not found by avoiding problems but by becoming excellent at solving them. Your financial abundance is directly proportional to the size and number of problems you can solve.

Life is like the seasons.

Jim Rohn taught one of life's most important lessons: life operates in seasons, just like nature. There are winters, springs, summers, and falls—and each requires different wisdom. Understanding this transforms how you handle financial ups and downs.

Learn how to handle the winters. Economic winters will come—downturns, losses, lean times. They come as predictably as January. Don't wish them away. Instead, get wiser, stronger, and better. Use winter to develop skills, read more, and prepare for spring. Don't let winter destroy you—let it develop you.

Learn to take advantage of the spring. Spring is opportunity time—new chances, fresh starts, open doors. But you must take advantage. You must plant in the spring or beg in the fall. When opportunity appears, seize it swiftly. Life offers only a handful of springs—don't let them pass unused.

Learn to nourish and protect in the summer. Summer brings both promise and threat. Nourish what's good—your values, investments, relationships—like a mother. Defend against threats—bad influences, wasteful spending, destructive habits—like a father. Summer requires both nurturing and vigilance.

Learn to harvest in the fall without complaint or apology. Take full responsibility for your harvest. If it's small, accept it without complaint. If it's large, take it without apology. Your harvest reflects your efforts in previous seasons.

Today, recognize which season you're in financially. If winter, focus on growth. If spring, take action on opportunities. If summer, protect what you're building. If fall, accept your harvest and plan for the next cycle. The seasons will continue—your growth through them determines your financial future.

You cannot out give the universe.

The more you give—money, time, knowledge, support—the more comes back to you, often multiplied. This is not just spiritual philosophy; it's observable pattern.

Generous people tend to be more prosperous, not despite their generosity but because of it. Why? Because giving demonstrates abundance mindset. When you give freely, you're declaring to yourself and the universe: "I have more than enough. I can afford to share. Abundance flows through me." This mindset attracts more abundance.

When you hoard and withhold, you're declaring: "I don't have enough. I must protect what little I have. Scarcity defines me." This mindset attracts more scarcity. The universe operates on reciprocity. What you put out comes back, multiplied. But you must give first, before receiving, without expectation of return. Give because giving feels good and aligns you with abundance, not as a manipulation to get something back.

Today, practice giving generously. Tip more than expected. Donate to causes you believe in. Share your knowledge freely. Help someone in need. Give your time to meaningful service. As you give, feel the abundance mindset it creates. Notice how giving makes you feel rich rather than poor, abundant rather than scarce. Trust that what you give will return multiplied, though perhaps from unexpected sources.

You cannot out-give the universe—the more you give from a genuine abundance mindset, the more flows back to you. Giving is not depletion; it's circulation that attracts more flow.

Abundance is a decision, not a destination.

As we close this month on creating abundance, understand this crucial truth: abundance is not something you achieve; it's something you decide. It's not a destination you reach when you have enough money; it's a decision you make regardless of circumstances.

You can have millions and live in scarcity, constantly worried about loss and never feeling satisfied. You can have modest means and live in a mindset of abundance, grateful for what you have and confident more is coming. The difference is not circumstances, but a state of mind. It's your chosen perspective, your habitual thoughts, your emotional state, and your relationship with abundance.

An abundance mindset is the decision to see abundance rather than scarcity, to focus on what you have rather than what you lack, to trust rather than fear, to give rather than hoard, to celebrate rather than resent, to act from sufficiency rather than desperation. This decision is available to you right now, regardless of your bank balance.

Today, decide to live in a mindset of abundance. Not when you have more money—now. Decide to see opportunities instead of obstacles. Decide to feel grateful instead of deprived. Decide to trust that the universe supports you. Decide to give freely and receive graciously. Decide to celebrate others' success. Decide to think and act from abundance rather than scarcity.

This decision—made and renewed daily—transforms your entire experience of life and, over time, transforms your circumstances to match your mindset.

August

Daily Disciplines

Consistent Practices for Growth

August 1

Success is built one day at a time through consistent daily disciplines.

Extraordinary results don't come from extraordinary actions done once. They come from ordinary actions done consistently.

Excellent health isn't created through occasional intense workouts. It's built through daily, moderate exercise practiced over months and years. Significant wealth isn't created through lucky breaks. It's built through daily financial disciplines practiced over decades. Deep knowledge isn't gained by cramming once in a while. It's developed through daily reading over a lifetime.

This is the power of daily disciplines. Small actions, repeated consistently, compound into remarkable results. Yet people often underestimate the power of consistency and overestimate the power of occasional intensity. They work out intensely for a week, then stop for a month. They save aggressively for a short period, then spend carelessly for months. They read enthusiastically for a few days, then abandon the habit altogether. This pattern produces minimal results and unnecessary frustration.

Today, trade intensity for consistency. Don't ask, "What big thing can I do?" Ask instead, "What small thing can I do every single day?" Identify one daily discipline that, if practiced consistently, would transform an important area of your life. Make it so small you can't fail. Then do it today, tomorrow, and every day after. This is how you build success—one disciplined day at a time.

August 2

Your morning routine sets the tone for the entire day.

How you start your day shapes how you live your day. If you wake up rushed, reactive, and chaotic, your day tends to unfold the same way. If you wake up calm, intentional, and centered, your day reflects that state.

Your morning routine is not just about the first hour—it's about establishing the energetic and mental frequency that colors everything that follows. Successful people understand this, which is why they guard their mornings fiercely. They don't check email first thing. They don't scroll social media. They don't immediately react to the world's demands.

Instead, they use morning time for disciplines that strengthen them—meditation, exercise, reading, planning, visualization. These practices aren't luxuries; they're strategic investments in daily success.

When you start your day by centering yourself, moving your body, feeding your mind, and clarifying your intentions, you enter the day from a position of power rather than reaction.

Today, audit your morning routine honestly. Do you wake up and immediately hand your attention to the outside world, or do you create intentional space to invest in yourself first? If you don't have a morning routine, create one. Even 30 minutes can transform your days. Include practices that strengthen you physically, mentally, emotionally, and spiritually.

This morning buffer is where you fill your own cup before pouring into others. Protect this time as sacred—it's where you set the tone for everything that follows. Win the morning, and you win the day.

August 3

> *What you do daily matters more than what you do occasionally.*

People often think about success in terms of big moments—the promotion, the breakthrough, the big win. But these moments are outcomes, not causes. The causes are the daily disciplines practiced in obscurity long before the big moment arrives.

The novelist who publishes a bestseller spent years writing every day before recognition. The entrepreneur who builds a successful company spent years working daily on their craft. The athlete who wins a championship spent years training consistently. The big moments receive the attention, but daily disciplines are what create them.

This truth is both challenging and liberating. Challenging because it means success requires sustained daily effort without immediate rewards. Liberating because it means success is available to anyone willing to commit to daily disciplines, regardless of talent, luck, or circumstances. You don't need to be exceptional; you need to be consistent.

Today, shift your focus from occasional big actions to consistent daily actions. What you do once in a while—whether positive or negative—has minimal impact. What you do daily shapes everything. Eating healthy occasionally doesn't create health; eating healthy daily does. Working on your goals occasionally doesn't create success; working on them daily does.

Choose one daily discipline and commit to it regardless of how you feel, regardless of whether you see immediate results. Trust the compound effect of daily consistency.

August 4

Discipline is doing what needs to be done even when you don't feel like it.

Motivation is fleeting—some days you feel motivated, other days you don't. If you only act when motivated, your results will be inconsistent and mediocre. Discipline is the ability to act regardless of how you feel. It's doing what needs to be done even when you don't feel like it.

This is the crucial distinction between amateurs and professionals. Amateurs wait for motivation. They exercise when they feel like it, work on goals when they're inspired, eat healthy when they're motivated. Their results reflect this inconsistency. Professionals have discipline. They exercise whether they feel like it or not. They work on goals whether they're inspired or not. They maintain healthy habits whether they're motivated or not. Their results reflect this consistency.

Discipline is not natural—it's developed through practice. Each time you act despite not feeling like it, you strengthen discipline. Each time you wait for motivation, you weaken discipline.

Today, notice when you're about to skip a commitment because you don't feel like it. Then do it anyway, specifically because you don't feel like it. This is how you build discipline—by overriding feelings with commitment. The more you practice discipline, the stronger it becomes, until disciplined action becomes your automatic response rather than an occasional effort. Motivation is nice; discipline is necessary.

August 5

Small daily improvements compound into massive results.

If you improve by just 1% each day, you'll be 37 times better after a year due to compounding. This is the power of marginal gains—small improvements that seem insignificant in the moment but compound into extraordinary results over time.

People often ignore marginal gains because they want dramatic transformation now. They dismiss 1% improvement as too small to matter. But this thinking misses how compounding works. Small gains are easy to achieve but easy to dismiss. That's why many people don't experience their power.

The person who reads 10 pages daily doesn't seem to be doing much compared to someone who tries to read an entire book in one sitting. But the daily reader completes 12+ books per year effortlessly while the binge reader completes maybe 2-3 through exhausting effort. The daily approach wins through consistency and compounding.

Today, stop looking for dramatic transformations and start embracing marginal gains. In what area do you want improvement? Instead of trying to overhaul everything at once, improve by 1% today. Read 10 pages instead of zero. Exercise 10 minutes instead of zero. Save $5 instead of zero. These tiny improvements feel almost insignificant, which is exactly why they're sustainable.

You can maintain them indefinitely without burnout. And as they compound over weeks, months, and years, they produce results that far exceed what dramatic but unsustainable efforts ever could. Small daily improvements compound into massive results.

August 6

*Your daily habits are either
compounding toward success or toward failure.*

Every habit is a vote for the kind of person you want to become. Good habits compound positively—each instance makes the next instance easier and moves you incrementally toward your goals. Bad habits compound negatively—each instance makes the next instance more likely and moves you incrementally toward outcomes you don't want.

There is no neutral. You're either compounding toward success or toward failure. You're either getting 1% better or 1% worse each day. The trajectory might not be visible today or even this month, but over years, the difference is dramatic.

The person with healthy eating habits compounds toward vibrant health. The person with poor eating habits compounds toward disease. The person with saving habits compounds toward wealth. The person with spending habits compounds toward debt. The habits seem small daily, but their direction is everything.

Today, audit your daily habits honestly. For each habit, ask: Is this compounding toward success or failure? Is this taking me closer to who I want to become or further away? You can't change everything at once, but you can start changing direction.

Eliminate one negative-compounding habit. Install one positive-compounding habit. As these new patterns compound over time, your life transforms. Remember: you don't need perfect habits, just directionally correct ones that compound toward your desired destination rather than away from it.

August 7

You don't rise to the level of your goals; you fall to the level of your systems.

Goals are important for setting direction, but systems are what actually create results. A goal is where you want to go. A system is the daily behaviors and processes that get you there.

In many cases people set ambitious goals but don't build systems to support them. They want to lose 30 pounds but don't create a daily eating and exercise system. They want to write a book but don't create a daily writing system. They want to build wealth but don't create a daily earning and saving system.

Without systems, goals remain wishes. With systems, goals become inevitable. The person with a goal of running a marathon might not achieve it. But the person with a system of running every morning will eventually be capable of running a marathon, whether that's their explicit goal or not. Focus on systems—the daily disciplines and processes—and let results take care of themselves.

Today, choose one important goal. Instead of obsessing over the goal, design a system—a set of daily disciplines—that would make achieving that goal inevitable given enough time.

Want to write a book? Create a system of writing 500 words daily. Want financial security? Create a system of saving 10% of income daily. Want better relationships? Create a system of meaningful daily connection. Then focus on following the system, not achieving the goal. Trust that consistent system execution will produce the desired goal eventually. You don't rise to your goals; you fall to the level of your systems.

August 8

*The chains of habit are too
light to be felt until they are too heavy to be broken.*

This quote, often cited by Warren Buffett, reveals the danger of bad habits and the power of good ones. When you first develop a habit—good or bad—it feels insignificant.

Eating unhealthy once doesn't create obesity. Skipping exercise once doesn't create poor fitness. Spending carelessly once doesn't create debt. The consequences are too light to feel, so you continue the behavior. But each repetition strengthens the habit slightly. After months and years, the habit becomes so entrenched that changing it feels nearly impossible. The chains you didn't feel forming are now heavy restraints.

The good news is that this principle can also work in your favor. The first time you exercise, meditate, or work on your goals, it may feel awkward and insignificant. But keep doing it daily, and eventually these positive habits become so automatic, so ingrained, so natural that not doing them feels wrong. The chains of good habits become comfortable routines that effortlessly support your success.

Today, recognize that your daily choices are forming chains, either helpful or harmful. Each time you repeat a behavior, you're strengthening that chain. While habits are still new and the chains are light, this is the time to break what no longer serves you and build what does. Don't wait until negative habits become heavy chains that require great effort to break. Start building positive chains now, while they are light and easy to form.

August 9

> *Every day is a new opportunity to start over and do better.*

One of the most damaging beliefs is that a broken streak means complete failure. You commit to daily exercise, miss a day, and conclude you've failed so you might as well quit. You commit to daily meditation, skip it once, and feel like you've lost all progress.

But this all-or-nothing thinking sabotages success. Missing one day doesn't erase the benefit of all previous days. A single mistake doesn't nullify months of discipline. What matters is not perfection but persistence—the ability to start again after setbacks.

The person who exercises daily for 30 days, misses day 31, then resumes on day 32 is far more successful than the person who exercises daily for 30 days, misses day 31, criticizes themselves up and quits entirely. One missed day is simply one missed day if you resume immediately. It only becomes failure if you let it derail you.

Today, if you've broken a commitment or missed a discipline, refuse to let it become complete abandonment. Don't waste energy on guilt or self-judgment. Simply start again today. Every morning is a fresh start, a clean slate, a new opportunity to recommit to your disciplines.

Yesterday's imperfection doesn't determine today's choices. This resilience, the ability to start over without drama or self-judgement, matters more than perfection. You will have setbacks. What separates success from failure is whether you use setbacks as excuses to quit or as opportunities to demonstrate commitment by resuming immediately.

August 10

Reading daily expands your mind and multiplies your opportunities.

Reading is one of the highest-leverage daily disciplines you can practice. Ten pages daily equals 3,650 pages yearly—about 12 full books. Through reading, you can learn from the wisdom of hundreds of experts, avoid mistakes others made, and discover opportunities you never would have thought of. Warren Buffett reads 500 pages daily. Mark Cuban reads for more than three hours almost every day.

The most successful people are voracious readers. They understand that reading is not leisure—it's strategic personal development. Each book contains distilled wisdom that took the author years to learn. In a few hours of reading, you gain access to insights that took someone decades to acquire. This accelerates your growth exponentially.

Beyond knowledge, reading disciplines your mind. It develops focus, expands vocabulary, enhances critical thinking, and builds patience—all valuable traits. It also keeps you learning, which keeps you relevant as the world changes.

Today, if you're not reading daily, start. Even 10 pages daily creates compound benefits. Choose books that serve your growth—not just entertainment, but books that teach, inspire, and expand. Biographies of successful people. Books on skills you want to develop. Books on philosophy and wisdom.

Make reading daily non-negotiable, perhaps part of your morning or evening routine. This simple daily discipline—reading 10-20 pages—can transform your life more than almost any other single habit.

August 11

Dream big — write down everything you want in the next 10 years.

Jim Rohn taught that if you have no 10-year goals, you're not thinking far enough into the future. People tend to limit their dreams to what seems immediately achievable, which keeps them thinking small.

Get a piece of paper and write this question at the top: "What do I want in the next 10 years?" Then list everything that comes to mind without concern for how likely it seems. Don't filter. Don't judge. Don't ask "how?" Just write what you truly want.

Want to travel the world? Write it down. Want to build a thriving business? Write it down. Want to master a skill? Write it down. Want financial freedom? Write it down. Want deeper relationships? Write it down. Want to write a book, own a home, learn a language, achieve excellent health? Write them all down.

The key is quantity and permission. Give yourself permission to want what you want without justifying it or figuring out how you'll achieve it. Aim for at least 20-30 goals. The longer your list, the better—it means you're accessing real desires rather than safe, pre-approved wishes.

This exercise isn't about committing to everything on your list. It's about discovering what you actually want when you remove the filters of "realistic" and "practical." Many people have lived so long within limitations that they've forgotten how to dream. This exercise reconnects you with authentic desire.

Today, spend 20-30 minutes on this exercise. Write freely. Let yourself want what you want. Don't worry about what comes next—we'll organize and prioritize tomorrow. For now, just dream. The act of writing goals down begins transforming them from vague wishes into tangible possibilities. What you write, you can pursue. What stays in your head remains a fantasy.

August 12

Categorize your goals and assign timeframes.

Yesterday you created a list of everything you want in the next 10 years. Today, you'll bring structure to those dreams by categorizing them and assigning realistic timeframes.

Jim Rohn taught specific goal categories that ensure balanced life development: Lifestyle, Family goals, Personal Development, Quality Time, Travel, Possessions, and Financial. Look at each goal on your list and label it with its category. This reveals whether your goals are balanced or heavily weighted in one area.

If all your goals are financial with nothing for relationships or health, you'll achieve wealth at the expense of connection and wellbeing. If all your goals are lifestyle with nothing for personal development, you'll remain the same person in a nicer setting. Balanced categories create balanced success.

Next, assign each goal a timeframe: 1 year, 3 years, 5 years, or 10+ years. Be honest about what's realistic. Some goals can be achieved within a year with focused effort. Others require three years of skill development. Some need five years of resource building. A few are 10-year visions that require sustained long-term effort.

Don't make everything a 1-year goal—that creates overwhelm. Don't make everything a 10-year goal—that creates no urgency. Distribute your goals across timeframes realistically. A goal to lose 20 pounds might be 6 months. A goal to build a million-dollar business might be 5-10 years. A goal to master a new skill might be 3 years.

Today, go through your list from yesterday. Label each goal with its category. Assign each goal a timeframe. This transforms a random wish list into a structured vision for your future. You now have organized goals distributed across different life areas and different time horizons.

August 13

Choose your top 4 major goals for each timeframe.

You now have a list of categorized goals with assigned timeframes. Today, you'll make the crucial distinction Jim Rohn taught between major goals and minor goals.

You cannot pursue everything with equal intensity. Trying to focus on 50 goals simultaneously guarantees scattered energy and minimal progress. Rohn's solution: choose 4 major goals for each timeframe. These are your priorities—the goals that matter most, that would create the biggest positive impact if achieved.

Look at your 1-year goals. Which 4 would make the biggest difference in your life if achieved this year? Highlight them. These are your major 1-year goals. The rest remain on your list as minor goals—things you'd like to achieve but won't prioritize. Do the same for your 3-year, 5-year, and 10-year goals, choose 4. This process forces clarity. You must decide what matters most. You must choose. And choosing creates power because focused energy produces results while scattered energy produces frustration.

Your major goals get your best time, attention, and resources. Your minor goals receive attention only after major goals are handled. This isn't abandoning your other goals—it's being strategic. As you achieve major goals, minor goals can become major goals. As new desires emerge, you can add them. But at any given time, you have clear priorities.

Today, review your goals from yesterday. For each timeframe (1yr, 3yr, 5yr, 10yr), choose your top 4 most important goals. Highlight or mark them clearly. These are your major goals. Everything else is minor. This clarity transforms overwhelming goal lists into manageable focus areas. You now know exactly what deserves your attention and what can wait.

August 14

Write WHY each of your major goals matters to you.

Having clear goals is important. Understanding WHY those goals matter is essential. The why provides fuel when motivation wanes. It sustains effort through difficulty. It connects goals to deeper values, making them compelling rather than merely desirable.

Jim Rohn taught his students to write a paragraph for each major goal explaining why they chose it. This exercise clarifies whether it's an authentic desire or an imported expectation.

Look at your four major 1-year goals. For each one, write a paragraph answering: Why does this goal matter to me? What will achieving this give me? How will my life be different? What deeper value does this serve? Why did I choose this over other possibilities? Be honest. If a goal is on your list because you think you "should" want it but don't actually care, this exercise will reveal that. Remove it. Replace it with something you genuinely want.

Some goals matter because they create freedom. Some matter because they develop you into someone you respect. Some matter because they serve people you love. Some matter because they align with your deepest values. Understanding these connections makes goals meaningful rather than arbitrary.

Today, get your goal list and a journal. For each of your major 1-year goals, write a paragraph explaining why it matters to you. If you have time, do the same for your 3-year, 5-year, and 10-year major goals. Don't rush this. Let yourself explore your real reasons. When you finish, you'll have goals connected to purpose rather than disconnected wishes. This connection will sustain you through the work required to achieve them.

August 15

Identify who you must BECOME to achieve each major goal.

Jim Rohn taught the most important principle about goals: "The major value in setting goals is to entice you into being the kind of person it takes to achieve them." The goal is not the real prize—the person you become while achieving it is the real prize.

If you focus only on achieving the goal, you might succeed through luck or temporary effort without real growth. But if you focus on becoming the kind of person who naturally achieves such goals, you transform permanently. The achievement becomes inevitable because you've become the person for whom that achievement is normal.

For each of your major goals, ask: What kind of person would I need to become to achieve this? What qualities, skills, habits, or knowledge would that person have that I currently don't?

Want financial freedom? You must become financially disciplined, knowledgeable about money, skilled at earning and investing. Want excellent health? You must become someone who values their body, exercises consistently, and eats well. Want to write a book? You must become a daily writer with developed skills and discipline.

This list is more valuable than the goal itself because it shows you what to focus on daily. Instead of obsessing over the goal, focus on becoming this person. Develop these qualities. Build these skills. As you do, the goal becomes a natural byproduct of who you've become.

Today, review your major goals. For each one, write a brief paragraph describing the kind of person who would naturally achieve that goal. What qualities would they have? What would you need to develop to become that person? This is your real work—not chasing goals but becoming the person who attracts them naturally.

August 16

Your evening routine determines the quality of tomorrow.

Many people focus on morning routines but neglect evening routines. Yet what you do before bed significantly impacts sleep quality, next-day energy, and mental state. If you scroll social media until you fall asleep, your mind processes negativity and stimulation all night. If you watch disturbing news, your subconscious marinates in fear and stress. If you only rehash the day's problems, you carry stress into sleep and wake with anxiety.

Your evening routine should prepare the mind and body for restorative sleep and tomorrow's success. This might include: conducting a daily inventory—reviewing what went well and what could have gone better without judgment, extracting lessons from both wins and mistakes, planning tomorrow to create clarity and reduce morning decision fatigue, reading inspirational material to seed positive thoughts in your subconscious, journaling gratitude to shift into an appreciative state, meditation or gentle stretching to release tension, and avoiding screens 30-60 minutes before bed to improve sleep quality.

The daily inventory is crucial. Ask yourself: What did I do well today? Where could I have done better? What did I learn? What will I do differently tomorrow? This honest reflection transforms each day from an event that happens to you into a lesson that develops you. You end the day with closure and clarity rather than unresolved tension.

Today, create an evening routine that sets you up for success. Even 20-30 minutes of intentional wind-down creates dramatic improvements in sleep quality and next-day performance. End each day by reviewing what went well, expressing gratitude, planning tomorrow, and calming your nervous system. Your evening routine is as important as your morning routine—it bookends your day with intention rather than leaving it to chance. Win the evening, and tomorrow starts with an advantage.

August 17

Meditation is not about stopping your thoughts; its about gaining perspective.

Many people try meditation and quit because they can't stop their thoughts. But meditation is not about having a blank mind—it's about changing your relationship with your thoughts. Through daily meditation, you learn to observe thoughts without being controlled by them.

You notice: I'm having an anxious thought, but I am not my anxiety. I'm having a negative thought, but I don't have to believe it. This observer perspective is tremendously powerful because people often are completely identified with their thoughts. When they think something, they believe it's truth. When they feel something, they believe it defines them.

Meditation creates space between you and your mental content. You start to recognize that you are not your thoughts, but the awareness that notices them. From this perspective, negative thoughts, anxious feelings, and limiting beliefs are seen as passing mental weather rather than fixed truths about who you are.

Daily meditation builds this observer capacity over time. Begin with just 5-10 minutes daily. Sit quietly, focus on your breath, and when thoughts arise (they will), simply notice them without judgment and return attention to your breath. You're not trying to stop thoughts— you're practicing noticing them without being swept away by them and letting them pass. This daily practice creates calm, clarity, and emotional resilience that benefit every area of life. Meditation is not luxury; it's essential mental training.

August 18

Plan your day the night before to maximize productivity.

One of the simplest yet most powerful daily disciplines is planning tomorrow tonight. When you plan your day in advance, you wake up with clarity and purpose rather than confusion and decision fatigue. You know exactly what needs to be done, in what order, and why. This eliminates the morning stress of figuring out priorities and the afternoon paralysis of deciding what to work on next.

Planning also gives your subconscious time to work. When you review tomorrow's tasks before bed, your mind continues processing them during sleep, often delivering insights or solutions by morning. Many people notice they wake up with clarity around problems they considered the night before.

Effective planning doesn't require much time—10 minutes is sufficient. Review tomorrow: What are your 3 most important tasks? What appointments or commitments exist? When will you exercise, read, or practice other disciplines? What potential obstacles might arise? How will you handle them? Write this plan down so you don't have to remember it.

Today, before bed, plan tomorrow. List your top 3 priorities—the tasks that, if completed, would make tomorrow a success. Schedule them for your peak energy times. Plan your disciplines—when and how you'll exercise, read, meditate. Anticipate obstacles and plan responses.

This 10-minute evening practice transforms next-day productivity. You wake with purpose rather than figuring out what to do. This clarity creates momentum that carries through the entire day.

August 19

Track your progress to maintain motivation and accountability.

What gets measured gets managed. When you track progress on your daily disciplines, you create accountability and motivation. A simple habit tracker—marking off each day you complete a discipline—provides powerful psychological reinforcement.

Seeing a streak of completed days motivates you to maintain the streak. Breaking a streak feels like loss, which you should allow to motivate you to restart. Tracking also reveals patterns. You might believe you're consistent when tracking shows you're actually somewhat inconsistent. You might think a discipline isn't working when tracking shows steady progress you hadn't noticed. Objective measurement reveals truth beyond subjective feeling.

The tracking method doesn't need to be complex. A simple calendar where you mark X for each completed day works perfectly. Or a spreadsheet. Or a habit-tracking app. The key is making tracking effortless so you actually do it. Include visual progress indicators—seeing your streak growing or watching a graph trending upward provides satisfaction that reinforces behavior.

Today, create a simple tracking system for your most important daily disciplines. It might be a calendar on your wall where you mark each day completed. Or a checklist you review each evening. Or an app designed for habit tracking. The specific method matters less than the act of tracking.

When you track progress, you become aware of your actual consistency versus your perceived consistency. This awareness creates accountability that strengthens discipline.

August 20

Schedule your disciplines as non-negotiable appointments.

Many people say they don't have time for important disciplines—exercise, reading, meditation, personal development. Yet they find time for television, social media, and other low-priority activities. The reality is not lack of time but lack of intentional scheduling. You make time for what you schedule.

When something is on your calendar as a non-negotiable appointment, it happens. When it's just an intention without scheduled time, it gets perpetually postponed. Treat your important disciplines with the same respect you treat important meetings. You wouldn't skip a meeting with your boss because you didn't feel like it.

Don't skip your exercise, reading, or meditation because you don't feel like it. Schedule these disciplines on your calendar as appointments with yourself. If you schedule exercise at 6am, you show up at 6am just as you would for any other appointment. If you schedule reading at 8pm, you read at 8pm.

Today, open your calendar and schedule your most important disciplines for the next week. Put exercise on the calendar. Put reading on the calendar. Put meditation, planning, learning—whatever disciplines matter most to you.

Treat these as seriously as you treat appointments with others. When someone asks if you're free during a scheduled discipline time, say no—you have an appointment. That appointment happens to be with yourself, which makes it no less important. Schedule your priorities or other people's priorities will fill your time.

Eliminate before you optimize.

People tend to try and optimize their time—finding more efficient ways to do everything on their list. But this often means becoming more efficient at tasks that maybe shouldn't be done at all. Before optimizing, try eliminating.

Look at your daily activities and ask: Does this need to be done at all? Does this support my most important goals? What would happen if I simply stopped doing this? Many tasks you do daily are unnecessary—habits from the past, obligations you haven't questioned, busywork that creates the illusion of productivity. Eliminating these creates time for what matters without requiring any optimization.

After eliminating the unnecessary, then optimize what remains. Make necessary tasks more efficient. Batch them. Delegate them. Systematize them. But don't optimize tasks that should be eliminated.

Today, audit your daily activities. List everything you do regularly. Then eliminate ruthlessly before optimizing. Which activities could you stop doing entirely without significant negative consequence? Stop doing them. Which could you do less frequently? Reduce the frequency. Which create no value toward your important goals? Eliminate them.

Only after you've eliminated the unnecessary should you spend energy optimizing the essential. This elimination-before-optimization approach creates more time and energy than any amount of optimization alone ever could. The most efficient way to do something unnecessary is to not do it at all.

August 22

Your inputs determine your outputs.

What you consume daily—food, media, conversations, content—directly affects what you produce. Consume junk food, and your body produces low energy and poor health. Consume junk media, and your mind produces anxiety and distraction. Consume negative conversations, and your attitude produces pessimism. Consume low-quality content, and your thinking produces mediocre ideas.

The principle is simple: garbage in, garbage out; excellence in, excellence out. People are commonly careless with their inputs. They consume whatever is readily available without considering consequences. They eat whatever is convenient, watch whatever is entertaining, scroll whatever appears in their feed, engage with whatever drama presents itself. This unconscious consumption creates unconscious outputs—poor health, scattered attention, negative emotions, unoriginal thinking.

Today, become conscious of your inputs. What are you consuming daily in terms of food, media, conversations, and content? Are these inputs creating the outputs you want? If you want energy, health, and vitality, consume nutritious food. If you want clarity, focus, and insight, consume high-quality educational or personal development content. If you want positivity and motivation, consume inspiring messages and associate with positive people. If you want original thinking, consume diverse ideas.

Your outputs are downstream from your inputs. Control your inputs consciously, and your outputs will automatically improve. You cannot consume junk and expect to produce excellence. Quality inputs create quality outputs.

August 23

The practice of daily review creates continuous improvement.

People commonly live the same day repeatedly for years, never learning from experience because they never reflect on experience. They encounter challenges, handle them somehow, then move on without extracting lessons. This means repeating the same mistakes, missing the same opportunities, and staying stuck in the same patterns.

Daily review changes this. Spending 10 minutes each evening reviewing the day creates continuous learning and improvement. Ask yourself: What went well today? What could I have done better? What did I learn? What will I do differently tomorrow? This reflection transforms experience into wisdom. You learn from successes, understanding what worked and why. You learn from mistakes, understanding what didn't work and how to improve. You identify patterns, recognizing recurring challenges that need systemic solutions.

Over time, daily review compounds into significant growth. Each day you extract lessons, and each day you apply yesterday's lessons. This creates a virtuous cycle of continuous improvement that accelerates development.

Today, commit to a daily review. Before bed, spend 10 minutes reflecting on the day. Write brief notes about wins, challenges, lessons learned, and improvements for tomorrow. Don't just replay the day— extract wisdom from it. This simple practice transforms each day from an event that happens to you into a lesson that develops you. Daily review is the discipline that converts time passing into growth happening.

August 24

Protect your peak hours for your most important work.

Everyone has peak hours—times of day when energy, focus, and creativity are highest. For most, this is morning, but some peak in the afternoon or evening. These peak hours are precious resources that should be protected jealously for your most important, creative, and strategic work.

Yet it's not unusual for people to waste peak hours on low-value activities. They check email during peak hours. They attend unnecessary meetings during peak hours. They scroll social media during peak hours. They save their most important work for later when energy and focus have declined.

This is backwards and wasteful. Your peak hours—perhaps 2-4 hours per day—are when you can do your best thinking, create your best work, and make your best decisions. These hours should be protected like gold. Block them on your calendar. Don't schedule meetings during them. Don't check email during them. Don't allow interruptions during them. Use them exclusively for your most important, high-value work. Save email, meetings, administrative tasks, and routine work for non-peak hours when they're appropriate for your lower energy state.

Today, identify your peak hours—when are you most energized, focused, and creative? Tomorrow, protect those hours ruthlessly. Use them for your most important work and nothing else. Notice how much more you accomplish and how much better the quality when you do important work during peak hours. This single strategy—protecting peak hours—can double your productive output.

August 25

Say no to good opportunities and yes to great ones.

One of the hardest disciplines is saying no to good opportunities because they prevent you from saying yes to great opportunities. Every yes to something is a no to something else because time and energy are finite.

When you say yes to a good opportunity, you're saying no to the great opportunity that might come along if you had capacity. The person who accepts every good opportunity ends up overwhelmed, scattered, and unable to pursue any opportunity excellently. The person who declines good opportunities to preserve capacity for great opportunities ends up focused, energized, and able to achieve excellence.

This requires discipline because good opportunities feel appealing and saying no feels like loss. But it's actually strategic. You're declining good to make space for great.

Today, audit your commitments. How many are good but not great? How many are you doing out of obligation, guilt, or inability to say no rather than genuine strategic choice? Consider which good opportunities you could decline to create capacity for great opportunities.

Practice saying no: "That sounds interesting, but it doesn't align with my current priorities." "I appreciate the opportunity, but I need to decline to focus on other commitments." "Thank you for thinking of me, but I'm not able to take that on right now." Saying no to good feels uncomfortable initially, but it becomes empowering as you realize it creates space for great. Don't let good opportunities crowd out great ones.

August 26

Daily journaling clarifies thinking and tracks growth.

Jim Rohn taught: "Don't use your mind as a filing cabinet. Use it as a thinking tool. Get your thoughts down on paper." Writing clarifies thinking. When thoughts swirl in your mind, they remain vague, confused, and easily forgotten. Your mind isn't designed to store everything—it's designed to process and create. When you write thoughts down, they must become concrete and organized. This process of translating thoughts into words on paper creates clarity that thinking alone cannot achieve.

Daily journaling—spending 10-20 minutes writing about your thoughts, experiences, challenges, and insights—provides multiple benefits. It processes emotions, helping you understand and release them rather than carrying them unconsciously. It clarifies problems, often revealing solutions that weren't apparent before writing. It tracks growth, allowing you to look back and see how far you've come. It identifies patterns, showing recurring challenges that need attention.

The format can be simple: What happened today? How do I feel about it? What did I learn? What am I grateful for? What challenges am I facing? What insights am I having? Just write freely without editing or censoring.

Today, start a daily journaling practice. You don't need a fancy journal—any notebook works. Spend 10 minutes before bed writing about your day, your thoughts, your feelings, your insights. Don't worry about grammar or coherence—this is for you, not an audience. Let the writing flow freely. Over time, you'll discover journaling becomes a powerful tool for processing life, clarifying thinking, and tracking growth. It's meditation in written form—a daily practice that brings order to mental chaos.

August 27

Invest the first hour of every day in yourself.

The first hour after waking is the most valuable hour of the day. Your mind is fresh, your willpower is full, and you haven't yet been pulled into the day's demands. This hour belongs to you before it belongs to anyone else.

Yet people often give this precious hour away immediately—checking email, scrolling social media, watching news, reacting to others' priorities. By the time they think about their own priorities, the best hour is gone.

Successful people protect the first hour zealously for personal development. They use it for exercise, meditation, reading, planning, visualization, journaling—activities that strengthen them and prepare them for the day. They don't check email in the first hour. They don't engage with others' demands in the first hour. They invest in themselves first. This isn't selfishness; it's strategic.

When you invest in yourself first, you're stronger, clearer, and more capable of handling whatever the day brings. When you give yourself away first, you enter the day already depleted.

Today, commit to investing your first hour in yourself tomorrow. Don't check phone, email, or social media. Instead, use that hour for activities that develop you—exercise, reading, meditation, planning. This single discipline—protecting your first hour for self-investment—can transform your life because it ensures that every day begins with growth rather than reaction.

August 28

Create keystone habits that cascade into other positive changes.

Some habits are more powerful than others because they create cascade effects—one positive habit naturally leads to other positive habits without additional effort. These are called keystone habits.

Exercise is a keystone habit. When people start exercising regularly, they often spontaneously eat better, sleep better, work more productively, and reduce harmful habits—all without consciously trying. The exercise habit triggers these other improvements naturally. Morning routine is a keystone habit. People with strong morning routines often find their entire days become more structured and productive. Reading is a keystone habit. Regular readers often develop other good habits because books expose them to ideas that inspire change.

The power of keystone habits is leverage—you focus on one habit that automatically improves multiple areas of life. Instead of trying to change everything at once (which is overwhelming), you establish one keystone habit and let it cascade into other improvements.

Today, identify potential keystone habits for your life. Exercise is the most common because physical discipline creates mental and emotional discipline. Morning routine is powerful because it sets tone for everything that follows. Reading is valuable because learning inspires growth.

Choose one keystone habit to establish. Focus all your discipline on making this one habit consistent. As it becomes established, watch for cascade effects—other areas of life improving without direct effort. This is the power of keystone habits: one discipline creates multiple benefits.

August 29

> *Discipline in the small things creates discipline in all things.*

How you do anything is how you do everything. If you're disciplined about small, seemingly insignificant things—making your bed, keeping your space organized, being punctual, following through on minor commitments—you develop discipline that extends to everything. If you're undisciplined about small things—leaving messes, being chronically late, breaking minor commitments—this lack of discipline extends to everything.

Small disciplines matter not because making your bed changes your life directly, but because the act of making your bed builds the discipline muscle you'll need for bigger challenges. Each small act of discipline proves to yourself that you're someone who does what they commit to, even when it's inconvenient. This builds self-trust and self-efficacy.

Conversely, every small act of undiscipline proves you don't follow through, eroding self-trust. Over time, these small proofs accumulate into your identity.

Today, focus on discipline in small things. Make your bed even when you're rushed. Keep your workspace organized even when you're busy. Be on time even when you're tempted to run late. Honor minor commitments even when no one would notice if you didn't.

These small disciplines might seem inconsequential, but they're building the discipline foundation that will support major achievements. Discipline is not situational—it's a character trait developed through consistent practice in small things that extends naturally to big things.

August 30

Consistency beats intensity every time.

The person who exercises intensely for two weeks then quits will be less fit than the person who exercises moderately for two years. The person who studies intensely for a weekend will learn less than the person who studies moderately for a semester. The person who works frantically for a month will accomplish less than the person who works steadily for a year.

Intensity feels productive and creates the illusion of progress. But intensity without consistency is ultimately ineffective because gains fade when practice stops. Consistency might feel less impressive—moderate daily effort seems boring compared to heroic bursts. But consistency compounds. Each day's modest effort builds on previous days. Progress might be invisible daily, but over months and years, it's dramatic.

Additionally, consistency is sustainable. You can maintain moderate daily effort indefinitely. You cannot maintain intense effort indefinitely—it leads to burnout and quitting.

Today, if you've been approaching goals with intensity rather than consistency, adjust your strategy. Reduce the intensity if necessary to create a pace you can sustain indefinitely. It's better to exercise moderately forever than intensely for a month. Better to write one page daily than ten pages once. Better to save consistently than save aggressively then stop.

Choose consistent moderate effort over intense temporary effort. Trust that consistency, given enough time, produces far greater results than intensity ever could. Slow and steady wins the race.

August 31

Daily disciplines are the bridge between dreams and accomplishments.

As we close this month on daily disciplines, understand this: dreams without disciplines remain fantasies. Accomplishments without disciplines are lucky accidents. Disciplines are the bridge that reliably transforms dreams into accomplishments.

You can dream of any achievement—wealth, health, success, mastery. But dreams alone create nothing. Action creates results, and sustained action requires discipline. The person who dreams of writing a book but never develops the discipline of daily writing never writes the book. The person who dreams of financial freedom but never develops the discipline of daily saving and investing never achieves freedom. The person who dreams of excellent health but never develops the discipline of daily exercise and nutrition never achieves health. Dreams show you the destination. Disciplines provide the vehicle.

Today, acknowledge that every significant accomplishment in your life came through some form of discipline, not luck. Most failures to accomplish something you desired came from lack of discipline, not lack of ability. Going forward, when you set new goals, immediately ask: What daily disciplines would make this goal inevitable? Then commit to those disciplines more than the goal itself. Focus on showing up daily to practice your disciplines. Trust that if you maintain your disciplines consistently, accomplishments will follow inevitably.

You don't need perfect disciplines—just consistent ones. Small daily disciplines, maintained over time, build the bridge between where you are and where you want to be. Walk that bridge daily through disciplined action, and eventually you arrive at your dreams transformed into reality.

September

Breaking Old Patterns

Release and Transformation

September 1

Awareness is the first step to breaking any pattern.

You cannot change what you're not aware of. Most limiting patterns operate unconsciously—you repeat them automatically without noticing. You react the same way to stress. You make the same poor decisions. You sabotage success in the same ways. These patterns feel like 'just how you are' rather than learned behaviors you can change.

Breaking patterns requires first becoming aware of them. This means observing yourself with curiosity rather than judgment. Notice when you're engaging in the pattern. What triggered it? What thought preceded it? What emotion accompanied it? What need was it attempting to meet? This observation creates space between trigger and response. Instead of automatically reacting, you pause to notice: "I'm about to engage in this pattern." That pause is where change becomes possible.

Today, identify one limiting pattern you want to break. It might be emotional—reacting with anger when criticized. Behavioral—procrastinating when faced with challenging tasks. Relational—withdrawing when you need connection. Mental—thinking negatively about yourself. Don't try to change it yet. Just observe it. Notice when it happens, what triggers it, how it feels.

This awareness practice might seem passive, but it's actually the essential first step. You're bringing the unconscious pattern into conscious awareness. Once aware, change becomes possible. Without awareness, you're trapped in automatic repetition.

September 2

Your brain automates patterns – good and bad.

The brain is focused on efficiency. It automates as much as possible to conserve energy for essential functions. Each time you repeat a behavior, thought, or emotional response, your brain strengthens a neural pathway. With enough repetition, that pathway becomes automatic. A pattern is formed.

This efficiency mechanism is useful for beneficial patterns like brushing your teeth or driving. But it also automates limiting patterns. If you repeatedly respond to stress with overeating, your brain automates that response to save energy. If you repeatedly think "I'm not good enough," your brain automates that thought. If you repeatedly sabotage success, that behavior becomes automatic.

These patterns persists not because you want them, but because your brain has made it automatic. Breaking patterns requires understanding this mechanism. You're not weak or flawed, you're experiencing your brain's natural tendency to automate repeated behaviors.

The good news is that you can create new patterns. When you consistently practice a new response, your brain creates new neural pathways. Over time, the new response becomes just as automatic as the old one.

Today, recognize that limiting patterns are simply well-worn neural pathways, not permanent traits. They can be changed through consistent practice of new responses. This understanding removes shame and creates possibility. You're not broken. You're running old programs, and those programs can be updated.

September 3

Patterns persist because they once served a purpose, even if they no longer do.

Every pattern you have—even limiting ones—was originally created to serve you in some way. The person who developed a pattern of people-pleasing did so to gain approval and avoid rejection, which felt necessary for survival. The person who developed a pattern of emotional withdrawal did so to protect themselves from pain. The person who developed a pattern of perfectionism did so to avoid criticism.

These patterns made sense in the context where they originated. They were adaptive responses to real challenges. The problem is that patterns tend to persist long after the original situation has changed. The adult continues people-pleasing even though they no longer need others' approval for survival. The person continues withdrawing even though they're now in safe relationships. The perfectionist continues striving even though they're no longer facing harsh criticism.

Understanding the original purpose of your patterns creates compassion rather than self-judgment. You weren't stupid or weak—you were adapting the best way you knew how at the time.

Today, examine one limiting pattern with curiosity instead of judgment. Identify it clearly and ask what purpose it once served and what it was protecting you from. Acknowledge that it helped you cope when you needed it, and offer it gratitude for that support. Then recognize that it no longer fits your current life. Choose a new response that better serves who you are now, and mentally rehearse yourself using it the next time the old trigger appears. Each time you practice the new response, the old pattern weakens and the new one strengthens. Change doesn't require force. It requires awareness, compassion, and consistent practice.

September 4

You cannot break a pattern
with willpower alone; you must replace it with a new pattern.

People tend to try to break patterns through willpower by resisting urges, fighting the impulse, and forcing themselves to stop. This approach is exhausting and usually fails because you're creating a vacuum. When you remove a pattern without replacing it, the mind pulls you back to the old pattern because your brain needs something to fill that space.

The effective approach is replacement rather than resistance. Instead of trying to stop the old pattern, focus on starting a new one. Instead of "stop procrastinating," practice "start immediately on small tasks." Instead of "stop negative thinking," practice "redirect to empowering thoughts." Instead of "stop emotional eating," practice "take a walk when stressed."

When you consistently practice the new pattern, several things happen. First, you're building a new neural pathway. Second, you're weakening the old pathway through lack of use. Third, you're filling the space the old pattern occupied, eliminating the vacuum that pulls you backward. With continued practice, the new pattern becomes just as automatic as the old one was.

Today, identify one pattern you want to change. Rather than focusing on stopping it, design a replacement. Choose a new behavior you will practice when the old trigger appears. Make it specific and actionable, then commit to practicing it consistently.

Each time you successfully execute the replacement pattern instead of the old one, you're building the new neural pathway while weakening the old one. This replacement strategy works better than resistance because you're building something new rather than fighting what already exists.

September 5

Breaking the habit of being yourself.

Joe Dispenza teaches that your personality, how you think, act, and feel, creates your personal reality. To change your reality, you must change your personality by breaking old mental patterns and installing new ones. This requires more than willpower. You must consciously interrupt automatic patterns at the neurological level.

Here's how the process works: First, become aware of your habitual thoughts and emotional responses through meditation and self-observation. Notice when you're thinking the same thoughts, feeling the same feelings, and making the same choices as yesterday.

Second, catch yourself in old patterns and refuse to continue them. When you notice yourself beginning the familiar thought pattern, emotional reaction, or behavior, pause. Every time you interrupt the old pattern, you weaken its automatic programming.

Third, mentally rehearse your new self. In meditation, vividly imagine and feel yourself as the person you want to become. See yourself thinking new thoughts, feeling new emotions, and making new choices. When you mentally rehearse being your new self with emotional intensity, you create new neural pathways.

Fourth, live from this new identity. Throughout your day, embody the person you rehearsed in meditation. Think their thoughts. Feel their feelings. Make their choices. This repetition strengthens new neural pathways and stabilizes change.

Today, begin breaking the habit of being yourself. Spend 10-20 minutes in meditation observing your habitual thoughts and feelings without judgment. Notice old patterns as they arise. Mentally rehearse your new self, who you want to become. Then embody that new self throughout your day. You're not fighting your old patterns with willpower; you're creating new neural pathways through conscious repetition until your new self becomes your automatic self.

The story is the pattern.

Every pattern has a story attached to it, an explanation of why you do what you do. These stories either empower change or prevent it. Limiting stories sound like: "This is just how I am. I've always been this way. I can't help it. It's in my genes. Everyone in my family is like this." These stories make patterns feel permanent and unchangeable. If you believe "this is just how I am," you won't try to change because change seems impossible.

Empowering stories sound like: "This is a pattern I learned. I can unlearn it. This behavior is not my identity. I'm capable of change. Others have overcome this, and so can I." These stories make patterns feel temporary and changeable. If you believe "this is a learned pattern," you'll work to unlearn it because change seems possible. The pattern itself is the same, but the story determines your response to it.

Today, examine the stories you tell yourself about your limiting patterns. Are they stories of permanence or possibility? Do they define patterns as your unchangeable nature or as learned behaviors you can modify? If your stories are limiting, consciously rewrite them. Change "I've always been anxious" to "I learned to respond with anxiety, and I can learn new responses." Change "I can't help it" to "I haven't learned to manage this yet, but I can learn."

Your stories about your patterns are more important than the patterns themselves because stories determine whether you try to change.

September 7

Repetition before results.

Research shows it takes an average of 66 days to form a new habit, the point at which a behavior becomes automatic rather than requiring conscious effort. This means breaking an old pattern and installing a new one requires approximately two months of consistent daily practice.

People often give up too soon. They practice a new behavior for a week or two, don't see dramatic results, and conclude it's not working. But neural pathways take time to form. The old pathway has been reinforced through years of repetition. The new pathway is just emerging and requires deliberate practice to strengthen.

For roughly the first 30 days, the new behavior feels unnatural and requires significant willpower. You're pushing against the momentum of the old pattern. Around day 30-45, it usually starts to feel easier as the new pathway strengthens. By day 66, the new behavior often feels natural and automatic, requiring little conscious thought.

Today, commit to 66 days of consistent practice for one new pattern you're installing. Don't evaluate success before 66 days. Don't give up because it feels hard at day 20. Trust the process. Mark your calendar for 66 days from now. Each day, practice the new behavior regardless of how you feel. Track your progress to maintain accountability.

After 66 days, evaluate. You'll likely find the new pattern has become automatic while the old pattern has weakened significantly. Lasting change requires patience and consistency over weeks, not just days.

September 8

Your identity determines your patterns more than your willpower.

Every behavior is preceded by a belief about identity. You don't just smoke cigarettes—you identify as a smoker. You don't just procrastinate—you identify as a procrastinator. You don't just get anxious—you identify as an anxious person.

These identity-level beliefs make patterns extremely difficult to change because changing behavior that contradicts identity creates cognitive dissonance. The mind works hard to maintain consistency between who you believe you are and how you act. The person who identifies as a smoker will find reasons to keep smoking because not smoking contradicts their identity. The person who identifies as anxious will find reasons to remain anxious because calm contradicts their identity.

To break patterns permanently, identity must shift. Instead of identifying as someone who has a problem, identify as someone who is transforming. Not "I'm a procrastinator trying to stop procrastinating" but "I'm becoming someone who takes immediate action." Not "I'm anxious" but "I'm developing calm resilience." Not "I'm a smoker trying to quit" but "I'm a non-smoker."

Today, examine how you identify yourself regarding your limiting patterns. Do you claim these patterns as core parts of your identity? If so, consciously shift your identity. You are not your patterns. You are someone capable of change who temporarily exhibits certain patterns. Claim a new identity aligned with who you're becoming, not who you've been. As your identity shifts, your behaviors will shift naturally to maintain consistency with the new identity.

September 9

Stress and fatigue weaken your ability to resist old patterns.

Old patterns tend to resurface under stress and fatigue because these states drain the willpower and mental resources needed to maintain new behaviors. When you're rested and calm, practicing new patterns feels manageable. When you're stressed and exhausted, old patterns return because they're automatic and require little effort.

This is why people relapse into old behaviors during difficult times. The recovering addict uses again during a crisis. The person building healthy eating habits returns to comfort food during stress. The person developing assertiveness reverts to people-pleasing when tired. This isn't weakness—it's how the brain responds under duress.

Understanding this pattern allows you to plan for it. First, prioritize stress management and adequate rest. When you're managing stress well and sleeping enough, you have the resources to maintain new patterns. Second, don't be too hard on yourself if old patterns resurface during particularly stressful periods. Rather than seeing it as failure, see it as valuable information about your need for better self-care. Third, create a crisis plan. Identify your high-risk situations for pattern relapse and plan specific strategies for how you will respond in those moments.

Today, examine when your old patterns tend to resurface. Is it during stress? When you're tired? During an emotional upheaval? Create strategies for these high-risk times: stress management practices, earlier bedtimes during difficult periods, or additional support during challenges. Protect your pattern-breaking progress by managing stress and fatigue that would otherwise sabotage it.

September 10

> *The pause between trigger and response is where freedom lives.*

Viktor Frankl taught that between stimulus and response there is a space, and in that space is your power to choose your response. This is the key to breaking reactive patterns. Old patterns operate automatically: a trigger appears and is followed immediately by a habitual response. You receive criticism and immediately become defensive. You face a challenge and immediately procrastinate. You feel anxious and immediately reach for food. There's no space between trigger and response—just automatic reaction.

Breaking patterns requires creating space. When triggered, instead of immediately responding, pause. Breathe. Notice: "I'm being triggered. I'm about to engage in my old pattern." This pause creates the space where choice becomes possible. In that space, you can ask: "What would a new response look like? How does the person I'm becoming respond to this?" Then choose deliberately rather than react automatically.

Initially, you might not catch the trigger until you're already responding. That's part of the process. Awareness develops gradually. Over time, you'll notice the trigger sooner, creating more space. Eventually, you'll pause automatically before responding.

Today, practice creating pause. When you notice a trigger for an old pattern, take three deep breaths before responding. This simple practice creates space between stimulus and response. In that space, your freedom to choose a new response exists. The old pattern says: trigger → automatic response. The new pattern says: trigger → pause → conscious choice → new response. Master the pause, and you master pattern change.

September 11

Forgive yourself for past patterns; shame makes change harder.

People frequently carry tremendous shame about their patterns. They judge themselves harshly for repeating behaviors they wish they could stop. This self-judgment creates a painful cycle: you engage in the pattern, feel shame, use the pattern to cope with the shame, feel more shame, and repeat.

Shame is especially destructive for pattern change because it reinforces the identity of being broken or flawed. When you shame yourself for overeating, you strengthen the identity of someone who can't control eating. When you shame yourself for anxiety, you reinforce the identity of someone who's anxious. Shame creates more of what you are shaming yourself for.

The antidote is self-compassion. You developed these patterns for reasons that made sense at the time. You've been doing your best with the awareness and tools you had. The patterns don't make you bad or weak. They make you human.

Today, practice self-forgiveness for your patterns. Say to yourself: "I forgive myself for engaging in this pattern. I was doing my best to cope. I release shame and choose compassion. I am not my patterns. I am someone capable of change." This self-compassion, paradoxically, makes change easier. When you're not weighed down by shame, you have more energy for transformation. When you accept yourself as you are, you're more capable of becoming who you want to be. Forgive yourself for past patterns, and free yourself to create new ones.

September 12

The company you keep reinforces or breaks your patterns.

If you're trying to break a pattern while surrounded by people who engage in and encourage that pattern, you're fighting an uphill battle. Your social environment powerfully influences behavior. We unconsciously mirror the people around us.

If everyone around you complains, you'll tend toward complaining. If everyone around you procrastinates, you'll tend toward procrastination. If everyone around you thinks negatively, you'll tend toward negative thinking.

Conversely, surrounding yourself with people who model the patterns you want to develop makes change natural. If you're around people who take action, you'll tend toward action. If you're around positive thinkers, you'll tend toward positivity. If you're around disciplined people, you'll tend toward discipline. This doesn't mean abandoning all friends who don't support your growth. It means being intentional about who you spend the most time with and whose influence you allow to shape you.

Today, audit your social environment. Who do you spend the most time with? What patterns do they model? Do they reinforce the patterns you want to break or support the patterns you want to build? Then make strategic adjustments. Spend more time with people who model the behaviors you want. Join groups where desired behaviors are normal. Reduce time with people who reinforce unwanted patterns. Your social environment is either supporting your transformation or undermining it. Choose your influences consciously.

September 13

Small pattern changes create cascading transformations.

You don't need to change every pattern at once. In fact, attempting total transformation usually leads to overwhelm and failure. Instead, focus on changing one small pattern. One change often creates a cascade, where progress in one area naturally leads to others.

When people begin exercising, they often start eating better without consciously trying. The exercise pattern cascades into healthier choices. When people start making their bed, they often find other areas of their life becoming more organized. The small discipline cascades into broader discipline. When people begin meditating, they often respond more calmly throughout the day. One small discipline can quietly reshape many others.

This happens because patterns are interconnected. Changing one pattern affects the system, creating natural momentum for other changes. Success also builds self-efficacy. When you prove to yourself that you can change one behavior, other changes feel more possible and less intimidating.

Today, identify one small pattern to change. Pick something manageable rather than overwhelming. Not "completely transform my life" but "meditate five minutes daily" or "make my bed each morning" or "take a five-minute walk after lunch." Focus all your energy on establishing this one small pattern. As it becomes automatic, notice what else begins to shift naturally.

Trust that small pattern changes create cascading transformations throughout your life without requiring force or perfection.

September 14

> *Your patterns are maintained by the payoffs they provide.*

Every pattern persists because it provides some payoff, a benefit that makes the pattern worth maintaining, even if the overall cost is high. The person who procrastinates gets the payoff of avoiding discomfort, even though procrastination creates bigger problems later. The person who people-pleases gets the payoff of avoiding conflict, even though it means sacrificing authenticity

These payoffs are often unconscious. You may not realize you're maintaining a pattern because of what it provides. This is why self-awareness is essential. Noticing when the pattern emerges allows you to interrupt it consciously and choose a new response. Once you identify the payoff, you can find healthier ways to meet the same need. If procrastination's payoff is avoiding discomfort, build discomfort tolerance by intentionally facing it, such as having a difficult conversation or starting the task you've been avoiding. If people-pleasing's payoff is conflict avoidance, practice saying no to small requests first.

The key is catching yourself when the pattern emerges, then consciously choosing the new response that meets the need more directly.

Today, identify the payoff behind a pattern you want to break. Ask yourself: What do I get from this pattern? What need does it meet? What discomfort does it help me avoid? What benefit makes it worth maintaining?

Be honest. There's always a payoff, even for destructive patterns. Once you identify the payoff, ask: How can I meet this need in a healthier, more direct way? When you find alternative ways to receive the payoff without the pattern, releasing the pattern becomes far easier.

September 15

Visualization accelerates pattern changes by rehearsing new responses.

Your brain learns from both actual experience and vividly imagined experience. This means you can accelerate pattern change through visualization by mentally rehearsing new responses to old triggers.

If you have a pattern of reacting defensively to criticism, visualize receiving criticism and responding with openness and curiosity instead. See yourself in that situation, feel the temptation to defend, then watch yourself pause and choose a new response.

If you have a pattern of procrastinating on important tasks, visualize encountering an important task and immediately beginning work on it. Experience the satisfaction of taking action.

Make these visualizations vivid and emotional. The more real they feel, the more your brain treats them like actual experience, creating neural patterns for the new response. Practice this visualization daily. 5-10 minutes of mentally rehearsing your new response to typical trigger situations.

Today, identify a common trigger for an old pattern. Then create a detailed visualization of encountering that trigger and responding with your new pattern instead. Visualize it from first-person perspective, making it as real as possible. Practice this visualization daily. When the actual trigger occurs in real life, you'll find yourself more prepared to execute the new response because you've already practiced it mentally dozens of times.

Visualization is like a flight simulator for behavior change. You practice in a safe environment before encountering the real situation.

September 16

Track your pattern interruptions to build momentum.

When breaking patterns, it's easy to focus on failures, the times you didn't catch the trigger, the times you responded with the old pattern. This focus on failure is demoralizing and can make change feel impossible.

Instead, track your successes, the moments you successfully interrupted the pattern and chose a new response. Keep a journal or simple tally. Each time you notice the trigger and choose differently, mark it down. Each time you pause before reacting, note it. Each time you replace the old pattern with the new one, celebrate it.

Tracking success provides several benefits. First, it shifts your focus from failure to progress, creating positive momentum. Second, it provides evidence that change is happening, even when it doesn't feel dramatic. Third, it builds motivation, seeing your successes accumulate inspires you to continue. Fourth, it reveals patterns. You may notice you're more successful at certain times of day or in certain situations, helping you understand what supports your progress.

Today, create a simple system to track pattern interruption. It might be a journal where you note each success. Or a habit tracker where you mark successful days. Or simply a tally in your phone. Each time you successfully interrupt an old pattern and choose a new response, record it.

At the end of each week, review your successes. Celebrate progress, even if it's not perfect. This approach turns pattern change from an overwhelming project into a series of small, measurable wins you can acknowledge and build upon.

September 17

Patterns can be stored in your body, not just your mind.

Patterns aren't just mental. They're also stored in the body. The person who tenses their shoulders when stressed has a somatic pattern. The person who holds their breath during anxiety has a somatic pattern. The person whose stomach clenches during conflict has a somatic pattern.

These body-level patterns often drive mental and emotional patterns. You tense your shoulders, which triggers stress thoughts, which reinforces the tension. Pure cognitive approaches to pattern change miss this body component. You might understand your pattern intellectually but still feel pulled by somatic cues.

Somatic practices help release body-held patterns. These can include: breathwork that releases tension and resets nervous system responses; body scanning that brings awareness to physical patterns; gentle movement that releases stored stress; progressive muscle relaxation that teaches the body how to release tension; and somatic therapy that addresses trauma stored in the body.

Today, notice the somatic component of a pattern you want to break. Where do you feel it in your body? What physical sensations accompany the pattern? Then experiment with somatic practices. When you notice the body sensation, take several deep breaths. Consciously relax the area of tension. Move your body gently and deliberately.

These practices interrupt the pattern at the body level, which makes interrupting it at the mental level far easier. Lasting pattern change often requires working with the body as much as the mind.

September 18

Celebrate small wins to reinforce new patterns.

Your brain learns through rewards. When a behavior is followed by something pleasurable, the brain strengthens the neural pathway for that behavior. This is how patterns form. Repeated behavior plus positive reinforcement leads to automation.

You can leverage this mechanism consciously by celebrating small wins in pattern change. Each time you successfully interrupt an old pattern and choose a new response, celebrate it. This doesn't mean making a big deal out of it. It simply means acknowledging the win and allowing yourself to feel good about it.

Say to yourself: "Yes! I did it! I caught the trigger and chose differently!" Feel the pride and satisfaction. This positive emotion reinforces the new neural pathway, making the new response more likely to repeat.

In many cases people do the opposite. They minimize small wins and fixate on failures. They successfully interrupt a pattern 3 times and slip once, then focus entirely on the slip while dismissing the successes as "not enough." This focus on failure strengthens the old pattern rather than building the new one.

Today, commit to celebrating every small win in pattern change. When you notice a trigger and pause instead of reacting automatically, celebrate it, even if you eventually respond with the old pattern. The pause alone is progress. When you choose a new response even once, celebrate it, even if you don't do it perfectly.

Each small win is building the new pattern. Acknowledge it, feel good about it, let that positive emotion reinforce the new neural pathway. Small celebrations, practiced consistently, create meaningful change.

September 19

You must grieve the loss of old patterns, even destructive ones.

Even patterns you desperately want to break have been with you a long time. They're familiar. They've been your coping mechanism, your default response, your comfort zone. Letting them go, even when they're destructive, involves loss.

People tend to resist pattern change unconsciously because they haven't acknowledged this loss. They try to break a pattern while holding onto it emotionally, because releasing it feels like losing part of themselves. This creates internal conflict that quietly sabotages change. The solution is to consciously grieve the pattern you're releasing.

Acknowledge this truth: "This pattern has been with me for years. It helped me cope when I didn't know better ways. Letting it go feels like saying goodbye to part of my past." This isn't romanticizing the pattern or wanting to keep it. It's acknowledging the emotional reality of release. When you allow yourself to grieve what you're letting go, you free yourself to fully commit to something new.

Today, if you're struggling to release an old pattern despite genuinely wanting to change, practice conscious closure. Write a goodbye letter to the pattern. Thank it for serving you when you needed it. Acknowledge that letting it go is difficult. Express what you'll miss about the familiar comfort of the pattern, even knowing it doesn't serve you. This may feel uncomfortable or unfamiliar, but it honors the emotional process of change. Once you grieve what you're losing, you create space to fully embrace what you are becoming.

September 20

The moment you feel the urge to engage in an old pattern, do something-anything-else immediately.

When the urge to engage in an old pattern arises, there is a brief window, usually 10 to 15 minutes, where the urge peaks and then naturally subsides. If you can avoid acting on the urge during this window, it will often pass on its own. The key is having a plan for that moment.

When you feel the urge to procrastinate, immediately do something else—take a walk, call a friend, or do five minutes of work on anything. When you feel the urge to emotionally eat, immediately do something else—drink water, stretch, or journal. When you feel the urge to react defensively, immediately do something else—take deep breaths, count to ten, or excuse yourself briefly.

The "something else" doesn't need to be perfect or profound. It just needs to be immediate and different. This interrupts the automatic trigger-to-response pathway. It creates space between urge and action. Often, after doing something else for 10-15 minutes, the urge has passed and you can respond more consciously.

Today, create a list of 5-10 things you can do when you feel the urge to engage in an old pattern. Make them simple and immediately accessible. Post this list where you'll see it. Next time the urge arises, immediately do one item from your list. Don't negotiate, don't think about it, just do it immediately. This interrupt-and-redirect strategy is one of the most effective tools for breaking reactive patterns.

September 21

Your underlying beliefs create and maintain your patterns.

Beneath every pattern is a belief. The person who people-pleases believes "My worth depends on others' approval." The person who procrastinates believes "I'm not capable of doing this well." The person who sabotages success believes "I don't deserve good things." The person who reacts defensively believes "Criticism means I'm inadequate."

These beliefs operate unconsciously, driving patterns that seem irrational on the surface. But once you identify the belief, the pattern makes perfect sense, it's a logical response to that belief. Changing the pattern without changing the underlying belief is like treating symptoms without addressing the disease. The pattern might shift temporarily, but it returns because the belief recreating it remains active. Lasting pattern change requires changing underlying beliefs.

Today, identify a persistent pattern. Ask yourself: What would I have to believe for this pattern to make sense? If I engage in this pattern, what does that imply I believe about myself, others, or the world? Write down the beliefs you uncover. Then examine them: Are they actually true? Where did they come from? Do I want to continue believing them?

Create alternative beliefs that support new patterns instead. "My worth is inherent, not dependent on approval." "I'm capable and can learn what I don't know." "I deserve good things." When you change beliefs, patterns change naturally because the old behaviors no longer make sense.

September 22

Relapse is part of the pattern breaking process, not evidence of failure.

People often expect pattern change to be linear, a steady improvement from old pattern to new pattern without setbacks. In reality, change is rarely linear. It involves progress, setbacks, renewed progress, occasional relapses, and gradual overall improvement. The trajectory is upward, but the path zigzags.

When people experience a relapse, reverting to the old pattern after a period of success, they often interpret it as total failure. They think: "I'm back to square one. All my progress is lost. I can't change." This interpretation leads many to give up entirely.

But relapse is a normal part of change, not evidence of failure. Old neural pathways are deeply ingrained. They don't disappear the moment a new pathway is created. They weaken gradually over time. During stress or challenge, it's natural to occasionally fall back into familiar patterns.

Today, if you've experienced relapse, reframe it. You haven't failed; you've learned. Each relapse provides information: What triggered the relapse? What were the warning signs? What can I do differently next time? Extract the lessons, then return to your new pattern immediately.

Don't waste energy on shame or despair. Relapse is only failure if you allow it to stop you permanently. When you treat relapse as feedback and resume your new behavior quickly, it becomes a temporary detour on an ultimately successful path. Expect relapse, plan for it, learn from it, and keep moving forward.

It's not "Can I change?" but "What needs to change for me to change?"

It's common for people to doubt their ability to change patterns, asking themselves "Can I really change? Am I capable of this?" These questions focus on personal capacity, often leading to doubt and discouragement.

A more empowering question is: "What needs to change for me to change successfully?" This shifts the focus away from your capability and toward the conditions and supports required for success. Maybe you need more knowledge about how patterns change. Maybe you need stronger social support. Maybe you need to address underlying beliefs. Maybe accountability structures are missing. Maybe you need to start smaller or take a different approach.

This question assumes you are capable of change. The issue is not your ability, but identifying the right conditions for success. It opens the door to problem-solving rather than self-doubt.

Today, if you've been struggling to change a pattern while questioning your capability, shift the question. Instead of "Can I change?", ask "What needs to change for me to change successfully?" List potential answers: What knowledge do I need? What support? What beliefs need shifting? What smaller starting point? What different strategy? Then implement one of these changes. This shifts you from powerless questioning to empowered problem-solving.

You are capable of change. You just need to discover what conditions and supports allow change to happen consistently for you.

September 24

> *Meditation strengthens the observer*
> *part of you that can witness patterns without engaging them.*

One of meditation's most valuable benefits for pattern change is strengthening your capacity to observe thoughts, urges, and patterns without automatically acting on them.

People are often completely identified with their patterns. When the urge arises, they become the urge. When the pattern triggers, they become the pattern. There's no separation between observer and observed. Meditation creates this separation. Through regular practice, you develop the ability to notice: "There's an urge to procrastinate" without becoming that urge. "There's anxiety arising" without becoming the anxiety. "There's a pattern triggering" without becoming the trigger.

This observer perspective is transformative because it creates space between urge and action. You're not trying to suppress or fight the urge. You're simply observing it with curiosity, knowing it will pass. Often, when you observe patterns without engaging them, they naturally weaken over time.

Today, if you don't already meditate, begin a simple practice. Sit quietly for 10 minutes. Focus on your breath. When thoughts, urges, or emotions arise, simply notice them without judgment: "There's a thought. There's an urge. There's an emotion." Then return your attention to the breath. You're not trying to stop thoughts or urges. You're practicing observing them without automatically acting on them.

This observer capacity transfers to daily life, making pattern interruption easier. Meditation is training for witnessing patterns without being controlled by them.

> *Your self-talk either reinforces old patterns or supports new ones.*

The way you talk to yourself about your patterns has a powerful impact on whether they change. Negative self-talk reinforces patterns: "I always do this. I never learn. I'm so stupid. I'll never change. What's wrong with me?" This self-talk strengthens the identity of someone who has this pattern, making change harder.

Empowering self-talk supports change: "I'm learning new responses. I'm making progress. This is challenging, but I'm capable. Each day I'm getting better. I caught myself this time, that's progress." This self-talk strengthens the identity of someone who is actively changing, making change easier.

Often, self-talk about patterns is unconsciously negative. They criticize themselves harshly every time the pattern appears, unknowingly reinforcing it.

Today, pay attention to your self-talk when a pattern shows up. What do you say to yourself? Is it harsh criticism or compassionate encouragement? If it's harsh, consciously change it. When the pattern appears, say: "I notice this pattern. I'm working on changing it. I'm making progress even if it's not perfect yet. I'm capable of change." This shift in self-talk doesn't excuse the pattern, but it supports transformation rather than reinforcing old behavior.

Speak to yourself the way you'd talk to a close friend who's genuinely trying to grow, with encouragement, compassion, and confidence in their ability to change. Your self-talk is powerful. Make sure it supports change rather than sabotaging it.

Change happens gradually, then suddenly.

Pattern change follows a specific trajectory. Initially, change is invisible. You're putting in effort by practicing new responses, interrupting patterns, and building new neural pathways, yet you see little outward change. The old pattern still triggers easily. The new behavior still requires a lot of effort. Progress seems minimal. This is the gradual phase where people tend to give up. They don't see results proportional to effort, so they conclude it's not working.

But beneath the surface, neural pathways are forming, old connections are weakening, and change is underway, even if not visible yet. Then, after weeks or months of gradual invisible change, suddenly it clicks. The new pattern feels natural. The old pattern loses its grip. What required enormous effort now happens easily. This is the sudden phase where change becomes obvious. It feels like overnight transformation, but it's actually the accumulated result of consistent, invisible work. Understanding this trajectory prevents premature quitting.

Today, if you've been working on pattern change without seeing dramatic results, trust the process. You're in the gradual phase where change is invisible but real. Keep practicing your new responses. Keep interrupting old patterns. The neural pathways are forming even though you can't see it yet.

If you persist through the gradual phase, you'll reach the sudden phase where change becomes obvious and easy. Don't quit during the invisible growth period. Change is happening gradually, and soon it will become unmistakable.

September 27

Make the new pattern easier and the old pattern harder.

Every behavior has friction, the effort required to do it. Low-friction behaviors happen easily. High-friction behaviors happen rarely. You can engineer pattern change by adjusting friction levels. Make the new pattern as low-friction as possible so it's easy to do.

If your new pattern is exercising daily, put workout clothes beside your bed so they're the first thing you see. Keep equipment readily accessible. Remove barriers that make exercise harder. If your new pattern is eating healthy, prep healthy meals in advance. Keep healthy snacks visible and convenient. Make healthy choices the path of least resistance.

At the same time, make the old pattern as high-friction as possible so it's difficult to engage in. If your old pattern is scrolling social media, delete the apps from your phone so you must consciously reinstall them to use them. If your old pattern is unhealthy eating, don't keep tempting foods in your home. If your old pattern is procrastinating with TV, put the remote in a drawer instead of leaving it within easy reach.

Today, examine a pattern you're trying to change. Ask: How can I make the new pattern easier? What barriers can I remove? What preparations can I make? How can I make the old pattern harder? What barriers can I add? What temptations can I remove? Then implement these friction adjustments. This strategy leverages human tendency toward low-friction behaviors, making change feel effortless rather than forced.

September 28

When you change patterns, expect others to resist your change.

Your patterns exist within relationship systems. Others have adapted to your patterns and often unconsciously benefit from them. When you change, it disrupts these systems, and others may resist, sometimes overtly, sometimes subtly.

The person who changes from people-pleasing to assertiveness might encounter resistance from those who benefited from the pleasing. The person who stops enabling might face anger from those they enabled. The person who sets boundaries might face guilt-trips from boundary-violators. This resistance doesn't mean your change is wrong, it means systems resist change. Expect this resistance, and don't let it deter you.

Others' discomfort with your growth is their process to navigate, not your responsibility to prevent. Some relationships will adjust to your new patterns. Others might end, which can be painful but necessary. Not everyone can support the person you're becoming, and that's okay.

Today, if you're changing patterns and experiencing resistance from others, recognize this as normal systems dynamics rather than evidence you're doing something wrong. Stay committed to your change. Communicate clearly about your new boundaries or behaviors. Allow others to have their reactions without taking responsibility for managing their feelings.

Some will adjust; some won't. Focus on becoming who you're meant to be, and trust that relationships aligned with your growth will adapt, while relationships incompatible with your growth may naturally fall away.

September 29

Breaking patterns is an act of self-love, not self-punishment.

People tend to approach pattern change from self-rejection: "I hate this about myself. I need to fix this. I'm so messed up." This self-punishing energy makes change feel like punishment, which creates resistance and makes success unlikely.

A more effective approach is recognizing pattern change as self-love: "I deserve better than these old patterns. I love myself enough to release what no longer serves me. I'm committed to my wellbeing." This self-loving energy makes change feel like self-care rather than self-punishment.

You're not changing because you're broken; you're changing because you value yourself. You're not fixing defects; you're evolving toward your highest potential. This reframe transforms the entire experience of pattern change. Instead of gritting your teeth and forcing yourself to stop doing things you judge yourself for, you're compassionately releasing patterns that once served you but no longer align with who you're becoming.

Today, examine your motivation for pattern change. Is it rooted in self-rejection or self-love? If it's self-rejection, consciously shift it. Tell yourself: "I'm not changing because I'm bad or broken. I'm changing because I love myself enough to release patterns that limit me. This is self-care, not self-punishment." This shift in energy makes change far more likely to succeed because you're moving toward something positive rather than fleeing from something negative. Break patterns from love, not judgment.

September 30

You are not your patterns; you are the awareness that can change them.

As we close this month on breaking patterns, embrace this liberating truth: you are not your patterns. Your patterns are learned behaviors, conditioned responses, habitual reactions, but they are not your essence.

You are the awareness that can observe these patterns, understand them, and choose to change them. This distinction is crucial. When you believe you are your patterns, saying "I am anxious, I am a procrastinator, I am reactive," change feels like trying to become a different person, which is overwhelming and often impossible.

But when you recognize patterns as learned behaviors separate from your essential self, change becomes simply a matter of learning new behaviors. You're not changing who you are; you're changing what you do. Your spirit—the awareness observing all of this—remains constant and unchanged. This awareness is already whole, already perfect, already free. Your patterns are just clouds passing across the clear sky of your awareness. They don't define you; they temporarily obscure you.

Today, practice this distinction. When a pattern arises, notice: "There is anxiety" rather than "I am anxious." "There is procrastination happening" rather than "I am a procrastinator." "There is a reactive pattern" rather than "I am reactive." This subtle shift in language creates space between essence and behavior, making change possible.

You are not your patterns. You are the vast, aware, capable consciousness that can witness patterns and choose to change them. This is your power. This is your freedom. Claim it.

October

Desire & Definiteness of Purpose

Clarity and Focus

October 1

The starting point of all achievement is desire.

Napoleon Hill taught that every great achievement begins with burning desire. Not mild interest. Not casual hoping. Not vague wishing. Burning desire. An intense, consuming want that dominates your thoughts and drives your actions.

Weak desires produce weak results or no results. You might want something casually, but without burning desire, you won't persist through obstacles. You'll quit when things get difficult because the desire wasn't strong enough to fuel persistence.

Strong desires produce strong results. When you burn with desire for something, obstacles become challenges to overcome rather than reasons to quit. Setbacks become learning opportunities rather than stopping points. Sacrifices become acceptable because the desired outcome is worth the cost.

Today, examine your primary goals honestly. Do you have a burning desire for them, or just a casual interest? If you're not achieving what you say you want, the problem might not be your strategy or effort. It might be insufficient desire. Burning desire cannot be forced through willpower, but it can be intensified by reconnecting with your reasons. What would achieving this goal mean to you? How would it change your life? Who would you become?

Visualize the outcome vividly and emotionally until desire strengthens. The starting point of all achievement is desire. Make sure yours burns hot enough to fuel the journey ahead.

October 2

Definiteness of purpose is the foundation of all success.

It's common for people to drift through life without a clear, definite purpose. They have vague desires, wanting to be happy, successful, wealthy, but no specific, definite purpose that guides their decisions and actions.

This vagueness almost guarantees mediocrity because without a definite target, you cannot create a plan to reach it. You cannot measure progress toward it. You cannot focus energy on it. Definiteness of purpose means knowing exactly what you want, when you want it, what you're willing to give in return, and creating a specific plan for getting it. Not "I want to be successful" but "I will achieve X specific result by X specific date through X specific actions."

This precision transforms vague hoping into focused pursuit. When you have definiteness of purpose, decisions becomes clearer. Does this action move me toward my purpose or away from it? Does this opportunity align with my purpose or distract from it? Should I say yes or no to this request based on my purpose? Without definiteness, you're pulled in every direction by others' purposes. With definiteness, you have a compass that guides every decisions.

Today, define your purpose with precision. What exactly do you want to achieve? By when? What specific actions will you take? Write it out in detail. This definiteness is the foundation upon which all success is built. Vague purposes produce vague results. Definite purposes produce definite results.

You become what you think about most of the time.

Earl Nightingale called this the strangest secret: we become what we think about. Your dominant thoughts determine your destination. If you think about your goals, you move toward them. If you think about your fears, you create them. If you think about success, you become successful. If you think about failure, you fail. This is not mysticism. It's how the mind operates.

Your thoughts direct your attention, which determines what you notice. Your thoughts create emotions, which determine your energy. Your thoughts influence decisions, which determine actions. Your actions create results. The person who consistently thinks about their business builds a successful business. The person who thinks consistently about their health creates excellent health. The person who thinks consistently about their goals achieves their goals.

Yet many people spend most of their time thinking about what they don't want: problems, fears, complaints, and worries. Then they wonder why their lives reflect these same conditions.

Today, audit your dominant thoughts honestly. What do you think about most throughout the day? Your goals or your problems? Possibilities or limitations? What you want or what you fear? If your dominant thoughts don't align with your desired outcomes, consciously redirect them.

Each time you notice yourself thinking about what you don't want, redirect to what you do want. Over time, this shifts your dominant thoughts, which shifts your trajectory. You become what you think about most. Choose your thoughts with intention.

A burning desire backed by faith knows no such word as impossible.

The combination of burning desire and unwavering faith creates an unstoppable force. Desire without faith becomes frustration. You want something intensely but don't believe you can have it. Faith without desire becomes passive. You believe things are possible but don't want anything specific enough to pursue. But desire combined with faith creates the mindset of achievers: "I know exactly what I want, and I absolutely believe I will achieve it."

This combination eliminates the word impossible from your vocabulary. Obstacles become temporary challenges. Setbacks become learning experiences. Other people's doubts become irrelevant. You persist until you succeed because failure is not an option you accept.

History demonstrates this principle repeatedly. Every great achievement came from someone who combined burning desire with absolute faith. They wanted something intensely and believed unwaveringly they would achieve it, despite contrary evidence, despite skepticism, and despite obstacles.

Today, examine your primary goal. Do you have both burning desire and unwavering faith? If you have desire but doubt, work on building faith through small successes, visualization, and studying examples of others who achieved similar goals. If you have faith but weak desire, work on intensifying desire by connecting more deeply with why this goal matters to you.

When you combine burning desire with unwavering faith, impossible becomes irrelevant. You know you will find a way because quitting is not an option.

October 5

Write down your definite major purpose and read it daily.

Unwritten goals remain wishes. Writing crystallizes vague desires into concrete intentions. When you write your definite major purpose, you're making a commitment to yourself, to your future, and to your potential. Napoleon Hill insisted that writing your purpose and reading it daily is essential for achievement.

This daily reading serves multiple functions. It keeps your purpose at the forefront of your mind, preventing drift. It reinforces commitment, making the purpose feel more real. It programs your subconscious, which then works continuously toward the goal. It reminds you why you're making sacrifices and doing difficult things.

Without daily reading, even written purposes fade into background noise, lost among daily distractions. With daily reading, your purpose remains alive, active, and directing your actions.

Today, if you haven't already, write your definite major purpose. Include: what you want to achieve, when you will achieve it, what you will give in return, and the specific plan for achievement. Write it in present tense as if already achieved: "I am..." or "I have..." Then commit to reading this statement at least twice daily—once upon waking, once before bed.

As you read it, visualize it as already accomplished. Feel the emotions of achievement. This daily practice keeps your purpose definite rather than letting it become vague and forgotten.

October 6

Your purpose must be specific, measurable, and time-bound.

Vague purposes produce vague results. "I want to be successful" is not a purpose. It's a wish. "I will build a business generating $500,000 in annual revenue by December 31, 2030" is a purpose—specific, measurable, and time-bound. Specificity provides clarity. You know exactly what you're working toward. Measurability provides feedback. You can track progress and know whether you're on track. Time-bound provides urgency. Without a deadline, there's always tomorrow, which becomes never.

People often resist making their purpose this specific because specificity feels like commitment and commitment feels like risk. What if I fail? What if I set the wrong goal? But vagueness is actually riskier because it guarantees you won't achieve anything specific. At least with specificity, you have a real chance at success.

Today, if your purpose is vague, make it specific. What exactly do you want? How will you measure achievement? By what specific date will you achieve it? Write it down with precision.

This might feel uncomfortable. That's a good sign. Discomfort means you're making a real commitment rather than entertaining comfortable fantasies. Specific, measurable, time-bound purposes create accountability and urgency that vague purposes never do. Your purpose should be so specific that when the deadline arrives, there's no question whether you achieved it or not.

October 7

Where there is no vision, the people perish.

This ancient wisdom remains true: without vision, without a clear picture of where you're going, you drift aimlessly, eventually perishing in mediocrity or worse.

Vision is what separates those who create their future from those who merely react to circumstances. Vision provides direction when you're lost. It provides motivation when you're tired. It provides meaning when you're questioning why you're making sacrifices. It provides hope when circumstances are difficult.

People without vision live day-to-day, reacting to whatever comes, following the path of least resistance. They end up wherever circumstances take them rather than where they want to go. People with vision live purposefully, making decisions aligned with where they're heading. They end up creating the future they envisioned rather than accepting whatever circumstances deliver.

Today, clarify your vision. Not just what you want to achieve, but who you want to become and how you want to live. Paint a detailed mental picture of your ideal future. Five years from now, what does your life look like? What have you achieved? Who have you become? What does a typical day involve? Make this vision vivid and emotionally compelling. Write it down. Review it regularly. Let it guide your decisions and fuel your efforts.

Without vision, you perish—not physically, but in terms of potential. With vision, you thrive, creating a future worthy of your capabilities.

October 8

Desire, backed by faith, is magnetic—it attracts the means for its realization.

When you hold a clear desire backed by unwavering faith, something remarkable happens: the means for achieving that desire begin appearing. The right people show up. Opportunities emerge. Resources materialize. Information arrives. This isn't magic. It's a combination of psychological and energetic factors working together.

Psychologically, clear desire combined with faith sharpens your focus. You notice opportunities you would have missed. You recognize resources you would have overlooked. You make connections you would have dismissed. Energetically, clear desire backed by faith broadcasts a frequency that resonates with similar frequencies, drawing in matching circumstances.

Additionally, clear desire backed by faith creates confidence and enthusiasm that others find attractive. People want to help, invest in, and collaborate with someone who knows what they want and believes they'll achieve it.

Today, examine whether your desires are truly backed by faith or shadowed by doubt. If doubt dominates, work on building faith. Study examples of people who achieved similar goals, proof that it's possible. Visualize your success daily until it feels real. Take small actions that prove to yourself you're capable.

As faith strengthens and combines with clear desire, you'll notice the universe beginning to respond. Opportunities appear. Help arrives. Resources manifest. Your desire, backed by faith, becomes magnetic, attracting everything needed for its realization.

You must know where you're going before you can plan the best way to get there.

Imagine trying to navigate to a destination without knowing what destination you're seeking. You might move, even move quickly, but you're just as likely to go in the wrong direction as the right one. This is how many people approach life: lots of motion, little direction.

Before you can create an effective plan, you must have absolute clarity about your destination. What exactly are you trying to achieve? What does success look like specifically? Until you know this with precision, any plan you create is guess-work. Once you know your exact destination, planning becomes straightforward.

You can work backwards from the goal: To achieve X by this date, what must happen the month before? The month before that? What actions are required? What resources are needed? What skills must be developed? This reverse engineering creates a roadmap from where you are to where you want to go.

Today, if you've been making plans without absolute clarity on your destination, pause. Get clear on exactly where you're going first. What is your ultimate goal? What does achievement look like specifically? Once this is crystal clear, then create your plan. But destination must precede plan. You cannot plan an effective route to a destination you haven't clearly defined. Know where you're going with precision, then the plan becomes obvious.

October 10

Small desires bring small results; great desires bring great results.

Your desires act as a thermostat for your results. If you desire small things, you will exert small effort and achieve small results. If you desire great things, you will exert greater effort and achieve greater results. Many people set small goals because they feel realistic and achievable. But small goals create small motivation. You will not push through significant obstacles for small rewards. You will not make meaningful sacrifices for minor gains. Small desires keep you safe, but stuck.

Great desires might seem unrealistic, but they generate great motivation. You'll push through obstacles for rewards you deeply want. You'll make sacrifices for gains that truly matter. Great desires force you to grow into someone capable of achieving them. This doesn't mean being delusional. It means being ambitious. There's a difference between impossible (defying physics) and improbable (requiring significant effort and growth). Improbable goals that inspire you are better than easily achievable goals that leave you uninspired.

Today, examine whether your desires are proportional to your potential. Are you playing small to stay comfortable? Are your goals inspiring or merely realistic? Consider expanding your desires. What would you attempt if you knew you couldn't fail? What would truly excite you even if it seems improbable?

Give yourself permission to desire greatly. Small desires produce small results. Great desires produce great results. Match your desires to your potential, not to your current circumstances.

Your purpose must be worthy of your life.

You have limited time on earth. Decades if you're fortunate, but finite nonetheless. Your definite purpose is how you invest this irreplaceable resource. Is your purpose worthy of this investment?

People tend to pursue purposes that are too small for their capabilities or too shallow for their souls. They chase money without considering what they'll do with it. They pursue status without considering whether it brings fulfillment. They build careers without considering whether the work matters. Then they achieve their purpose and feel empty because it wasn't worthy of their life investment.

A worthy purpose is one that, when achieved, you can look back on with satisfaction knowing your time was well spent. It challenges you to grow. It serves something beyond yourself. It utilizes your unique gifts. It creates value that outlasts you. It aligns with your deepest values.

Today, examine whether your purpose is worthy of your life. If you achieve it, will you feel your time was well invested? Does it challenge you to become more? Does it serve others, not just yourself? Does it utilize your unique capabilities? If your purpose feels unworthy—too small, too selfish, too meaningless—expand it. You have one life to invest.

Make sure you're investing it in a purpose worthy of that sacrifice. Your purpose should be something you'd be proud to define your life, something worth the years of effort required to achieve it.

Definiteness of purpose gives meaning to every action.

Without definite purpose, activities feel arbitrary and disconnected. You do things because you should, because others expect it, because it's what you've always done. But you lack the energizing sense of meaning that comes from knowing each action serves a greater purpose.

With definite purpose, even mundane activities gain meaning. You're not just exercising—you're building the energy needed to achieve your purpose. You're not just reading—you're acquiring knowledge essential for your purpose. You're not just working—you're earning resources to fund your purpose. You're not just networking—you're connecting with people who can support your purpose.

The same activities that felt meaningless without purpose become meaningful with purpose. Everything connects to something larger than itself. This transformation from meaningless to meaningful creates energy and motivation. Tasks that required willpower when purposeless become natural when purposeful.

Today, if daily life feels meaningless or draining, the problem might not be the activities themselves but lack of connection to definite purpose. Clarify your purpose, then consciously connect each daily activity to it. How does this serve my purpose? How is this investment moving me toward my goal?

When you see the connection, activities that felt burdensome become meaningful. Definiteness of purpose transforms random actions into purposeful steps toward a meaningful destination.

October 13

The majority of people drift without aim or purpose.

It's common for people to never define a clear purpose. They drift through life, reacting to circumstances, following the path of least resistance, accepting whatever comes. They work jobs they don't love because they need money. They live where they live because of happenstance or convenience. They pursue goals others set for them— parents' expectations, society's definitions of success, or peer pressure. They reach old age never having consciously chosen their direction.

This drifting is the default path. It requires no decision, no effort, no risk. You simply float wherever the current takes you. But drifting guarantees mediocrity at best, misery at worst. You end up wherever life takes you rather than where you want to go.

The minority who succeed are those who refuse to drift. They define clear purpose, create specific plans, and pursue goals deliberately. They might start from the same circumstances as drifters, but they end in completely different places because they navigated rather than drifted.

Today, decide whether you'll be part of the drifting majority or the purposeful minority. If you've been drifting, going through motions without clear direction, pause. Define your purpose. Create your plan. Start navigating deliberately. The majority will continue drifting, and you'll leave them behind not because you're more talented but because you know where you're going while they don't. Choose direction over drifting. Choose purpose over chance. Choose navigation over floating.

October 14

Your purpose must be your own, not what others expect from you.

It's common for people to pursue purposes that aren't truly theirs. They chase careers their parents wanted, lifestyles society values, or goals that would make others proud. They achieve these external purposes and feel empty because they were never aligned with their authentic desires.

Success without authenticity is sophisticated failure. You can achieve someone else's purpose for your life and still feel unfulfilled because it wasn't your purpose—it was theirs. Your purpose must emerge from your own values, desires, and vision. Not what would make your parents happy. Not what would impress your peers. Not what society defines as success.

What do you genuinely want? Who do you authentically want to become? What legacy do you want to leave? This requires courage because your authentic purpose might disappoint others. Your parents might not understand. Your peers might not respect it. Society might not value it. But living someone else's purpose is a waste of your one precious life.

Today, examine whether your purpose is authentically yours or adopted from others' expectations. Are you pursuing this because you genuinely want it or because others want it for you? If your purpose isn't authentically yours, give yourself permission to redefine it. What would you pursue if no one's approval mattered? What would you do if you knew you couldn't disappoint anyone? Define your purpose based on your authentic desires, then pursue it regardless of others' reactions. Your life. Your purpose.

October 15

Success requires burning the bridges behind you.

True commitment requires eliminating retreat options. This principle has been used throughout history by leaders who understood that when retreat is impossible, you find ways forward you never would have discovered otherwise.

In 1519, Hernán Cortés scuttled his ships upon landing in Mexico, forcing his men to conquer or die—leading to the fall of the Aztec Empire. In 207 BCE, Chinese general Xiang Yu destroyed his army's boats and cooking pots after crossing a river, creating the idiom "Break the kettles and sink the boats" for total commitment. Ancient Greek generals burned their boats upon landing to ensure fierce determination. The principle is simple: as long as you have easy fallback plans, you'll retreat when things get difficult.

This doesn't mean recklessness. It means commitment. The person who keeps their corporate job while half-heartedly starting a business has a retreat option that prevents full commitment. The person who quits to pursue the business full-time burns that bridge, creating urgency that drives success. The person who dabbles in their purpose while maintaining comfortable alternatives never experiences the creativity and resourcefulness that emerge when success is the only option. When retreat is impossible, you innovate. You persist. You find ways. Burning bridges transforms "I'll try" into "I will succeed."

Today, examine whether you're keeping retreat options that prevent full commitment to your purpose. Are you hedging bets? Maintaining fallbacks? Playing it safe? Consider what would change if retreat wasn't an option. What would you do differently if you had to make this work?

Sometimes, the key to success is eliminating the option of not succeeding. Burn the bridges behind you. Make success the only option. Watch how this forces you to discover capabilities you didn't know you had.

October 16

Your subconscious mind will work tirelessly on goals you emotionalize.

Your subconscious doesn't respond to logical arguments or rational goals. It responds to emotion. When you emotionalize a goal—feeling the desire intensely, experiencing the joy of achievement in imagination—your subconscious accepts it as important and works continuously toward it, even while you sleep.

The subconscious operates 24/7 processing problems, recognizing opportunities, and generating solutions. But it only works on goals you've emotionalized. Merely writing a goal logically doesn't engage subconscious power. But visualizing that goal with intense emotion— feeling the pride of achievement, the joy of success, the gratitude of realization—activates subconscious processing.

This is why visualization with emotion is so powerful. You're not just seeing the goal mentally; you're feeling it emotionally, which programs your subconscious to work toward it continuously.

Today, take your primary goal and emotionalize it through visualization. Don't just see yourself achieving it; feel the emotions intensely. How will you feel when you succeed? Pride? Joy? Relief? Gratitude? Freedom? Generate those emotions now, as if success is already yours. Do this daily, spending 10-15 minutes really feeling the emotions of achievement.

This emotional practice programs your subconscious, which then works tirelessly solving problems, recognizing opportunities, and moving you toward the goal without conscious effort. Emotionalize your goals to activate your subconscious mind's unlimited power.

Clear purpose attracts support.

Purpose radiates energy that attracts and inspires. When you're clearly pursuing something meaningful, people want to help, collaborate, and support you. Your purposeful energy is magnetic and uplifting.

People without purpose tend to drain energy. They complain, drift, seek endless entertainment or distraction, and pull others into their aimlessness. Their lack of direction creates a vacuum that sucks energy from those around them. This creates a self-reinforcing cycle. Purpose attracts support, which facilitates achievement, which strengthens purpose. Purposelessness repels support, which prevents achievement, which reinforces purposelessness.

If you want to attract high-quality people and opportunities, develop clear purpose. People are drawn to those who know where they're going. They want to be part of something meaningful, contribute to something worthwhile, associate with someone headed somewhere.

Today, recognize that your purpose—or lack of it—affects everyone around you. If you have a clear purpose, share it. Let people know what you're building. Invite them to participate. Your purposeful energy will inspire and attract support. If you lack purpose, recognize this is affecting your relationships and opportunities negatively. Others sense the absence of direction and either avoid you or try to impose their purposes on you.

Define your purpose, pursue it visibly, and watch how this changes the quality of people and opportunities that enter your life.

October 18

Your purpose should stretch you beyond your current capabilities.

If your purpose is easily achievable with current skills and resources, it's not a purpose—it's a task. True purpose requires you to grow, to become more than you currently are, to develop capabilities you don't yet have. This stretching is uncomfortable but essential.

Easy goals don't require growth. You achieve them with current capabilities and remain the same person. Stretching goals force growth. You must develop new skills, expand your capacity, and become someone capable of achieving them. The achievement is valuable, but the person you become in pursuit is more valuable.

If your purpose doesn't require growth, you're setting it too small. You should look at your purpose and think: "I'm not sure I'm capable of this. I'll have to grow significantly to achieve this." That uncertainty is perfect—it means your purpose is big enough to require transformation.

Today, examine whether your purpose stretches you or merely extends your current path. Does it require significant growth, or could you achieve it with current capabilities? If it doesn't stretch you, expand it. Make it big enough that you're not quite sure you can do it, big enough that you'll have to grow to achieve it.

The person you become in pursuit of a stretching purpose is worth more than any comfortable goal you could easily achieve. Set purposes that force growth, that demand you become more than you currently are.

October 19

> *Whatever the mind can conceive and believe, it can achieve.*

This Napoleon Hill principle reveals the power of combining conception (imagination) with belief (faith). You can conceive many things—wild fantasies, impossible dreams, random ideas. But conception without belief produces nothing. You can believe in many things—yourself, universal principles, possibilities. But belief without clear conception has no specific target.

When you combine conception and belief—when you imagine something specific and believe you can achieve it—you activate the creative power of your mind. Your brain treats this believed conception as a problem to solve, working continuously to find ways to make it real. History proves this principle. Every breakthrough began with someone conceiving something that didn't exist and believing it could be achieved. Others said it was impossible, but the conceiver-believer persisted until conception became reality.

Today, apply this principle to your purpose. First, conceive it clearly—imagine specifically what you want to achieve. Second, believe it's achievable for you—not easy, but possible with effort. The combination of clear conception and genuine belief activates creative forces in your mind that will find ways to make your conception real. Don't worry about how it will happen. Conceive what you want clearly and believe in it genuinely. When conception and belief unite, achievement becomes inevitable.

You must give before you get.

Many people approach their purpose with a getting mindset: What can I get? How much can I earn? What's in it for me? This mindset creates resistance and limits achievement. The universe responds more readily to giving than getting.

When your purpose centers on contribution—what you'll give, how you'll serve, what value you'll create—resources flow more freely. You attract support more easily. Success arrives more naturally. The marketplace rewards value creation. The more value you give, the more reward you receive. But you must give first, before expecting return. The person focused on creating value attracts abundance. The person focused on extracting value repels it.

Today, examine your purpose. Is it primarily about getting or giving? About extracting value or creating it? About what you can earn or what you can contribute? If your purpose is getting-focused, transform it to giving-focused. Instead of "I will earn $1 million," consider "I will create $10 million in value for others, earning $1 million in return." Instead of "I will become successful," consider "I will serve 10,000 people excellently, becoming successful in the process."

This shift from getting to giving transforms your energy from taking to contributing, which paradoxically increases what you receive. Give before you get. Create value before extracting reward. Serve before seeking success. This is the path of greatest achievement.

October 21

Clarity eliminates confusion and creates confidence.

Confusion about purpose creates hesitation, doubt, and scattered effort. You're not sure where you're going, so you don't move decisively. You try multiple directions simultaneously, making little progress in any. You question whether you're on the right path because you never clearly defined the path. Clarity eliminates all of this.

When you're crystal clear about your purpose—what you want, why you want it, how you'll achieve it—confusion vanishes. You know what to do, when to do it, and why you're doing it. This clarity creates confidence because you're no longer guessing or hoping. You're executing a clear plan toward a definite goal.

Clarity also eliminates wasted effort. With vague purpose, you pursue opportunities that might be relevant. With clear purpose, you immediately recognize which opportunities align with your purpose and which don't. You say yes to aligned opportunities and no to distractions.

Today, if you're experiencing confusion or lack of confidence, the root cause is likely lack of clarity. Get clear about your purpose. Write it out in detail. Clarify what you want, why you want it, and how you'll get it. Eliminate vagueness, generalities, and maybes. Make your purpose so clear that confusion has nowhere to hide. As clarity increases, confidence naturally follows because you know exactly where you're headed and how you'll get there.

October 22

Your purpose should make you willing to do what others won't.

Average purposes produce average effort, which produces average results. If your purpose is not compelling enough to make you willing to do things others won't do, you'll achieve what everyone else achieves—mediocrity. Exceptional purposes inspire exceptional effort.

When you're deeply committed to a compelling purpose, you become willing to work harder, sacrifice more, persist longer, and do difficult things that others avoid. You wake up earlier. You work when others rest. You study when others relax. You persist when others quit.

This willingness doesn't come from superhuman discipline—it comes from a purpose compelling enough to make sacrifices worthwhile. The person with a weak purpose struggles to do hard things because the purpose isn't worth the effort. The person with a strong purpose finds hard things acceptable because the purpose is worth any effort.

Today, examine whether your purpose inspires willingness to do what others won't. Are you willing to work harder for this purpose? Make sacrifices for it? Do difficult things in pursuit of it? If not, either your purpose isn't compelling enough or you haven't connected deeply enough with why it matters.

Strengthen your purpose or deepen your connection to it until you're genuinely willing to do what others won't. That willingness is what separates those who achieve exceptional results from those who achieve average ones.

Every adversity carries the seed of equivalent advantage.

When pursuing your purpose, you'll encounter adversity: obstacles, setbacks, failures, and disappointments. People often see adversity as purely negative, something to avoid or lament. But Napoleon Hill taught that every adversity contains the seed of an equal or greater benefit, though that seed is usually hidden. When that benefit is recognized and applied, it becomes an advantage.

The person who loses their job might discover their true calling. The business that fails might teach lessons essential for the next successful venture. The rejection might redirect toward a better opportunity. The adversity itself is not the advantage—the advantage is what you can extract from it if you look. Finding it requires shifting perception. Instead of asking "Why did this happen to me?" ask "What can I learn from this? How can I use this? What advantage might be hidden here?" This shift transforms adversity from pure loss to potential gain.

Today, if you're facing adversity in pursuit of your purpose, deliberately search for the seed of advantage. What can you learn? How might this redirect you to something better? What strength is this building? What weakness is this revealing that you can now address?

Every adversity contains a hidden advantage, but it will not reveal itself automatically. You must actively look for it. Don't waste adversity by seeing only the setback. Extract the lesson, claim the advantage, and use it as fuel. What feels like an obstacle today may prove to be the very thing that makes your ultimate success possible.

October 24

Your purpose becomes clearer through action, not just through thinking.

People often wait to take action until their purpose is perfectly clear. But clarity often comes through action rather than before it. You take a step, learn from it, and adjust. You try something, discover what you don't want, and refine. You act, receive feedback, and clarify based on results.

Waiting for complete clarity before acting keeps you stuck in analysis paralysis. You think endlessly about your purpose, reading books, taking assessments, journaling about possibilities. But thinking alone has limited power to create clarity. Action creates data. You learn what energizes you by doing things, not just thinking about them. You discover your strengths by applying them. You clarify your values by making decisions. You define your purpose by pursuing possibilities and eliminating what doesn't fit.

Today, if you're waiting for perfect clarity before acting, reverse the sequence. Act first, even with incomplete clarity. Choose a direction that seems promising and move. Pay attention to what you learn, how you feel, what works and what doesn't. Let this information refine your understanding of your purpose. Over time, through cycles of action and reflection, clarity emerges. Not through thinking alone, but through acting, learning, adjusting, and acting again.

Your purpose becomes clear through engaged exploration, not passive contemplation. Start acting, and clarity will emerge from your experience.

October 25

Associate with people aligned with your purpose.

Your associations powerfully influence your pursuit of purpose. People aligned with your purpose support, encourage, and inspire you. People misaligned with your purpose discourage, distract, and drain you.

If you're pursuing ambitious goals while surrounded by people who think small, you'll face constant resistance. They'll question your choices, express doubt, and pull you toward their comfort zone. If you're pursuing meaningful purpose while surrounded by people chasing superficial success, you'll feel pressure to abandon meaning for status.

Conversely, surrounding yourself with people who have similar purposes creates a supportive environment. They understand your choices because they're making similar ones. They encourage rather than discourage. They inspire through their example. They provide practical help and strategic advice.

Today, audit your closest associations. Are the people you spend the most time with aligned with your purpose? Do they support your goals or question them? Do they inspire you forward or pull you backward?

Then make strategic adjustments. Seek out people who are pursuing similar purposes or who have achieved what you're pursuing. Join groups, attend events, engage in communities where these people gather. Gradually shift your associations toward those aligned with your purpose. This doesn't mean abandoning all current relationships, but it does mean being strategic about who influences you most.

October 26

Your purpose must be backed by persistence.

Desire and definite purpose are essential, but they're not sufficient. Without persistence—the quality of continuing despite obstacles, setbacks, and discouragement—purpose remains unrealized potential.

Every meaningful purpose meets resistance. Results don't arrive on schedule. Plans break. Support wavers. Progress slows. In these moments, persistence becomes the difference between achievement and abandonment.

The person without persistence quits when challenges arise. They interpret obstacles as signs to stop or change direction. The person with persistence continues. They adjust strategy without abandoning purpose. They stay in motion long enough for results to compound.

But persistence must be paired with inner awareness. There's a difference between persisting through resistance on an aligned path and forcing yourself forward on a path that isn't truly yours. Persistence is powerful when your heart and mind are unified—when effort feels demanding but meaningful. When persistence feels like constant inner conflict or self-betrayal, it's often a signal to reassess alignment, not effort.

True persistence listens inward while continuing forward. It refines direction without abandoning commitment. It distinguishes between resistance that strengthens you and misalignment that drains you.

Today, examine both your persistence and your alignment. When obstacles arise, ask whether they require endurance or course correction. Stay persistent, but stay conscious. Purpose pursued with persistence and alignment becomes inevitable. Purpose without persistence remains unrealized. Persistence without alignment becomes exhaustion.

October 27

Review and revise your purpose regularly.

While definiteness of purpose is essential, flexibility is equally important. Growth changes you. Learning refines you. The purpose that inspired you five years ago might no longer fit who you've become. The goal that mattered at 25 might feel hollow at 35. Wisdom means revisiting your purpose regularly to ensure it still aligns with your authentic values and desires.

Rigid attachment to outdated purposes creates misery. You keep pursuing something that no longer serves you simply because you committed to it years ago, even though you are no longer the same person. Flexible evolution allows course correction. Sometimes you discover your purpose was too small and you are capable of more. Sometimes you realize it was misaligned and rooted in someone else's definition of success. Sometimes the core remains true, but the form and specifics need adjustment.

This isn't quitting or inconsistency. It's maturity.

Today, commit to regular purpose reviews, quarterly or annually. Ask: Does this still inspire me? Does it align with who I'm becoming? Does it reflect what I now value? If yes, continue with renewed commitment. If no, revise without guilt.

Definiteness does not mean rigidity. Be fully committed to your current purpose while remaining open to its evolution. Your purpose should grow as you grow, serving who you are becoming, not who you used to be.

October 28

> *Your purpose should leave you better than you found yourself.*

Purpose isn't just about achievement, it's about transformation. The person who achieves their purpose should be fundamentally different than when they started. The goal itself matters, but who you become in pursuit matters more.

A worthy purpose develops qualities you didn't have: discipline you lacked, courage you needed, wisdom you sought, compassion you cultivated, resilience you built. It stretches you beyond comfort zones, forcing growth. It challenges you to overcome weaknesses. It requires you to develop strengths. If you achieve your purpose but remain essentially the same person, was it truly a worthy purpose? The achievement might bring temporary satisfaction, but lasting fulfillment comes from transformation. Becoming someone you're proud to be.

Today, examine your purpose through this lens. If you achieve it, who will you have become? What qualities will you develop? How will you be better than you are now? If the answer is "not much different," your purpose might not be challenging enough. A worthy purpose should require you to become more capable, more disciplined, more wise, more courageous than you currently are.

The achievement is valuable, but the person you become in achieving it is invaluable. Choose purposes that transform you, that leave you better than you found yourself.

Burn your goals into your consciousness through daily reading and visualization.

Most goals are written once and forgotten, lost in journals or files, having no impact. But goals burned into consciousness through daily reinforcement become powerful directing forces in your life.

The process of burning in requires: writing your purpose and primary goals clearly and specifically, reading this written statement at least twice daily—morning and evening, visualizing achievement in vivid detail while reading, feeling the emotions of success intensely, and repeating this process without fail every single day.

This daily ritual serves multiple purposes. It keeps your purpose at the forefront of consciousness rather than buried under daily distractions. It programs your subconscious mind through repetition and emotion. It strengthens desire and belief through regular connection. It aligns daily choices with long-term purpose.

After weeks and months of daily reading and visualization, your purpose becomes so deeply embedded that you think about it unconsciously. It influences decisions automatically. It attracts opportunities naturally. You don't need to consciously remember it, it's become part of your operating system.

Today, commit to this daily practice. Write your purpose and primary goals if you haven't already. Read them twice daily. Visualize achievement vividly. Feel success emotionally. Do this every day without exception. This consistent practice burns your purpose into your consciousness so deeply that achievement becomes inevitable. Your goals must dominate your thoughts if they're to materialize in your life. Daily reading and visualization creates this domination.

October 30

Obstacles are tests for how badly you want your purpose.

Every purpose worth pursuing attracts obstacles. These aren't punishments or signs you're on the wrong path—they're tests of commitment. The universe is essentially asking: Do you really want this? How badly? Will you persist despite difficulty? These tests separate those who achieve from those who merely wish.

The person with weak desire sees the first obstacle and quits, concluding it wasn't meant to be. The person with burning desire sees obstacles as challenges to overcome, proof that the goal is worth pursuing. If it was easy, everyone would achieve it. Obstacles ensure only the committed succeed. Each obstacle you overcome strengthens your commitment and capabilities. You prove to yourself that you're serious. You develop resilience and resourcefulness. You become someone capable of achieving your purpose.

Today, if you're facing obstacles in pursuit of your purpose, interpret them correctly. They're not signs to quit—they're tests of commitment. The question isn't whether obstacles appear but how you respond when they do. Do you give up or persist? Do you find excuses or find solutions? Do you interpret obstacles as stop signs or speed bumps?

Your response to obstacles reveals how badly you want your purpose. If you want it badly enough, no obstacle will stop you—you'll go through, around, over, or under it. Use obstacles as opportunities to prove your commitment to yourself and to demonstrate that your desire is strong enough to fuel success.

October 31

*The person with definite purpose owns
their life; the person without it is owned by circumstances.*

As we close this month on desire and definiteness of purpose, embrace this fundamental truth: purpose is what separates those who create their lives from those who merely react to life. Without definite purpose, you're at the mercy of circumstances, other people's agendas, and random events. You react to whatever comes, accepting whatever circumstances provide, following paths others lay out. Your life is shaped by external forces rather than internal direction. You're owned by circumstances because you have no clear vision guiding you toward something better.

With definite purpose, you become the owner of your life. Circumstances still occur, but you respond to them through the lens of your purpose. Does this serve my purpose or distract from it? Does this move me forward or backward? Should I say yes or no based on my purpose? Your purpose becomes the North Star guiding all decisions. You're no longer reacting to life—you're creating life according to your vision.

Today, claim ownership of your life through definite purpose. If you've been drifting, define your purpose now. If you have vague desires, make them definite. If you have definite purpose, recommit to it. Write it clearly. Feel it deeply. Read it daily. Visualize it vividly. Let it dominate your consciousness. Take ownership of your life by knowing exactly what you want, why you want it, and how you'll achieve it.

This definiteness transforms you from passenger to driver, from victim to creator, from one who is owned by circumstances to one who owns their destiny. Definite purpose is your declaration of ownership over your life.

November

Gratitude & Present Moment

Appreciation Practices

November 1

Gratitude turns what we have into enough.

People often live in a state of perpetual dissatisfaction, always focused on what they lack. No matter how much they have, it never feels like enough. More money, more success, more possessions—the goalposts keep moving, and satisfaction remains elusive.

Gratitude breaks this cycle by shifting focus from what's missing to what's present. When you genuinely appreciate what you have, it suddenly becomes enough. Not because circumstances changed, but because your perception changed.

The same life that felt insufficient yesterday feels abundant today through the lens of gratitude. This isn't about settling or lowering your standards. It's about recognizing that dissatisfaction with what you have doesn't fuel achievement, it fuels misery. You can be grateful for what you have while simultaneously working toward more. In fact, gratitude for what is creates positive energy that attracts more.

Today, practice the gratitude shift. Instead of focusing on what you lack, inventory what you have. Health, relationships, opportunities, shelter, food, freedom—when you truly appreciate these, they become enough. Not forever enough, but enough right now.

This sense of sufficiency creates peace and paradoxically opens you to receive more. Gratitude turns scarcity into abundance without changing external circumstances, it changes your internal experience of those circumstances. What you have becomes enough when you're grateful for it.

November 2

The present moment is all you ever have.

Your life is not lived in the past or the future. It's lived only here, only now. The past exists as memory. The future exists as imagination. Neither can be entered or experienced. The only place life actually happens is this present moment.

Yet many people miss their lives because their attention is rarely here. They eat while replaying yesterday or worrying about tomorrow, barely noticing the flavors, textures, and nourishment arriving in the moment. They breathe thousands of times a day without ever feeling the life-giving breath move through their body. They sit in conversations while planning what to say next, hearing words but not truly meeting the person in front of them. Moments pass not because life is fast, but because attention isn't present.

There are times when stepping out of the present moment is intentional and useful. Visualization, meditation, and morning or evening rituals are dedicated spaces for reflection and inner work. These practices shape direction and align intention. But outside of those moments, presence is the gift. Life is meant to be lived, not mentally rehearsed while it's happening.

Living outside the present creates the feeling that life is slipping by. When attention returns to now, everything changes. Experience becomes richer. Conversations deepen. Ordinary moments reveal quiet beauty. You stop living in memory and anticipation and start living where life actually exists.

Today, practice returning to the present moment. Pause throughout the day and notice what is here now. What are you seeing, hearing, feeling in your body? Not what you're thinking about, but what's actually happening. You don't need a better moment. This is the only moment you ever have. Use your rituals to shape your direction, then give yourself fully to the moments in between. Life isn't happening somewhere else. It's happening here.

November 3

Gratitude is the antidote to negative emotions.

You can't simultaneously feel genuine gratitude and negative emotions. Try it—feel truly grateful for something while also feeling angry, anxious, or depressed. It's impossible. Gratitude and negativity occupy the same mental space; one displaces the other. This makes gratitude a powerful tool for emotional regulation.

When anxiety arises, shift to gratitude—what are you grateful for right now? When anger surfaces, shift to gratitude—what blessings do you have despite this frustration? When depression looms, shift to gratitude—what good exists in your life even though you're struggling? This isn't about suppression or denial. The negative circumstances might be real. The difficult emotions might be valid. But gratitude provides perspective and relief. It reminds you that even in difficulty, good exists. Even in struggle, blessings remain. This perspective doesn't solve problems, but it prevents you from drowning in negativity while solving them.

Today, when negative emotions arise, use gratitude as medicine. Don't fight the negative feeling, that creates resistance. Instead, redirect attention to something you're grateful for. Feel genuine appreciation. Notice how this shifts your emotional state. The negative emotion might return, but you've proven you're not trapped in it. You can shift your state through gratitude. Practice this repeatedly, and gratitude becomes your default emotional antidote to life's inevitable difficulties.

November 4

> *Yesterday is history, tomorrow is a*
> *mystery, and today is a gift, that's why they call it the present.*

This wisdom reminds us that the present moment is literally a present, a gift. Yesterday is gone, unchangeable, existing only as memory. Tomorrow has not arrived, unpredictable, existing only as imagination. But today, this moment, is here, real, and yours to either experience or waste.

People often treat the present as something to get through on the way to the future. "I'll be happy when..." "Life will be good once..." "I'll enjoy things after..." Appreciation is postponed until conditions improve, while the gift of now quietly passes by unnoticed.

But now is all you have. If you can't find something to appreciate in this moment, you won't suddenly develop that capacity when circumstances improve. The person who can't be present with what is will not be present with what will be. They remain focused on the next thing, perpetually postponing life.

Today, receive the present moment as a gift. Not because it's perfect, but because it's yours. It's the only moment you will ever actually experience. Everything else is mental abstraction. Open this gift by being fully here. Notice what is present right now, sights, sounds, sensations, experiences. Appreciate the quiet miracle of being alive in this moment. The past gave you lessons. The future holds possibilities. But the present is your gift, the only time you're truly alive. Unwrap it through presence and gratitude rather than letting it pass unopened while your mind drifts to yesterday or tomorrow.

November 5

A grateful heart is a magnet for miracles.

Gratitude doesn't just make you feel better, it changes what you attract into your life. The frequency of gratitude aligns with abundance, synchronicity, and positive circumstances. When you live in gratitude, you notice opportunities you would have otherwise missed. You attract supportive people. Resources appear. Solutions emerge. What seem like miracles are often the natural response of the universe to your grateful state of being.

Conversely, the frequency of ingratitude aligns with lack, struggle, and negative circumstances. The ungrateful mind focuses on problems and, in doing so, attracts more problems. It fixates on what's missing, which reinforces more lack. Complaining becomes a signal that repels the very things it seeks.

Your emotional state is always broadcasting a signal. Gratitude broadcasts "I have abundance, I notice blessings, I appreciate life." The universe responds by providing more to appreciate. Ingratitude broadcasts "I have lack, I notice problems, I'm dissatisfied." Life responds with more dissatisfaction.

Today, cultivate a grateful heart intentionally. Begin a simple gratitude practice. Each morning or evening, list 5 to 10 things you're genuinely grateful for. Feel the appreciation rather than merely naming it. Consistency matters more than perfection. As this practice deepens, notice what shifts. Opportunities increase. Support shows up. Circumstances begin to align.

Your grateful heart becomes a magnet for miracles, not because gratitude forces outcomes, but because it aligns you with an abundance-based way of seeing and experiencing life.

November 6

Worry is prayer for what you don't want.

Worry is a misuse of creative imagination. Rather than visualizing desired outcomes, many people vividly imagine feared outcomes. Rather than emotionalizing goals, they emotionalize potential disasters. The mind doesn't distinguish between imagining what is wanted and imagining what is feared—both act as instructions to the subconscious and broadcasts to the universe.

When you worry, you are effectively rehearsing negative outcomes with emotional intensity. You're doing the same inner work required to create results, but aimed in the wrong direction. This is why chronic worriers often experience what they worry about, not because worry predicts the future, but because it conditions perception, behavior, and expectation toward it.

Worry programs your inner world for struggle while broadcasting a frequency of fear and lack. It keeps attention fixed on problems, which makes solutions harder to see. It trains the mind to anticipate difficulty rather than opportunity.

Today, recognize worry as misdirected creative power. When you catch yourself worrying, interrupt the pattern. Ask: Am I using my imagination to create what I want or what I fear? If worry continues, consciously redirect it.

Take the worried thought and reverse it. If you're worrying about failure, imagine success. If you're worrying about loss, imagine stability. If you're worrying about rejection, imagine acceptance. Feel the emotion of the desired outcome as vividly as the worry once felt.

Stop using your imagination to rehearse what you don't want. Use it deliberately to create what you do.

November 7

The more grateful you are for what
you have, the more you'll have to be grateful for.

Gratitude creates a virtuous cycle. When you're grateful, you begin to notice more things to appreciate. As awareness of blessings increases, gratitude naturally deepens. As gratitude deepens, you attract more experiences, people, and circumstances that reinforce it. The cycle spirals upward toward greater appreciation and abundance.

Ingratitude creates the opposite effect. When attention rests on lack, more lack becomes visible. As problems dominate focus, dissatisfaction grows. As dissatisfaction grows, life begins to feel heavier and more difficult. This downward spiral leads toward frustration, scarcity, and discontent.

The turning point is gratitude now, regardless of circumstances. You don't wait to feel grateful until life improves. You choose gratitude for what already exists, and that choice begins the upward spiral.

Today, commit to the gratitude spiral. Each day, deliberately notice what is already there to appreciate: the ability to breathe, the life-giving warmth of the sun, people who care about you, food on your plate, a roof over your head, and a body that carriers you through the day. Let your attention rest there long enough for gratitude to be felt, not just acknowledged.

As this practice continues, you'll notice more blessings appearing in your life. They may seem new, but often they were present all along, unseen because your attention was elsewhere. Gratitude sharpens perception. As you notice more, you feel more grateful. As you feel more grateful, more reveals itself. The cycle continues.

Over time, life shifts from scarcity-focused to abundance-aware, from problem-centered to appreciation-filled. The principle remains true: the more grateful you are for what you have, the more you'll have to be grateful for.

November 8

Presence is the greatest gift you can give to yourself and others.

In a distracted world, presence is rare. People tend to be physically present but mentally absent—scrolling social media while sitting with loved ones, checking scores during conversations, or escaping into screens at the first hint of stillness. Modern devices have trained us to fragment our attention almost constantly.

When you give someone your full presence—undivided attention without a phone, without glancing at screens, without mental escape—you offer something increasingly rare and valuable. You make them feel seen and heard in a way partial attention never does. Similarly, when you give yourself full presence—experiencing this moment rather than escaping into devices—you give yourself the gift of actually living your life instead of watching it pass by on a screen.

Presence is challenging because the mind has been conditioned to seek constant stimulation and quick dopamine hits. Attention naturally drifts toward checking notifications, catching game highlights, or endless scrolling. It's now common for a person to sit at the dinner table physically present while attention wanders to a phone, half-engaged in conversation while waiting for the next alert. This fractured way of being has become so normalized that it often goes unnoticed.

Today, practice giving the gift of presence. When with others, try putting your phone in another room. Turn off notifications. Make eye contact. Listen fully. When alone, resist filling every quiet moment with screens or scrolling. Notice when your hand reaches for your phone out of habit, and choose to be present instead.

Presence is not a state you achieve once; it's a practice of continuously choosing this moment over digital escape. The gift of presence—to yourself and others—is among the most valuable gift you can give. Everything else is enhanced by presence and diminished by the constant pull of distractions.

November 9

Gratitude transforms ordinary days into thanksgivings.

The external world doesn't change through gratitude—what changes is your experience and perception of that world. The same job that felt like drudgery yesterday becomes meaningful work today when viewed through the lens of gratitude. The same daily routine that felt monotonous becomes precious when you appreciate it. The same ordinary opportunities that seemed insignificant become recognized blessings.

Gratitude is not about the objective quality of circumstances but about the subjective experience of those circumstances. Two people can have identical lives, but the one with gratitude experiences joy while the other experiences dissatisfaction. The difference isn't in what they have but in how they perceive what they have. This is empowering because it means you don't need to change your life to transform your experience— you need to change your perspective. When you view your life through the lens of gratitude, everything shifts.

Today, take one aspect of your life you've been viewing negatively— perhaps your job, your home, or your routine. Deliberately shift to viewing it through gratitude. What's positive about this that you've been overlooking? What blessings does it provide that you've been taking for granted? What would you miss if it were gone?

This gratitude lens transforms your experience of that aspect without changing the aspect itself. Ordinary becomes extraordinary. Routine becomes meaningful. Common becomes blessed. Gratitude is the lens that transforms perception and therefore experience.

November 10

The past can't be changed, but your relationship with it can.

Many people remain trapped in the past, replaying regrets, reliving grievances, or wishing things had been different. They give mental and emotional energy to what cannot be changed, unknowingly draining themselves without benefit. You cannot change what happened. But you can change your relationship with what happened.

You can shift from victim to survivor, from bitter to grateful, from traumatized to transformed. You can extract wisdom from mistakes rather than dwelling in shame. You can forgive or let go of those who hurt you, freeing yourself from resentment's prison. You can find meaning in suffering rather than being defined by it.

This shift doesn't require denying or minimizing what happened. It requires choosing a relationship with the past that serves your present rather than sabotages it. The person who remains identified with past victimization stays victimized forever. The person who uses past difficulty as fuel for growth transforms victimization into victory.

Today, examine your relationship with the past. Are you replaying it endlessly? Using it as an excuse? Letting it define you? If so, consciously shift your relationship. The events cannot change, but your interpretation and response can. What can you learn? How can you grow? What meaning can you create? How can you let go? Shift from being controlled by the past to being informed by it.

The past happened, but it doesn't have to keep happening in your mind. Change your relationship with it, and free yourself to be present.

November 11

Begin and end each day with gratitude.

How you bookend your day determines the quality of your waking hours and your sleep. Beginning with gratitude sets positive tone for the day. Before checking devices, before engaging with demands, spend five minutes in appreciation. What are you grateful for? Your health, your relationships, opportunities available today? Feel genuine gratitude. This practice primes your mind to notice blessings rather than problems throughout the day. You enter the world from abundance rather than scarcity, from appreciation rather than complaint.

Ending with gratitude ensures peaceful sleep and positive subconscious programming. Before bed, review your day and find things to appreciate. Even difficult days contain moments worth gratitude. This practice prevents you from sleeping on negativity, which creates restless sleep and programs your subconscious negatively. Instead, you sleep in gratitude, which creates restful sleep and programs your subconscious for abundance.

Today, implement this morning and evening gratitude practice. Upon waking, before anything else, spend five minutes feeling grateful for something in your life. List things mentally or write them down. Feel the appreciation deeply. Before sleep, review the day and find things to be grateful for. Feel appreciation for them. Let gratitude be the first and last emotional state of each day.

This simple practice transforms your days because you're operating from the frequency of gratitude more hours of each day. Begin and end with gratitude and watch how it colors everything between.

November 12

The future is created in the present moment.

People frequently believe the future is created by planning alone, by thinking about what they'll do someday. But the future is actually created by what you do now. The seeds you plant today become the harvest you reap tomorrow. The choices you make now create the circumstances you'll inhabit later.

The person you're becoming today is the person you'll be tomorrow. If you want a different future, create it now through present choices and actions. Thinking about the future without taking present action is merely daydreaming. Acting in the present while aligned with your desired future is creating that future. This is why presence paradoxically creates the best future.

When you're fully present, you make better choices because you're not distracted. You take wiser actions because you're paying attention. You build stronger relationships because you're fully engaged. These present-moment choices and actions compound into the future you desire.

Today, recognize that your future self is depending on your present self. What you do today matters immensely because it's literally creating tomorrow. Don't postpone important actions until someday. Don't waste today while dreaming about tomorrow.

Invest in today wisely, and tomorrow will thank you. The future isn't only created by planning—it's created by doing. And doing only happens now, in this present moment. Create the future you want by being present and intentional now.

November 13

> *Gratitude for challenges transforms obstacles into opportunities.*

It's easy to be grateful for blessings, but advanced gratitude includes challenges. When you can genuinely appreciate difficulties—not because you enjoy suffering but because you recognize their value—you've mastered gratitude.

Every challenge carries gifts: strength developed, wisdom earned, character forged, resilience built. When you're grateful for challenges, you extract their value rather than just enduring their difficulty. You ask: What is this teaching me? How is this making me stronger? What capability am I developing? The same challenge that defeats the ungrateful person strengthens the grateful person. The difference isn't the challenge but the relationship with it. Gratitude transforms obstacles into opportunities for growth.

Today, identify a current challenge. Instead of resenting it, practice gratitude for it. What might this challenge be developing in you? What are you learning? How might you be better for having faced this? This doesn't mean liking the challenge or wanting more challenges. It means recognizing that since you have this challenge anyway, gratitude helps you extract maximum value from it.

The challenge might not change, but your experience of it transforms. Obstacles become opportunities when gratitude is your lens. Instead of "Why is this happening to me?" ask "What is this teaching me?" That shift from victim to student changes everything.

November 14

Mindfulness is the practice of returning to the present moment, again and again.

People often think mindfulness is achieving a state of constant presence. But this misunderstands the practice. Your mind will wander— that's what minds do. Mindfulness is not preventing wandering; it's noticing when you've wandered and gently returning to the present.

Each time your mind drifts to the past or future and you bring it back to now, you're practicing mindfulness. Each return strengthens your capacity for presence. Think of it like training a puppy. The puppy wanders off repeatedly. You don't punish it; you gently guide it back. Eventually, with patient repetition, the puppy learns to stay near.

Your mind works similarly. It wanders to the past or future repeatedly. You don't judge yourself; you gently guide attention back to now. Eventually, with patient repetition, your mind wanders less and presence increases. The practice isn't achieving perfect presence but developing the habit of noticing absence and returning to presence.

Today, practice mindfulness. Throughout your day, notice when your mind has wandered. Are you thinking about the past? Worrying about the future? Mentally absent while physically present? When you notice, simply return your attention to the now without judgment. What are you experiencing right now? This repeated returning is the practice. Don't expect to stay present constantly. Expect to wander and return, wander and return. Each return strengthens your presence.

November 15

Comparison is the thief of joy and gratitude.

You can be deeply grateful for what you have until you start comparing yourself to someone who has more. Suddenly, what felt abundant feels insufficient. What you appreciated becomes something you take for granted. What brought contentment brings dissatisfaction.

Comparison steals joy by shifting focus from what you have to what you lack relative to others. Social media amplifies this—you're constantly exposed to highlight reels of others' lives, which you may unconsciously compare to your behind-the-scenes reality. They have more success or a better relationships or nicer things or more excitement. Your life feels lacking by comparison.

But comparison is based on incomplete information. You're comparing their external highlights to your internal experience. You don't know their struggles, their private pain, what they sacrificed for what they have. The comparison is inherently false. Additionally, there will always be someone with more. No matter how much you have, comparison finds someone with more and makes you feel insufficient.

Today, when comparison arises, interrupt it. Catch yourself comparing and consciously redirect to appreciation. Instead of "They have what I don't," shift to "I'm grateful for what I do have." Practice genuine happiness for others' success and joy—when you celebrate their wins instead of envying them, you free yourself from comparison's grip. Instead of measuring yourself against others, measure yourself against your past self. Are you growing? Improving? Moving forward? That's what matters. Stop letting comparison steal your joy. Comparison to others is irrelevant. Gratitude for what you have is essential.

The present moment is neutral;
your thoughts about it create your experience.

The present moment itself—the raw sensory experience of now—is neutral. It's not good or bad, pleasant or unpleasant. It simply is. Your thoughts about the present moment create your experience of it as positive or negative.

Two people can be in identical circumstances. One thinks "This is terrible" and suffers. The other thinks "This is an opportunity" and finds meaning. Same present moment, completely different experience based on thoughts about it. This reveals tremendous power: since thoughts create experience, changing thoughts changes experience without changing circumstances. You don't need life to be different to feel differently about life. You need thoughts about life to be different.

Today, practice observing the difference between the present moment and thoughts about it. When experiencing something challenging, separate the raw experience from your thoughts about it. What is the actual sensory experience right now? Then notice: what am I thinking about this experience? How are these thoughts coloring my experience? Often, you'll discover the thoughts are more painful than the actual experience.

The present moment might be uncomfortable but tolerable. Your thoughts about it ("This is awful! This shouldn't be happening! I can't stand this!") create suffering beyond the discomfort. The present moment is neutral. Your thoughts about it create your experience. Change your thoughts, and you change your experience without changing the moment.

Express gratitude outwardly, not just internally.

Feeling gratitude internally is valuable, but expressing gratitude outwardly multiplies its power. When you thank someone, you strengthen the relationship. You make them feel valued. You create positive emotion in both of you. You reinforce the behavior you appreciated, making it more likely to continue.

Unexpressed gratitude is like an undelivered gift—valuable to you but not received by the intended recipient. Many people feel grateful but never express it. They assume people know they're appreciated. But people need to hear it. They need the explicit acknowledgment that they matter, that their efforts are valued, that their presence is a gift.

Today, express gratitude to someone. Thank someone who made your life easier. Acknowledge someone whose presence enriches your life. Appreciate someone whose service you've taken for granted. Be specific—don't just say "thanks" but explain what you're grateful for and why it matters. Watch how this expression impacts the other person. Notice how it strengthens your connection. Observe how it amplifies your own gratitude.

When you express appreciation outwardly, you feel it more deeply yourself. Make expressing gratitude a daily practice. Look for opportunities to acknowledge and thank. This outward expression creates ripples of positive emotion, strengthens relationships, and deepens your own gratitude practice. Express gratitude, don't just feel it.

November 18

Regret lives in the past;
anxiety lives in the future; peace lives in the present.

Your mental time travel determines your emotional state. When your mind dwells in the past—replaying mistakes, reviewing regrets, reliving grievances—you experience the emotions of the past: shame, guilt, sadness, regret. When your mind projects into the future—imagining worst cases, anticipating problems, catastrophizing possibilities—you experience the emotions of the future: anxiety, fear, worry, dread.

But when your mind inhabits the present—experiencing what's actually happening now—you experience peace. Not because the present is always comfortable, but because most present moments are actually okay when separated from past regrets and future anxieties. The present moment usually contains challenges you can handle, not catastrophes overwhelming you. It contains what is, not what you fear might be. Most suffering comes from mental time travel, not from the present moment itself.

Today, notice the connection between mental time travel and emotional state. When you feel regret, check: are you thinking about the past? When you feel anxious, check: are you thinking about the future? Then practice returning to the present. What's actually happening right now? Not what happened or might happen, but what is happening? Usually, you'll discover the present moment is manageable, even if not perfect. The problems you're suffering over are memories or imagination, not present reality. Peace lives in the present. Return there whenever you notice yourself suffering in the past or future.

November 19

Gratitude is not a feeling to wait for but a practice to cultivate.

Often, people wait to feel grateful. They think gratitude arises spontaneously when good things happen. While spontaneous gratitude does occur, relying on it means gratitude is sporadic and circumstance dependent.

Gratitude as a practice is different. You don't wait to feel it; you cultivate it deliberately through daily practice. Even when you don't feel particularly grateful, you practice finding things to appreciate. This might feel forced initially—you're consciously looking for positives rather than spontaneously feeling grateful. But that's okay. The practice is what matters. Like any skill, gratitude strengthens through practice. The more you practice, the more natural it becomes. Eventually, gratitude shifts from something you do to something you are. It becomes your default lens rather than an occasional practice.

Today, practice gratitude deliberately, whether you feel like it or not. Set aside time—perhaps morning or evening—to list things you're grateful for. Force yourself if necessary. Find at least five things daily, even on difficult days. Feel appreciation for them as best you can. This consistent practice, maintained over weeks and months, transforms gratitude from a sporadic feeling to a constant state. You're not waiting for life to give you reasons for gratitude; you're training yourself to find reasons regardless of circumstances. Gratitude is not a feeling to wait for; it's a practice to cultivate daily.

November 20

Every moment contains both
blessing and burden; you choose which to see.

No moment is purely positive or purely negative. Every situation contains both challenges and gifts, both difficulties and opportunities, both burdens and blessings. Your focus determines which dominates your experience. The same job contains frustrations and benefits. The same relationship contains conflicts and joys. The same day contains problems and privileges. Which aspect you focus on creates your experience of it.

Two people in identical circumstances can have completely different experiences based solely on focus. One focuses on burdens and experiences suffering. The other focuses on blessings and experiences gratitude. Same circumstances, different experience. This is empowering because it means you don't need circumstances to change for experience to change. You need your focus to change. When you deliberately focus on blessings rather than burdens, gratitude increases even though circumstances remain the same.

Today, practice conscious focus selection. When you notice yourself focusing on burdens—what's wrong, what's difficult, what's lacking— consciously redirect to blessings. What's right? What's working? What are you grateful for? This isn't denying difficulties. It's choosing not to let difficulties dominate your attention to the exclusion of positives. Every moment contains both. You choose which to see. Choose blessings over burdens, not because burdens don't exist but because focusing on blessings creates a fundamentally different experience of life.

November 21

The breath is an anchor to the present moment.

Your breath only happens now. You cannot breathe in the past or future—only this breath, this moment. This makes the breath the perfect anchor to bring you into the present whenever your mind has wandered into the past or future.

When you notice you're mentally absent—lost in thoughts about what was or what might be—return your attention to your breath. Feel the sensation of air entering and leaving. Notice the rise and fall of your chest or belly. Follow one complete breath cycle. This simple practice instantly returns you to the present because the breath only exists now. Attention placed on breathing naturally pulls attention away from past and future thinking.

Today, use your breath as your anchor throughout the day. When you notice yourself drifting—during meetings, conversations, routine activities, moments of stress—return to your breath. Take three slow, conscious breaths, feeling each fully. This creates a reset, bringing you from wherever your mind was back to where your body is: here, now. The breath is always available, always present, always guiding you home to this moment. Let it become your steady companion for presence. Whenever you feel lost in thought, return to your breath. It's the simplest, most accessible doorway to the present moment.

November 22

Gratitude for health becomes most apparent when health is threatened.

When healthy, people rarely pause to appreciate their health. They take for granted that they can walk, breathe easily, sleep well, or move without pain. Health is invisible until it's compromised. The person with a toothache would trade significant money for the absence of pain. The person with breathing difficulty would give anything to breathe easily. The person with mobility issues would treasure the ability to walk freely. Yet before the problem, these capabilities seemed so ordinary as to not warrant appreciation.

Don't wait for health to be threatened to appreciate it. Today, if you're relatively healthy, take time to deeply appreciate this blessing. You can breathe without effort. You can move your body. You can see, hear, touch. Your body is performing millions of functions automatically, keeping you alive without your conscious management. This is miraculous, yet easily overlooked.

Today, practice gratitude for your health. Notice your breath and the ease with which it flows. Move your body and recognize its capabilities. Use your senses and appreciate their presence. Let genuine gratitude arise for these capabilities. Don't wait for illness or limitation to reveal the value of your health. Appreciate it now, while it's here. This awareness brings peace and may even support continued wellbeing by creating emotional states that nurture the body. Gratitude for health is wisdom.

November 23

Multitasking is a myth; presence with one thing is reality.

The brain cannot truly multitask. It can only rapidly switch between tasks, giving each partial attention. What people call multitasking is actually task-switching, and it comes at a cost. Attention becomes fragmented. Quality declines. Satisfaction disappears. You may get things done, but you're never fully engaged in any of them. Life becomes something you manage rather than experience.

This divided attention creates a subtle sense of stress and emptiness. You're always elsewhere. Eating while scrolling. Working while monitoring messages. Listening while preparing your response. Nothing receives your full presence, including your own experience.

The alternative is single-tasking with full attention. Do one thing at a time, completely. When eating, just eat. When working, just work. When speaking with someone, be fully there. This isn't about slowing down. It's about removing friction. With full presence, tasks are completed more efficiently because energy isn't lost to constant switching. And life feels richer because you're actually here to experience it.

Today, practice presence through single-tasking. Choose one activity and give it your full attention. When the mind pulls toward something else, gently return to the one thing in front of you. Notice the difference in clarity, quality, and satisfaction.

Multitasking creates surface-level living. Presence creates depth. Reality is not doing many things at once. Reality is doing one thing fully.

Gratitude shifts your perception.

Your attention is like a spotlight—wherever you point it determines what you see. For many people, spotlight habitually points toward problems. They notice what's wrong, what's lacking, what's not working. This creates the subjective experience that life is problematic, even when objectively many things are going well.

Gratitude shifts the spotlight toward what's right. When you practice gratitude, you train your attention to notice what's working, what's present, and what's positive. Suddenly the same life that felt problematic reveals abundant blessings. Nothing changed except where your attention is pointed. This shift doesn't deny problems, they still exist. But it prevents problems from dominating your entire experience. Yes, you have challenges. You also have blessings. Which receives your primary attention determines your experience of life.

Today, consciously shift your attention spotlight from what's wrong to what's right. Make a list of everything working in your life. Health functioning? Roof over your head? Food available? People who care? Opportunities present? Freedom to choose? When you deliberately point attention toward what's right, you'll be amazed how much is working that you've been ignoring while focused on problems.

This doesn't solve problems, but it prevents problems from defining your entire experience. Shift your attention from what's wrong to what's right, and watch your experience of life transform.

November 25

Now is the only time you can act or change anything.

People often say "I'll start tomorrow" or "I'll change someday." But tomorrow never comes—when it arrives, it's today. Someday never arrives—it's always today. The only time anything can actually happen is now.

You can't act yesterday—it's gone. You can't act tomorrow—it hasn't arrived. You can only act now.

You can't choose yesterday—those choices are made. You can't choose tomorrow—it doesn't exist yet. You can only choose now.

You can't change yesterday—it's unchangeable. You can't change tomorrow—it hasn't manifested. You can only change now.

This makes now infinitely valuable. It's the only time you have power. When you postpone action to tomorrow, you surrender that power. When you wait for the perfect time, you wait for something that does not exist. The perfect time is always now.

Today, recognize the power of now. What action have you been postponing? Take it now. What choice have you been avoiding? Make it now. What change have you been delaying? Begin it now. Not perfectly, not completely, but now. Because now is the only time it can happen.

Tomorrow is just another now that will require the same decision to act or postpone. Stop waiting for someday. Act now. Choose now. Change now. This is the only moment you have power. Use it.

November 26

Keep a gratitude journal to train your brain to notice blessings.

The brain's default mode is to notice problems. This is a survival mechanism. Problems signal potential threats, so the brain evolved to scan for what could go wrong. While useful for survival, this habit creates constant low-level stress and causes you to overlook how much is actually going well.

A gratitude journal retrains the brain. When you commit to writing 5-10 things you're grateful for each day, your brain begins actively searching for things to appreciate. Throughout the day, you start noticing moments, interactions, and small wins that could become gratitude entries. This gradually shifts the brain from problem-scanning to blessing-noticing.

At first, gratitude journaling may feel forced. You're consciously searching for positives rather than naturally noticing them. But with consistent practice, noticing gratitude becomes automatic. Your brain rewires to notice blessings as readily as it once noticed problems.

Today, start a gratitude journal if you haven't already. Get a dedicated notebook or use a digital tool. Each evening, write 5-10 specific things you're grateful for. Be specific rather than generic—not just "family" but "the conversation I had with my daughter today." Feel genuine appreciation as you write. Do this daily without exception.

Within weeks, you'll notice your brain spontaneously identifying things to appreciate throughout the day. The gratitude journal isn't just recording blessings—it's training your brain to notice them. Keep a gratitude journal, and watch how it transforms your automatic attention patterns from problem-focused to blessing-focused.

November 27

Acceptance of what is creates space for what can be.

People often confuse acceptance with resignation. They believe accepting the present means giving up on change. In reality, acceptance is what makes meaningful change possible.

Resistance to what is drains enormous energy. When you deny reality, resent it, argue with it internally, or wish it were different, you're fighting something that already exists. That fight consumes emotional and mental resources while accomplishing nothing. Reality doesn't change because it's resisted. The only result is exhaustion.

Acceptance is the clear acknowledgment of present reality: "This is how things are right now." It doesn't mean approval. It doesn't mean passivity. It doesn't mean staying stuck. It simply means stopping the internal battle with what already exists. The moment resistance ends, energy is released.

That freed energy can now be used where it actually matters: deciding what to do next. Once you accept reality as it is, you can respond intelligently rather than react emotionally. You can assess options, set boundaries, make plans, take corrective action, or remove yourself from harmful situations. Acceptance shifts you from powerless struggle into purposeful action.

Change can't begin from denial. It begins from clarity. You must see what is before you can effectively shape what can be.

Today, notice where you are resisting reality. A situation, a limitation, a behavior, a circumstance. Practice acceptance: "This is how it is right now." Feel the internal tension release. Then ask the only question that creates progress: Given that this is the current reality, what is the most effective action I can take?

Acceptance isn't inaction. It's the foundation of all wise action. When you stop wasting energy fighting reality, you gain the power to change it.

November 28

Gratitude is a superpower.

Gratitude is not a personality trait or a polite habit. It's a powerful internal state that changes how your brain and body function. When you practice genuine gratitude, your nervous system shifts out of stress and into regulation. Your perception sharpens. Your responses soften. You gain access to clarity instead of reactivity.

Gratitude also affects the body. It improves heart rate variability, supporting the nervous system's ability to recover from stress. This leads to better impulse control, improved sleep, lower inflammation, and greater resilience overall. Gratitude doesn't just feel good, it restores balance.

But gratitude does more than regulate your internal state. It changes what you notice. When you practice gratitude, attention moves away from constant problem-scanning and toward what is already working. Opportunities become easier to see. Support becomes more visible. Life feels less hostile and more cooperative, not because everything changed, but because perception did.

That's why nearly every spiritual tradition teaches gratitude as a foundational practice. Sacred texts across cultures repeat the same message in different language: appreciation opens doors, thanksgiving leads to guidance, gratitude invites more. Whether you view this as neuroscience, psychology, grace, karma, or coincidence, the pattern is consistent. Gratitude creates more to be grateful for.

Today, treat gratitude as a practice, not a mood. Pause and consciously appreciate something real: your breath, your body, a moment of calm, a small comfort, a person who supports you. Stay with the feeling long enough for it to register in your body, not just your thoughts.

Gratitude does not require perfect circumstances. It works best precisely when things are imperfect. Practiced consistently, it becomes one of the most reliable tools for peace, clarity, and quiet transformation. The more you give thanks, the better your life will be.

November 29

> *The quality of your presence determines the quality of your life.*

Two people can live identical lives externally but have completely different quality of life based on presence. The person who is present—fully experiencing each moment—has a rich, meaningful life even with simple circumstances. The person who is absent—mentally elsewhere while being physically present—has an empty, unsatisfying life even with ideal circumstances.

Presence determines quality of experience. When present, you enjoy conversations deeply, appreciate beauty profoundly, and feel connections genuinely. When absent, everything is muted, experienced through the fog of distracted attention. You go through motions without experiencing them. The tragedy is that people commonly spend their lives mentally absent, then wonder why life feels unsatisfying despite having many blessings. They're not experiencing the blessings because they're not present to experience them.

Today, commit to improving the quality of your presence. Not perfectly, just better. During meals with family, give them your full attention and presence. Put away devices, hear about their day, ask engaging questions, feel the connection. When outside, let yourself be present to nature's beauty. During conversations, give people the gift of your complete presence rather than planning your response while they speak. Your attention is one of the most valuable things you can give another person, and most people rarely receive it. During routine activities, be present to the experience rather than mentally elsewhere.

Each moment of presence increases life quality. You don't need better circumstances—you need better presence. The quality of your presence determines the quality of your life. When you give others your full attention, you give them something rare and precious, and you enhance your own experience simultaneously.

November 30

Live each day as if it's precious, because it is.

As we close this month on gratitude and present moment awareness, integrate this truth: each day is precious and irreplaceable. You have limited days on earth, you don't know how many. Each one that passes is gone forever, never to return.

When you truly recognize that today is precious, you relate to it differently. You stop wasting it in complaint, resentment, or mental absence. You stop postponing life until conditions improve. You live now, fully and consciously. You appreciate the ordinary moments. You connect deeply with people. You pursue what matters because tomorrow isn't guaranteed.

People who live as if time is infinite tend to squander days carelessly. They assume there will always be another opportunity to appreciate, to connect, to be present. Then one day, looking back, they realize how valuable each ordinary day actually was. Don't wait for hindsight to teach you what awareness can teach you now.

Today, live this day as if it's precious, because it is. Be present to it. Appreciate it. Make it count. Not through frantic achievement but through full presence and deep gratitude. Experience this day rather than thinking your way through it. Connect genuinely rather than superficially. Appreciate what is rather than focusing on what's lacking.

Each day is a gift that, once given, cannot be recovered. Receive it fully. Live it completely. Appreciate it deeply. Because this day, like every day, is precious beyond measure.

December

Mastery & Integration

Bringing It All Together

December 1

Mastery is not a destination but a path of continuous growth.

It's common for people to think mastery means reaching perfection—a final state where nothing more needs to be learned or improved. But true masters understand that mastery is not a destination; it's a commitment to continuous growth. The beginner thinks they know little and has much to learn. The intermediate thinks they know much and has little to learn. The master knows how much they don't know and embraces perpetual learning.

Mastery is characterized not by having arrived but by being committed to the journey. The master remains a student, always curious, always refining, always growing.

Today, as you begin this final month integrating the year's lessons, adopt the master's mindset. You've learned much this year, but there's infinitely more to learn. You've grown significantly, but growth never ends. You've achieved progress, but the path continues forward. Embrace this endless journey. Don't seek the comfort of thinking you've arrived. Find joy in knowing you're still growing.

Mastery is not claiming expertise; it's committing to continuous improvement. As you move through this month, integrate what you've learned while remaining open to deeper understanding. The journey of mastery has no end point—only continuous evolution toward greater wisdom, capability, and consciousness. Welcome to the path of mastery, where every achievement opens doors to new challenges, and every answer reveals new questions.

December 2

Integration means living the principles not just knowing them.

Knowledge without application is just information. Throughout this year, you've learned powerful principles about thought, responsibility, intention, visualization, abundance, discipline, pattern-breaking, purpose, gratitude, and presence. But learning principles is not the same as living them.

Integration is the process of moving principles from intellectual understanding to embodied practice. It's when visualization becomes your daily habit rather than an interesting concept. When gratitude becomes your default lens rather than an occasional practice. When presence becomes your natural state rather than a conscious effort.

In many cases, people consume endless personal development content without ever integrating it into their lives. They know principles intellectually but don't live them practically. This knowing without doing creates frustration rather than transformation.

Today, begin the integration process by choosing one principle from this year that you understand intellectually but haven't fully embodied. Commit to living this principle daily for the rest of this month. Not perfectly, but consistently. Make it a practice rather than just knowledge.

The goal of this month is integration—taking everything you've learned and weaving it into the fabric of your daily life. Knowledge is potential; integration is actualization. Transform knowing into being.

December 3

The master does the basics better than anyone.

Beginners seek advanced techniques, thinking mastery comes from complexity. But masters know that excellence comes from perfecting fundamentals. The master chef doesn't need exotic techniques—they execute basic techniques flawlessly. The master athlete doesn't need complex plays—they execute fundamentals perfectly. The master musician doesn't need complicated pieces—they play simple pieces beautifully.

In personal development, the fundamentals are: managing your thoughts, taking responsibility, setting clear intentions, maintaining discipline, practicing gratitude, and staying present. These aren't exotic or advanced—they're basic. But people often execute them inconsistently or poorly. The master returns to these fundamentals daily, refining execution, deepening practice, improving consistency. They don't seek new principles; they master existing ones.

Today, identify the most fundamental principle you've learned this year—perhaps taking responsibility, or practicing gratitude, or staying present. Commit to mastering this fundamental through perfect execution. Not learning something new, but doing something basic better.

The path to mastery is paved with fundamentals executed excellently. While others chase advanced techniques, master the basics. Simple principles, deeply integrated and consistently practiced, produce extraordinary results. Return to fundamentals and execute them with excellence. This is the master's way.

December 4

Knowledge is knowing; virtue is doing; mastery is being.

There are three levels of development. Knowledge is knowing what's right—understanding principles intellectually. Virtue is doing what's right—applying principles through action. Mastery is embodying principles so completely that aligned action flows naturally without conscious effort.

People frequently get stuck at knowledge, knowing without doing. Some progress to virtue, doing with effort. Few reach mastery, being without effort. The beginner knows they should be present but gets lost in distraction. The intermediate practices presence deliberately, pulling their attention back with effort. The master is presence—awareness flows naturally without having to try.

Throughout this year, you've gained knowledge—you know powerful principles. This month is about moving from knowledge to virtue to mastery. From knowing to doing to being. From intellectual understanding, to conscious practice, to embodied truth.

Today, honestly examine where you are on this spectrum with key principles. Are you at the level of knowledge—knowing but not doing? At the level of virtue—practicing with effort? Or approaching mastery—being naturally? For principles still at the level of knowledge, commit to deliberate practice. For those at the level of virtue, continue refining until effort softens into embodiment.

The goal of integration is reaching mastery—where principles are no longer techniques you apply but truths you live.

December 5

The integrated life aligns thoughts, words, and actions.

People tend to live fragmented lives where thoughts, words, and actions contradict each other. They think one thing, say another, and do something else entirely. This misalignment creates internal tension and external confusion. Energy is lost managing contradictions, and trust erodes both internally and in relationships.

Integration means bringing thoughts, words, and actions into coherence. What you think aligns with what you say. What you say aligns with what you do. What you do reflects what you truly believe. This coherence creates personal power and inner peace. You're no longer divided within yourself or maintaining multiple versions of who you are. When thoughts, words, and actions align, you become authentic, trustworthy, and powerful. People sense your integrity. You trust yourself because your actions match your intentions. Life simplifies because you're no longer managing inner contradiction. You're simply being authentic.

Today, examine your alignment honestly. Do your thoughts, words, and actions match? Or is there contradiction between what you believe, what you express, and how you behave? Where there's misalignment, create coherence. If you think something, speak it when appropriate. If you speak something, follow through. If you do something, let it reflect your true thoughts. This alignment might require difficult conversations, uncomfortable honesty, or changing behaviors. But the peace and power of integration are worth it.

An integrated life is one where thoughts, words, and actions move together as a single, coherent whole.

December 6

Mastery requires patience with the process and yourself.

One of the biggest obstacles to mastery is impatience. People want instant mastery, immediate transformation, and quick results. When mastery doesn't arrive quickly, frustration sets in. They give up, lose confidence, or conclude they're not capable. But mastery is measured in years and decades, not days or weeks.

The master understands this and develops patience—with the slow unfolding of skill, with inevitable setbacks, with the repetitions required for embodiment, and especially with themselves. They're patient with their mistakes, slow progress, and temporary regressions. This patience is not passive resignation but active acceptance of how mastery develops. Skills must be practiced thousands of times before becoming automatic. Neural pathways must be strengthened through countless repetitions. Understanding must deepen through years of application. This cannot be rushed. Impatience doesn't accelerate mastery; it prevents it by making you quit too soon.

Today, cultivate patience with your journey toward mastery. You've been integrating principles for one year—this is just the beginning. Some principles will take years to fully embody. Some lessons will require multiple learning cycles. Some growth will be invisible for long periods before suddenly becoming obvious. Be patient. Trust the process. Be gentle with yourself. Mastery isn't achieved through force but through patient, persistent practice over time. Patience with the process, and yourself, is essential for mastery.

December 7

The obstacle is the way.

Every obstacle you encounter on the path to mastery is not blocking the way—it is the way. The difficulty is not preventing growth; it's providing growth. The challenge is not an interruption of learning; it's the learning itself. People often think mastery means reaching a place beyond difficulties. But masters face difficulties constantly—they've just learned to use difficulties as development tools.

The obstacle reveals where you need to grow. The challenge shows what capacity you need to develop. The difficulty exposes which belief needs changing. When you embrace obstacles as the path rather than interruptions of the path, everything changes. You stop wishing for easy and start welcoming challenge. You stop resenting difficulties and start appreciating their developmental value. You stop avoiding obstacles and start engaging them fully.

Today, identify an obstacle you're facing in your mastery journey. Instead of resenting it, ask: What is this obstacle teaching me? What capacity must I develop to overcome this? What is this revealing about where I need growth? The obstacle is not preventing your mastery—it's providing the very challenge that will create it. The smooth path develops nothing. The obstacle-filled path develops everything. The obstacle is the way. Embrace it, learn from it, let it forge your mastery.

December 8

*Integration happens through
consistent daily practice, not occasional effort.*

One of the most common obstacles to integration is relying on occasional intensity instead of daily consistency. A weekend may be dedicated to deep practice, followed by weeks of doing nothing. A few days of strong effort give way to abandonment once motivation fades. This pattern of sporadic intensity does not create integration.

Real integration comes from consistent daily practice. Five minutes of practice every single day integrates more deeply than five hours once per month. Daily practice, even when brief, creates changes in neural pathways, habit formation, and embodiment that occasional intensity simply can't. The compounding effect of daily consistency far exceeds periodic intensity. Think of it like watering a plant. Flooding it once per month doesn't work as well as watering it a little bit daily. Integration requires regular care, not occasional extremes.

Today, if you've been relying on bursts of intensity, shift to daily consistency. Choose one practice—gratitude, visualization, presence, or reflection—and commit to doing it for just 5-10 minutes every single day. Not when you feel like it, not when you have extra time, but every day without exception. This daily consistency, maintained over weeks and months, creates deep integration that occasional intensity never could.

Integration happens through the accumulation of daily practice, not through sporadic bursts of effort. Commit to daily consistency over occasional intensity.

December 9

The master knows when to apply effort and when to allow flow.

There's a balance between doing and being, between effort and allowing, between force and flow. The beginner hasn't yet learned this balance and often leans toward one extreme—either forcing everything through willpower or passively waiting for things to happen. The master has learned the wisdom of appropriate action: when to apply effort and when to allow flow.

Some situations require effort—taking action, making decisions, overcoming obstacles through determined work. Other situations require allowing—trusting the process, releasing control, letting things unfold naturally. The art is knowing which is which.

Trying to force what needs to flow creates resistance and exhaustion. Passively allowing what needs effort creates stagnation and missed opportunities. The master develops sensitivity to this distinction. They feel when effort is appropriate and apply it. They sense when allowing is appropriate and release. Throughout this year, you've learned both effort-based principles (discipline, responsibility, action) and allowing-based principles (surrender, trust, flow). Integration means learning when to use each rather than defaulting to one.

Today, cultivate this sensitivity. When facing a situation, ask: Does this require effort or allowing? Am I forcing something that needs to flow naturally? Am I passively waiting for something that needs my action? The master's wisdom is knowing when to push and when to trust, when to act and when to allow, when to control and when to surrender. Develop this discernment—it's the hallmark of an integrated life.

December 10

Teach what you're learning to deepen your own mastery.

One of the most powerful ways to deepen your understanding and integration of principles is to teach them. When you teach something, you must understand it more deeply than when you just practice it. You must clarify confusion, answer questions, and explain ideas clearly. This process deepens your own mastery. Teaching also creates accountability. The commitment to teach motivates you to live what you teach.

Teaching isn't just sharing information, it's sharing your experience. When you share your personal journey—the struggles you faced, the breakthroughs you experienced, the specific ways a principle transformed your life—you give others something more powerful than theory. Your story might be exactly what someone needs to hear to begin their own journey. They may have been stuck until they heard that someone like them—imperfect, learning, trying—found a way forward.

Many tend to think they need to achieve mastery before teaching. But the opposite is true—teaching is part of the mastery process, not something you do after mastering. You don't wait until you're perfect to share; you share what you're learning as you learn it.

Today, look for ways to teach the principles you've been learning. This might be formal—leading a workshop or writing about what you've learned. Or informal—sharing insights with a friend, mentoring someone, telling your story, or simply living these principles so visibly that others begin to ask about the changes they see.

You don't need to be an expert to teach. You only need to be honest about being a fellow traveler on the path. Share not just the principles, but your lived experience with them. As you teach, you'll find your own understanding deepening, your practice strengthening, and your integration accelerating. And you may discover that your story becomes the catalyst for someone else's transformation.

December 11

Mastery emerges from the integration of opposites.

Throughout this year, you've encountered apparent opposites: discipline and flow, effort and surrender, planning and spontaneity, desire and gratitude, ambition and contentment, structure and flexibility. The beginner sees these as contradictions, as either-or choices. The master understands they are complementary polarities meant to be integrated.

Mastery is not choosing one pole and rejecting the other. It's holding both, integrating them, knowing when each is appropriate. You need discipline and flow, structure that supports freedom. You need effort and surrender, working hard and then releasing attachment to outcomes. You need planning and spontaneity, clear direction paired with openness to change. You need desire and gratitude, a burning desire for your goals while being deeply grateful for what you already have. The master integrates these opposites, disciplined without rigidity, hardworking without force, intentional without inflexibility, ambitious without dissatisfaction.

Today, identify apparent opposites in principles you've been practicing. Instead of seeing them as contradictions, explore how they work together. How can you be disciplined and flowing? Committed and surrendered? Ambitious and content? Focused and present? Integration creates wholeness. Mastery is not one-sided living, but the ability to hold multiple truths at once and sense which one is needed in each moment. True mastery emerges through integration, the ongoing practice of balance, discernment, and inner coherence.

December 12

> *Your level of mastery is revealed in how you handle adversity.*

Anyone can practice principles when life is easy. The true test of integration is how you respond when life gets difficult. Do you abandon principles under stress? Or do principles support you through stress?

The beginner's practice is shallow not because they lack sincerity, but because the principles have not yet been embodied. They are understood intellectually but not yet integrated into automatic response. When stress arises, old habits take over and the practice collapses.

The master's practice is deep because the principles are no longer something they remember to use. They are lived. When facing adversity, the master doesn't abandon gratitude—they use it as medicine. They don't forget presence—they use it as an anchor. They don't release responsibility—they use it as power. The principles that seemed like nice ideas during easy times become essential tools during hard times.

Today, prepare for this test. Don't wait for adversity to discover whether your practice is integrated. Anticipate that difficulties will come and decide now how you'll respond. When stress arises, will you practice presence or lose yourself in mental chaos? When challenges appear, will you maintain gratitude or descend into complaint? When setbacks occur, will you take responsibility or make excuses?

Your level of mastery is revealed not when everything is going well but when everything is going wrong. Integrate principles so deeply that they become your automatic response to difficulty, not just your pleasant practice during ease. True mastery is tested by adversity and revealed through response.

December 13

Consistency beats intensity.

You've encountered certain principles repeatedly throughout this year—not by accident, but by design. The most important principles to master appear again and again because repetition emphasizes what's most critical to learn and practice. Consistency itself is one of those repeated themes, and it's fundamental to mastery.

People love intensity—the dramatic effort, the heroic push, the concentrated focus. Intensity feels productive and significant. But intensity without consistency produces minimal lasting change.

The person who practices intensely for a week then quits accomplishes less than the person who practices moderately for a year. The weekend warrior approach to personal development—intense seminars followed by weeks of no practice—doesn't create mastery. What creates mastery is showing up daily, even when you don't feel like it. Practicing when you're tired. Continuing when you're not seeing dramatic results. Maintaining discipline when motivation is absent. This consistent, unglamorous daily practice is what builds mastery.

Today, as you near the end of this year, recommit to consistency. Not intensity, not perfection, not dramatic transformation—just consistent daily practice. The principles you've learned this year won't integrate through occasional intense effort. They'll integrate through daily practice maintained over months and years. Choose 2-3 core practices and commit to doing them daily for the next year. Make them so simple you cannot fail. Then execute them consistently, regardless of how you feel or whether you see immediate results.

Consistency over time beats intensity in the moment. This is the master's secret: simple practices, done consistently, compound into extraordinary results.

December 14

Mastery is marked by simplicity, not complexity.

The beginner has a tendency to make everything complicated. They collect countless techniques, attempt to follow complex systems, and create elaborate practices. They think mastery requires complexity. But as you advance toward mastery, complexity gives way to simplicity. You realize you don't need hundreds of techniques—you need a few fundamentals practiced deeply.

The master's practice is remarkably simple: think constructively, take responsibility, act with intention, practice discipline, stay grateful, remain present. These aren't exotic or complex—they're fundamental. But the master executes them with depth that transforms simplicity into power.

Throughout this year, you've learned many principles. But mastery isn't accumulating more principles—it's integrating core principles deeply. As you move forward, resist the temptation to keep adding more. Instead, simplify. Identify the 3-5 most important principles for you. These become your practice focus. Release the rest, not because they're wrong but because mastery requires depth over breadth.

Today, identify your core principles—the ones that resonate most deeply, address your greatest challenges, or produce your best results. Let everything else fade to background while you focus on mastering these core principles. Simplify your practice. Deepen your execution. The master does a few things supremely well rather than many things adequately. Mastery is marked by simplicity.

December 15

The master serves others from overflow, not from depletion.

As you develop mastery, you'll naturally want to serve others—sharing insights, offering help, contributing to others' growth. This impulse is beautiful and important. But the master learns to serve from overflow, not from depletion.

Serving from depletion means giving when you're empty, helping when you're exhausted, contributing when you have nothing left. This creates martyr energy that ultimately helps no one. You burn out, resent others, and serve poorly. Serving from overflow means filling your own cup first, then sharing what overflows. You maintain your practices, honor your needs, and sustain your energy. From this full state, you serve others generously without depleting yourself.

Today, examine your service to others. Are you serving from overflow or depletion? If from depletion, give yourself permission to prioritize your own practice and wellbeing. This isn't selfishness—it's sustainability. You cannot pour from an empty cup. Fill yourself first through consistent practice. Maintain your energy through appropriate boundaries. Sustain your wellbeing through self-care.

Then, from this overflowing state, serve others generously. The master knows that the best service comes from those who serve themselves first, not in narcissistic indulgence but in wise sustainability. Serve from overflow, not depletion. Fill your cup, then share what overflows.

December 16

Integration requires regular reflection and course correction.

You cannot integrate what you don't evaluate. Without regular reflection, you continue patterns unconsciously, repeat mistakes unaware, and drift from intentions unnoticed. Integration requires periodic pause to reflect: What's working? What's not? Where am I succeeding? Where am I struggling? What needs adjustment?

The master builds reflection into their rhythm—daily, weekly, monthly, annually. They review progress, celebrate wins, identify challenges, and adjust their approach. This reflection prevents drift and ensures continuous alignment with intentions.

Today, as you approach the year's end, establish a reflection practice. Begin with a brief daily reflection—5 minutes reviewing the day. What went well? What could improve? Add a weekly deeper reflection—20 minutes reviewing the week. What patterns emerged? What needs attention? Include a monthly comprehensive reflection—an hour reviewing the month. What progress occurred? What course corrections are needed? Finally, commit to an annual profound reflection—several hours reviewing the year. What changed? What was learned? What's next?

Without reflection, experience doesn't become wisdom. With reflection, every experience becomes a teacher. Integration requires this continuous feedback loop: practice, reflect, adjust, practice. Make reflection a regular discipline, not an occasional afterthought. The master reflects consistently, ensuring their path remains aligned with their intentions.

December 17

Mastery is not about perfection but about consistent improvement.

Perfectionism is the enemy of mastery. The perfectionist refuses to start until conditions are perfect, quits when mistakes occur, and judges themselves harshly for imperfection. This prevents mastery rather than creating it.

The master knows perfection is impossible and irrelevant. What matters is consistent improvement—being slightly better today than yesterday, slightly wiser this month than last month, slightly more capable this year than last year. The direction matters, not the perfection. Think of mastery as a compass pointing toward excellence rather than a destination of perfection. The compass guides you forward, but you never fully arrive. You're always improving, always growing, and always refining.

Today, release perfectionism if it's been holding you back. You don't need perfect practice—you need consistent practice. You don't need perfect execution—you need regular execution. You don't need perfect results—you need directional improvement. Are you better than you were six months ago? Are you more conscious, more disciplined, more grateful, and more present? That's what matters. Not whether you're perfect, but whether you're improving.

The master measures progress against their past self, not against an impossible ideal. Commit to consistent improvement over impossible perfection. Small gains, accumulated over time, create mastery.

The integrated life is authentic, coherent, and whole.

Integration creates wholeness—all parts of you working together rather than in conflict. You're no longer fragmented into multiple selves: the self you present at work versus the self at home, the self you show publicly versus the self you hide privately, the self you aspire to be versus the self you actually are.

The integrated person has brought all these parts into coherent wholeness. Who they are publicly matches who they are privately. What they believe inwardly reflects how they act outwardly. The values they profess are the values they live. This integration creates authenticity— you're genuine rather than performing. It creates coherence—your parts work together rather than against each other. It creates wholeness— you're complete rather than fragmented.

Today, examine where you're still fragmented. Where do you present one version of yourself while hiding another? Where do your stated values not match your actual choices? Where are you living inauthentically? Then begin the integration work: bring hidden parts into the light, align actions with values, be the same person in all contexts.

This is vulnerable and difficult, but it's essential for wholeness. The integrated life might be more challenging than the fragmented life, but it's infinitely more peaceful and powerful. Integration creates authenticity, coherence, and wholeness.

December 19

Celebrate how far you have come while staying hungry for growth.

There's a balance between appreciation and aspiration. If you only appreciate how far you've come, you might become complacent. If you only aspire to where you're going, you might never feel satisfied. The master maintains both: genuine appreciation for growth achieved and authentic hunger for growth remaining. They celebrate progress while pursuing more progress. They honor their current level while working toward the next level.

Today, practice this balance. First, appreciate your growth this year. How have you changed since January? What have you learned? What habits have you developed? What patterns have you broken? What consciousness have you gained? Truly acknowledge this growth. Allow yourself to feel genuine pride.

Then, maintain hunger for continued growth. What's next? What new level calls you? What further development awaits? What deeper mastery beckons? Feel genuine excitement about future growth. This combination, appreciation for what is and aspiration for what can be, creates sustainable motivation. You're not perpetually dissatisfied, always focused on what's missing. You're not complacent, satisfied with current achievement. You're balanced: grateful for growth while hungry for more growth. Celebrate how far you've come. Stay hungry for how far you can go. Both appreciation and aspiration are essential for mastery.

December 20

Your commitment to mastery
must be greater than your comfort with mediocrity.

Mastery requires leaving the comfortable mediocrity where it's common for most people to live. Mediocrity is seductive—it's easy, familiar, and socially acceptable. It requires no risk, no discomfort, and no discipline. You can coast in mediocrity indefinitely.

But mastery requires commitment that exceeds the comfort of mediocrity. You must be willing to be uncomfortable, to risk failure, to face judgment, to work when others rest, and to persist when others quit. The pull of comfortable mediocrity is strong. In moments of difficulty, you'll be tempted to settle for good enough, to stop pushing, to accept average. These are the moments that determine whether you achieve mastery or return to mediocrity.

Today, strengthen your commitment to mastery by clarifying why it matters to you. What will mastery give you that mediocrity won't? How will your life be different as a master versus remaining average? What legacy will mastery create versus settling? Make these answers so compelling that when mediocrity tempts you with comfort, your commitment to mastery is stronger.

You'll face countless moments where comfortable mediocrity offers relief from the difficult path of mastery. Your commitment must be strong enough to choose mastery in those moments. Not once, but again and again. Your commitment to mastery must exceed your comfort with mediocrity. Make this commitment now, before temptation arises.

December 21

The masters work is never done.

The beginner hopes for completion—a point where work is finished, growth is achieved, and they can finally rest. But the master knows the work is never done. There's always deeper understanding to gain, greater skill to develop, and higher consciousness to achieve. This might sound exhausting, but for the master, it's exciting.

The endless journey means endless possibility. There's always another level, another insight, or another breakthrough. Boredom is impossible because growth never ends. The master finds peace not in completion but in engagement. Not in arriving but in traveling. Not in achieving but in evolving.

Today, release any expectation that you'll reach a point where the work is finished. You won't master all principles, solve all challenges, or achieve perfect enlightenment in this lifetime. And that's perfect. The journey is the point. The growth is the reward. The process is the achievement.

Find peace in knowing the work never ends. This means you never run out of opportunity for growth, discovery, and evolution. Each level you reach opens a door to the next level. Each achievement reveals new possibilities. Each answer generates new questions. The master's work is never done, and the master wouldn't have it any other way. Embrace the endless journey. Find joy in perpetual growth.

December 22

Integration transforms knowing into being, practice into second nature, effort into ease.

The ultimate goal of integration is transformation: from knowing principles to being them, from practicing consciously to doing naturally, from effortful execution to effortless flow. Initially, principles require conscious attention. You must remember to practice gratitude, deliberately choose presence, intentionally take responsibility. This conscious practice is necessary and valuable—it's how integration begins.

But as integration deepens, something shifts. Principles that required effort become natural. Gratitude arises freely. Presence becomes your default. Responsibility is your automatic response. What you once practiced consciously becomes who you are unconsciously.

Today, notice where this transformation has already occurred. What practices that once required effort now flow naturally? What principles that you once had to remember are now automatic? Celebrate these integrations, they represent real transformation.

Then notice where you're still in the conscious practice phase. What still requires deliberate effort? What do you still forget? These are your ongoing integration opportunities. Continue practicing these consciously, trusting that with time, they too will become natural. Integration is the journey from knowing to being. From practice to second nature. From effort to ease. You're not trying to perform principles forever—you're transforming into someone who embodies them naturally.

> *The master remains humble because*
> *mastery reveals how much more there is to master.*

Itzhak Bentov understood this paradox: "I speak from my present level of ignorance. The more you know, the more ignorant you become, because ignorance grows exponentially—the more answers you get, the more new questions arise." Arrogance comes from limited knowledge—thinking you know more than you do because you don't know how much you don't know. Humility comes from expanded knowledge—recognizing how much remains unknown because you've learned enough to see the vastness beyond.

The beginner is often confident, even arrogant sometimes, because they don't know what they don't know. The intermediate becomes less confident as awareness expands and the depth of the unknown becomes clear. The master returns to confidence, but is tempered by humility—grounded in real capability while fully aware of infinite room for growth.

True mastery creates humility. The more you master, the more you realize how much more there is to master. Each answer reveals ten new questions. You're no longer impressed with yourself because you see clearly how far the path extends.

Today, let any arrogance dissolve into humility. If you've been proud of your growth, balance it with recognition of how much further you can grow. If you've been judging others who aren't as far along, remember you were there once too.

The master is simultaneously confident and humble—confident in real growth, humble about how much more remains. This balance creates openness to learning, compassion for others, and commitment to continued growth. Mastery reveals the vastness beyond mastery, creating the master's defining characteristic: humble confidence.

December 24

Create a personal operating system from your integrated principles.

Throughout this year, you've learned individual principles. Now it's time to integrate them into a personal operating system—a coherent set of principles that guide all decisions and actions.

Your personal operating system answers key questions: How do I think? I manage my thoughts, visualize my goals, and focus on what I want. How do I respond? I take responsibility, choose my response, and learn from every experience. How do I act? I practice daily disciplines, pursue my purpose, and maintain integrity. How do I relate? I practice gratitude, stay present, and serve from overflow. How do I grow? I break old patterns, embrace challenges, and commit to continuous improvement.

Today, create your personal operating system by identifying your core principles—the ones that will guide your life going forward. Write them down as a coherent system. These aren't aspirational principles you hope to live someday—these are the principles you're committed to living now.

Your personal operating system becomes your decision-making framework, your behavior guide, your life philosophy. When facing decisions, you reference your operating system: Which choice aligns with my principles? When facing challenges, you apply your operating system: Which principle addresses this situation? Create your personal operating system from your integrated principles. Make it explicit, concrete, and actionable. This operating system is your transformation codified.

Mastery is a gift you give yourself and the world.

Your commitment to mastery serves more than just yourself. Yes, you benefit from greater capability, deeper wisdom, and expanded consciousness. But the world benefits too. When you master yourself—your thoughts, emotions, patterns, and potential—you become a force for good. You create value for others. You model possibility. You inspire transformation. You serve from overflow. You contribute from capability.

Every person committed to mastery raises the collective consciousness slightly. You demonstrate that growth is possible, that change is achievable, that transformation is real. Others see your example and think: If they can do it, perhaps I can too. Additionally, the master serves the world more effectively than the unmastered person. You have more to give, fewer personal problems draining energy, greater clarity about contribution, and deeper capacity for service.

Today, recognize your mastery journey as a gift—to yourself and to the world. You're not just improving yourself for selfish reasons. You're developing yourself to serve more effectively. You're mastering yourself to model possibility. You're transforming yourself to contribute more fully.

The world needs people committed to mastery—not perfection, not superiority, but continuous growth toward greater wisdom, capability, and consciousness. Your mastery journey is a gift to yourself and everyone whose life you touch. Give this gift generously by committing fully to your ongoing mastery.

December 26

Review your year to extract wisdom from your journey.

You've traveled 360 days through twelve monthly themes, absorbing principles, practicing techniques, and growing in consciousness. But experience doesn't automatically become wisdom—reflection transforms experience into wisdom.

Today, review your entire year. Look back at January. Who were you then? What challenges did you face? What patterns limited you? Then trace your path through the months: your exploration of thought's power, your embrace of responsibility, your learning about intention and reality creation, your practice of visualization, your development of an abundance mindset, your commitment to discipline, your release of old patterns, your clarification of purpose, and your practice of gratitude and presence.

Who are you now compared to then? What have you learned? How have you grown? What patterns have you broken? What capabilities have you developed? What consciousness have you gained? Write a year-in-review reflection capturing: your biggest insights, your greatest challenges, your most significant changes, your proudest moments, your ongoing struggles, and your lessons learned.

This reflection isn't just looking backward—it's extracting wisdom that will guide you forward. The year's experiences contain teachings. Reflection extracts those teachings. Today, honor your journey by reviewing it thoroughly. Extract the wisdom from your year. Let the past twelve months become the foundation for your next level of mastery.

December 27

Commit to continuing the journey beyond this year.

This year of daily readings ends in a few days, but your mastery journey doesn't end. It's just beginning. You've built a foundation, established practices, developed awareness, and started transformation. But this is the starting point, not the destination.

Many complete programs or finish books and then stop practicing. The learning ends, the growth plateaus, and they gradually drift back toward old patterns. Don't let this happen.

Today, commit to continuing beyond this year. Not through daily readings necessarily, but through daily practice. Commit to maintaining the disciplines you've developed, living the principles you've integrated, and continuing the growth you've begun. Make specific commitments: Which daily practices will you continue? What principles will guide your decisions? How will you ensure continued growth? What accountability will you maintain? Write these commitments down. Make them concrete and specific. This prevents drift and ensures momentum continues.

The year of readings provided daily guidance and structure. Going forward, you must provide your own structure. But you're no longer the same person who started this journey—you're more aware, more conscious, and more disciplined. You now have the tools to maintain your practices and deepen your growth.

Today, commit to the journey beyond this year. Your mastery journey is lifelong, not year-long. This year planted seeds and built a foundation. Future years will deepen your mastery and expand your consciousness. Commit to continuing.

December 28

Share your journey to inspire others toward their own mastery.

Your transformation this year isn't meant to be hidden. When you grow, people notice. They see something different about you—more presence, more peace, and more purpose. They wonder what changed. This is your opportunity to share your journey and inspire theirs.

Sharing doesn't mean preaching or forcing principles on others. It means being willing to answer honestly when people ask about your transformation. Telling your story vulnerably, including struggles and successes. Living principles visibly so others see what's possible. Offering guidance when requested, not when unsolicited. Your journey—with its challenges, breakthroughs, and ongoing growth—might be exactly what someone else needs to see to believe their own transformation is possible.

Today, consider how you might share your journey. Maybe you'll have a conversation with friends. Maybe you'll post on social media about principles you're practicing. Maybe you'll give this book to someone who needs it. Maybe you'll simply live so authentically that people are drawn to ask your secret. Don't hide your growth. Let it show. Not from pride but from generosity—offering your experience as encouragement for others.

Your mastery journey can light the path for others beginning theirs. Share generously. Inspire openly. Model courageously. Your transformation might be the catalyst for someone else's transformation.

December 29

Trust the timing of your growth.

Throughout this year, you might have felt frustrated by the pace of growth. Some things integrated quickly, while others remained challenging. Some patterns broke easily, while others persisted stubbornly. Some principles felt natural while others required constant effort. This uneven growth is normal and perfect.

Some lessons require multiple cycles before integrating. Some patterns take years to fully release. Some capabilities develop slowly, invisibly, before suddenly becoming obvious. Growth can't be forced onto a preferred timeline. Growth has its own rhythm, its own timing, and its own season. Your job is not to control that timing, but to trust it while maintaining consistent practice.

Today, release any judgment about your pace of growth. If something hasn't integrated as quickly as you hoped, that doesn't mean you're failing—it means you need more time. If a pattern hasn't fully released, that doesn't mean you can't change—it means the change is still developing. Trust the timing. Continue the practice. Stay committed to the journey.

Some growth happens quickly, providing encouraging feedback. Other growth happens slowly, testing your commitment. Both are necessary. Both are valuable. Both are perfect timing. Trust that everything is unfolding as it should for your highest good. Your growth is right on schedule, even when it doesn't feel like it. Trust the timing. Keep practicing. Keep growing.

December 30

Tomorrow begins a new cycle on your spiral of growth.

Growth doesn't happen linearly—it happens in spirals. You revisit similar lessons at deeper levels, encounter similar challenges with greater capacity, and face similar questions with expanded consciousness.

Tomorrow, as this year ends and a new year begins, you're not starting over at the beginning. You're starting a new cycle on your upward spiral. You'll encounter familiar themes—thought, responsibility, intention, discipline—but from a higher level of understanding. What challenged you last January may feel effortless next January. What you learned intellectually last year might integrate experientially next year.

This is the spiral of growth: revisiting, deepening, and expanding. Each cycle takes you higher while covering similar territory. Don't be discouraged if next year brings challenges you thought you'd overcome. You're facing them from a higher level, which means they appear in more subtle forms requiring deeper mastery. This is progress, not perfection.

Today, prepare for tomorrow's new cycle. Acknowledge you're not where you were a year ago—you're higher on the spiral. Honor your growth. Then embrace the next cycle with curiosity rather than expectation. What will you learn in this next cycle? How will you deepen existing integration? What challenges will you overcome? What new levels of consciousness are waiting to emerge?

Tomorrow begins a new cycle on your spiral of growth. Each cycle builds on previous cycles, taking you higher while deepening mastery. Embrace the spiral. Trust the process.

December 31

You are becoming a master.

Today marks the completion of 365 days of daily readings, but not the completion of your journey. You've traveled through twelve transformative themes, absorbed hundreds of principles, practiced countless techniques, and grown in immeasurable ways. You're not the same person who began this journey. You think differently—more consciously, more intentionally, more powerfully. You respond differently—more responsibly, more purposefully, more effectively. You live differently—more gratefully, more presently, more authentically.

This transformation makes you a master-in-progress. Not a completed master, because mastery is never finished. But someone committed to the path of mastery, someone actively developing capability, someone continuously growing in consciousness.

The question now is simple: Will you continue? Will you maintain the practices you've developed? Will you live the principles you've integrated? Will you pursue the growth you've started? Your answer to this question determines everything. If you continue, this year becomes the foundation for decades of ongoing mastery. If you stop, this year becomes a pleasant memory with fading impact. The choice is yours, but consider this: You've already done the hardest part. You've built habits, overcome resistance, developed awareness, and proven capability. Continuing is easier than starting was. You have momentum. Use it.

Today, as you complete this year's readings, make one final commitment: to continue. Continue practicing. Continue growing. Continue becoming.

You are becoming a master. This is not an arrival—it's an ongoing journey. This is not a completion—it's a continuation. This is not an ending—it's an evolution. You are becoming a master. The path extends infinitely before you. Walk it with commitment, curiosity, and courage. You've proven you can.

Resources

Books, Tools, and Practices for Continued Growth

RESOURCES FOR YOUR JOURNEY

The principles in this book draw from many teachers and practices. This section provides additional tools, recommended reading, and resources to support your transformation. Use what resonates. Explore what calls to you. This journey is yours to customize.

I. RECOMMENDED BOOKS BY THE MASTERS

The following books have profoundly influenced my journey and form the foundation for many principles in this book. If you want to go deeper into specific teachings, start here.

Joe Dispenza - Neuroscience & Meditation

- *Breaking the Habit of Being Yourself: How to Lose Your Mind and Create a New One* - Essential reading on rewiring your brain and creating lasting change through meditation and mental rehearsal

- *Becoming Supernatural: How Common People Are Doing the Uncommon* - Advanced practices for transformation, including specific meditation techniques

- *You Are the Placebo: Making Your Mind Matter* - Scientific evidence and case studies demonstrating the mind's power to heal and transform

Vadim Zeland - Reality Transurfing

- *Reality Transurfing Steps I-V* (Complete series) - The complete system for understanding and navigating reality, including pendulums, importance, intention, and the alternatives space

- *Transurfing in 78 Days: A Practical Course* - A condensed, practical guide to applying Transurfing principles daily

Napoleon Hill - Achievement Principles

- *Think and Grow Rich* - Timeless principles of success, definiteness of purpose, and the power of organized thinking (Essential reading)

- *Outwitting the Devil* - Powerful insights on overcoming fear, procrastination, and self-sabotage

- *The Law of Success* - Comprehensive 16-lesson course on achievement principles

Jim Rohn - Personal Development

- *The Art of Exceptional Living* - Core teachings on personal responsibility, goal setting, and building life by design

- *7 Strategies for Wealth & Happiness* - Practical wisdom on creating prosperity and fulfillment

- *The Seasons of Life* - Understanding life's natural cycles and responding appropriately

Earl Nightingale

- *The Strangest Secret* - Classic recording/book on the power of thought and becoming what you think about

- *Lead the Field* - Comprehensive personal development program

James Allen

- *As a Man Thinketh* - Short, powerful book on thought as creative force (Essential reading - can be read in one sitting)

- *The Path to Prosperity* - Practical application of thought principles to daily life

Neville Goddard - Consciousness & Imagination

- *The Power of Awareness* - Understanding consciousness as the only reality

- *Awakened Imagination* – The creative power of imagination and how to use it to shape your experience

---

II. PRACTICES & TOOLS

Meditation Resources

- **Dr. Joe Dispenza Meditations** - Available at DrJoeDispenza.com - Guided meditations specifically designed for rewiring the brain and creating new states of being

- **BrainWave: 37 Binaural Series** - App for brainwave entrainment

- **Insight Timer** - Free meditation app with thousands of guided meditations

Journaling & Reflection

- **Reality by Design App** – Guided journal and reflection app aligned with this book's daily readings

- **Daily Reflection Notebook** – Blank journal for the daily review practice

- **Rooted in Gratitude Journal** - Structured gratitude and reflection practice book

Goal Setting & Planning

- **Goal Setting Worksheet** – RealityByDesign.net/resources Complete template for the goal setting process outlined in August 11-15

- **Vision Board Tools** - Canva.com for creating digital vision boards; Pinterest for collecting images

- **Habit Tracking Apps** – Reality by Design, Habitica, Streaks, or simple paper tracking

Breathwork & Body Practices

- **Wim Hof Method** - Breathwork and cold exposure for physical and mental transformation (wimhofmethod.com)

- **Essential Pranayama book** - Breathing techniques for balance, healing, and peace

---

III. WEBSITES & ONLINE COMMUNITIES

Teacher Websites

- **DrJoeDispenza.com** - Workshops, retreats, online courses, and meditations

- **Zelands.com** - Official Transurfing resources and community

- **JimRohn.com** - Audio programs, courses, and legacy content

General Resources

- **RealityByDesign.net**
  - Downloadable worksheets and templates
  - Blog posts expanding on key principles
  - Community forum access
  - Coaching session information

Online Communities

- **Reality Transurfing Facebook Groups** - Active communities discussing Transurfing principles

- **Joe Dispenza Community** - Online groups for meditation practitioners

- **Reality by Design** - Join our online community at RealityByDesign.net

  - o Connect with fellow readers

  - o Share experiences and insights

  - o Accountability partnerships

IV. WORKSHEETS & TEMPLATES

The following worksheets support key practices from the book. Download printable PDFs at RealityByDesign.net/resources:

1. **Jim Rohn Goal Setting Template** (August 11-15)

   - o 10-year vision brainstorm

   - o Goal categorization worksheet

   - o Top 4 major goals selector

   - o "Who must I become?" reflection

2. **Daily Reflection Template** (August 23, December 16)

   - o What went well today?

   - o What could improve?

   - o What did I learn?

   - o What will I do differently tomorrow?

3. **Monthly Review Worksheet** (December 16)

   - o Progress tracking

   - o Pattern identification

   - o Course corrections

   - o Celebration of wins

4. **Gratitude Journal Prompts** (November)

   o   Daily gratitude practice

   o   Appreciation exercises

   o   Reframing challenges

5. **Pattern Identification Worksheet** (September)

   o   Recognizing recurring patterns

   o   Identifying payoffs

   o   Creating new responses

6. **Visualization Script Template** (June)

   o   Guided visualization structure

   o   Future self meditation outline

   o   Mental rehearsal framework

V. EXPANDED PRINCIPLE GUIDES

Some principles warrant deeper exploration. The following expanded guides are available at RealityByDesign.net/resources:

- **Reality Transurfing Deep Dive** - Comprehensive guide to pendulums, importance, outer/inner intention, and the alternatives space

- **The Science of Meditation** - Neuroscience behind meditation practices and how they rewire the brain

- **Mental Rehearsal Mastery** - Step-by-step guide to effective visualization and mental rehearsal

- **Breaking Pattern Addiction** - Extended guide to identifying and changing stubborn patterns

- **The Art of Surrendered Action** - Balancing effort and surrender in daily life

---

VI. CONTINUE YOUR JOURNEY

If you've found value in this book and want to go deeper, I invite you to join our community of like-minded individuals committed to personal transformation.

Community Support

Join our online community where readers connect, share experiences, and support each other's growth:

- Group discussions and accountability partnerships

- Shared wins and breakthrough stories

- Ongoing encouragement and support

Visit RealityByDesign.net to join.

One-on-One Holistic Life Coaching

As a certified holistic life coach, I offer personalized support for integrating these principles into your specific circumstances:

- Customized action plans based on your unique situation

- Accountability and guidance through challenges

- Deeper work on specific patterns or blocks

- Support tailored to your goals and timeline

Transformation is personal work, but it doesn't have to be done alone. I'd be honored to support your journey.

Learn more or schedule a discovery session at RealityByDesign.net

---

VII. A FINAL NOTE

These resources are tools, not requirements. The daily entries in this book contain everything you need for transformation. But if you're drawn to explore further, if specific principles resonate deeply, if you want community support—these resources are here.

Use what serves you. Leave what doesn't. Trust your own wisdom about what your journey needs.

The principles work regardless of whether you read every recommended book or join every community. What matters is daily practice, consistent application, and the willingness to keep showing up for your own transformation.

You have everything you need within you. These resources simply help you access it.

The Seed of Life is a sacred geometric symbol of **creation, unity, and universal harmony**, forming the core of the Flower of Life, representing the seven days of creation and the blueprint for all existence.

ABOUT THE AUTHOR

Russell L. Powers is an entrepreneur, certified holistic life coach, and author. After nearly losing his life to addiction at twenty-seven, Russell discovered the transformative power of reprogramming the mind and taking full responsibility for creating his reality. His journey from despair to building a thriving family and purpose-driven life inspired him to dedicate himself to helping others achieve similar transformations.

Russell has spent over a decade studying consciousness, personal development, and reality creation, integrating wisdom from masters including Joe Dispenza, Vadim Zeland, Napoleon Hill, Jim Rohn, Earl Nightingale, James Allen, and Neville Goddard. Through finding his own daily practice, he transformed not only his internal world but also his external circumstances.

As a holistic life coach, Russell works with individuals navigating personal transformation, helping them break old patterns, reprogram limiting beliefs, and create lives aligned with their deepest desires. He understands firsthand the challenges of changing ingrained thought patterns and the power of consistent daily practice to create lasting change.

Reality by Design: 365 Principles for Transforming Your Mind and Reality represents Russell's commitment to making transformative wisdom accessible through daily practice. He created this book not only as a guide for others but as a legacy for his three sons—Jackson, Mason, and Michael—and anyone seeking to break free from unconscious patterns and design their reality with intention.

Russell lives in Missouri with his wife Shelley and their three sons. He continues his own daily practice of meditation, mindfulness, and conscious creation while building a community of like-minded individuals committed to personal transformation.

Connect with Russell:
- Website: RealityByDesign.net